Mathematics for Every Student

Responding to Diversity, Grades Pre-K–5

Mathematics for Every Student

A series edited by Carol E. Malloy

Mathematics for Every Student
Responding to Diversity, Grades Pre-K–5

Volume Editors

Dorothy Y. White
University of Georgia
Athens, Georgia

Julie Sliva Spitzer
San José State University
San José, California

Series Editor

Carol E. Malloy
University of North Carolina at Chapel Hill
Chapel Hill, North Carolina

NATIONAL COUNCIL OF
TEACHERS OF MATHEMATICS

Copyright © 2009 by
THE NATIONAL COUNCIL OF TEACHERS OF MATHEMATICS, INC.
1906 Association Drive, Reston, VA 20191-1502
(703) 620-9840; (800) 235-7566; www.nctm.org
All rights reserved

Library of Congress Cataloging-in-Publication Data

Mathematics for every student. Responding to diversity, grades pre-K–5 / volume editors,
Dorothy Y. White, Julie Sliva Spitzer.
      p. cm. — (Mathematics for every student)
   ISBN 978-0-87353-611-0
   1. Mathematics--Study and teaching (Preschool) —United States. 2. Mathematics—Study and teaching
(Elementary) —United States. 3. Multicultural education—United States. 4. Educational equalization—
United States. I. White, Dorothy Y. II. Spitzer, Julie Sliva. III. Title: Responding to diversity, grades pre-K–5.
   QA13.M35453 2009
   372.7—dc22
                              2008050998

The National Council of Teachers of Mathematics is a public voice of mathematics education,
providing vision, leadership, and professional development to support teachers in ensuring
equitable mathematics learning of the highest quality for all students.

Printed in the United States of America

Contents

Contents—*Continued*

Contents — *Continued*

Preface

The National Council of Teachers of Mathematics has demonstrated its dedication to equity in the mathematics education of *all students* through its publications, through regional and annual meeting programs, and through professional development programs. In clarification of what is meant by *all students*, in 1990 the NCTM Board of Directors endorsed the following statement, which set the mathematical education of every child as the goal for mathematics teaching at all levels.

> As a professional organization and as individuals within that organization, the Board of Directors sees the comprehensive mathematics education of every child as its most compelling goal.
>
> By "every child" we mean specifically—
>
> • students who have been denied access in any way to educational opportunities as well as those who have not;
>
> • students who are African American, Hispanic, American Indian, and other minorities as well as those who are considered to be a part of the majority;
>
> • students who are female as well as those who are male; and
>
> • students who have not been successful in school and in mathematics as well as those who have been successful.
>
> It is essential that schools and communities accept the goal of mathematical education for every child. However, this does not mean that every child will have the same interests or capabilities in mathematics. It does mean that we will have to examine our fundamental expectations about what children can learn and can do and that we will have to strive to create learning environments in which raised expectations for children can be met. (NCTM 1991, p. 4)

Through the Equity Principle in *Principles and Standards for School Mathematics* (2000), NCTM built on the challenging goal of the "every child" statement above and extended its vision of equity by stating, "Excellence in mathematics education requires equity—high expectations and strong support for all students" (p. 12). Specifically, the principle states that equity requires high expectations and worthwhile opportunities for all, requires accommodating differences to help everyone learn mathematics, and requires resources and support for all classrooms and all students (pp. 12–14). Guided by the Equity Principle and the charge of the NCTM Educational Materials Committee, the editors of this three-book series are pleased to feature instructional practices of teachers from diverse classrooms that embody this principle and the every-child statement.

The editors thank the authors, who were willing to share their experiences and successful strategies for teaching all students within diverse classrooms, the numerous reviewers for their contributions, and the NCTM Publications Department for its support, patience, and encouragement from our initial meeting through the publication phases of this project. I personally want to thank the volume editors, who worked tirelessly during the development of this series. It was a pleasure and an intellectual inspiration to work with them. They were my friends, critics, and colleagues.

—Carol E. Malloy
Series Editor

REFERENCES

National Council of Teachers of Mathematics (NCTM). *Professional Standards for Teaching Mathematics.* Reston, Va.: NCTM, 1991.

———. *Principles and Standards for School Mathematics.* Reston, Va.: NCTM, 2000.

Introduction

WE ARE teachers—teachers of mathematics. Every year, we are thrilled to meet the new students who are in our classrooms to learn about mathematics. On the first day of school, when we look around the room at the students' faces, we know that every student has the ability to learn mathematics. At the same time, students look at our faces for guidance through the mathematics content and to their mathematical understanding. Students' confidence in our skills is both our inspiration and our challenge, especially because we know, as Bobbie Poole stated in *I Am a Teacher* (Marquis and Sachs 1990),

> Every kid is different. What's exciting is to try to meet the needs of those individual kids. It is never boring. It is different from minute to minute, and there is no formula that works for everyone. (p. 20)

Knowing that no one strategy will work for all students, teachers have the responsibility to determine strategies, both affective and cognitive, that together support all students while they learn mathematics. Affective behaviors—which include students' beliefs about mathematics and self, teachers' beliefs, students' emotions, and students' attitudes—play a prominent role in achievement (McLeod 1991). The following vignette describes a situation that I experienced with a student, Alfred,[1] who was a behavioral challenge in my mathematics class because he lacked confidence in his academic skills.

Building Confidence through Caring

In my sixth year of teaching, my husband and I moved to a city that had hired him as a central office school administrator. During my interview for a teaching position in the district, the personnel officer encouraged me to take a position at Jefferson High School. She called Jefferson High an inner-city high school that was in transition from being the strongest high school in the city to becoming an average school. I decided to take that position. When I entered school on the first day that students attended, I was nervous. I am always nervous on the first day, but this experience was different. In some ways, I was a little scared because in my limited experience as a teacher, I had never taught in a school labeled "inner city." As a result of my preconceived notions of inner-city schools, I had visions of disruptive, unruly, and unmotivated students in the halls and in my classes.

The students whom I greeted at the door of my classroom were not disruptive or unruly. They were polite, very well dressed, and enthusiastic; and they seemed excited to be in my mathematics classes. I learned quickly that this school and its students were similar to the schools in which I had previously taught—normal schools with a diverse student population. I was comfortable. But in every perfect situation, an enigma can arise. My enigma the first few days of school was Alfred. He was a rather large tenth-

Teachers have the responsibility to determine strategies, both affective and cognitive, that together support all students while they learn mathematics.

---

1. This is a pseudonym.

1

grade boy who was enrolled in Algebra Concepts 2—the second year of a two-year course in Algebra I. Alfred looked like he played football—he was approximately six feet two, muscular, and very well developed. During the first few days of class, it became apparent that Alfred was testing me and my ability to control the class and teach algebra. Even though Alfred did not always have his homework ready for class, he did not refuse to do his work. His ability and motivation to complete classwork were not the problem; the problem was his behavior. He was disruptive, sarcastic, and in some situations demeaning to other students. I was therefore unsure of a strategy to use to diffuse his need to challenge both the students and me and to help him become serious about learning algebra.

It became apparent that Alfred was testing me and my ability to both control the class and teach algebra.

I thought about this problem for several days and then decided that I would demonstrate through my behavior that Alfred was special to me. I decided to say something special to him every day when he entered the room. Because this situation occurred at the beginning of the year, I knew nothing of Alfred's life or his aspirations. All I knew was that I wanted him to know that I wanted him in my class and that I cared about more than just his knowledge and performance in mathematics. My question or comment to Alfred varied from day to day. I generally asked him about the school's football games and professional ones, how his previous weekend or evening was, his view on something that I had seen in the newspaper or on the television news, or whether he had problems with the homework assignment. I just wanted to engage him in a brief conversation.

After about two weeks of my talking with him before class, I was surprised that Alfred started to come to my class earlier and earlier. His behavior in class improved, and he actually started completing his homework assignments with some concern about how well he achieved. He was certainly still playful in class, and we laughed a lot; but he no longer challenged me for direction of the class. What was more important was that Alfred began to learn algebra. He was motivated to do mathematics because he believed that he could be successful and he knew that he would have my support when he had difficulty. With his new efforts, I became aware that he was an average to above-average student in mathematics. Alfred became one of my successful students. He even requested to take geometry during the next school year.

Alfred was motivated to do mathematics because he believed that he could be successful.

As fate would have it, I was scheduled to teach geometry that year and was to be Alfred's teacher. I was surprised when he told me later that he had made sure that he was signed up for my course. I had the privilege of teaching Alfred in three mathematics classes in three years. Certainly the years were not totally without challenges. I can remember many situations in which I had to pull him out of the classroom for private conversations because of his interactions with other students. But Alfred received the conversations with respect and understanding of my concern for his achievement and emotional development. The relationship that Alfred and I forged had transcended his constant need to disguise his lack of confidence by trying to exert power and control in class and had become one of mutual respect in which he believed that he could be successful in mathematics. Alfred graduated from high school and was accepted into college. Our close relationship has lasted over the years and will last for our lifetimes. This relationship and his understanding of mathematics were influenced, in part, by my asking him one question a day to let him know that I cared about him and his learning.

The strategy that I used in this situation demonstrates the power of a teacher's care and concern for a student. Even though the preceding vignette is from a high school class, teachers can use this strategy at any grade level. The following quotation is from a sixteen-year-old student who remembered his third-grade teacher as a motivating factor in his life:

> My third-grade teacher was the best. She made sure I learned. She taught me right from wrong. And she kept me out of trouble. She told me to be a leader, not a follower. And that's what I've done. She gave me pride and self-confidence. She made me understand what life is all about and how important it is to plan your life. Today I believe in myself. I'm never going to let her down. (Burke 1996, p. 21)

It appears that this third-grade teacher demonstrated care and concern for her student, similar to the care and concern that I showed in my relationship with Alfred, that stayed with him throughout his schooling. Just as displaying care can inspire change in a student's reaction to learning and view of himself or herself, appropriate classroom instructional strategies that focus on the specific needs of students can result in academic success in heterogeneous mathematics classrooms.

> **Instructional strategies that focus on the specific needs of students can result in academic success in heterogeneous mathematics classrooms.**

Focus of This Three-Book Series

Whereas we strive to provide students in classrooms from prekindergarten to twelfth grade with opportunities to experience and learn mathematics that will serve them throughout their lifetimes, increasingly more teachers face classrooms of students with a range of needs and backgrounds, expertise, and experience, including students who lack prerequisite skills and students who may be able to move forward quickly and with deep understanding. Recognizing that all classrooms are diverse, this NCTM series of three books (for prekindergarten–grade 5, grades 6–8, and grades 9–12) addresses instructional strategies that meet the needs of all students and offer them high-quality mathematics. The mathematical instructional strategies presented in these books recognize that diversity can come in the form of language, culture, race, gender, socioeconomic status, and ways of learning and thinking, as well as cognitive and emotional characteristics.

Guided by the vision of NCTM's *Principles and Standards for School Mathematics* (2000), which states that "Equity … demands that reasonable and appropriate accommodations be made as needed to promote access and attainment for all students" (p. 12), we designed these books to help teachers meet the diverse needs of their students and to focus on helping teachers determine *how* to support high-quality mathematics learning for diverse student populations in a given classroom. The articles that follow are in the form of cases of classroom practice, instructional strategies, and teacher development.

> **Diversity can come in the form of language, culture, race, gender, socioeconomic status, and ways of learning and thinking, as well as cognitive and emotional characteristics.**

- Case articles describe classroom practice that promotes the learning of all students. They offer rich descriptions of teachers' practice, students' activity, and resulting students' learning.

- Instructional Strategies articles offer glimpses of the implementation or effect of particular instructional practices that support mathematical learning not only for one group of students but for students across many diverse needs or examples of instruction or mathematical tasks that are beneficial for all students but that are especially relevant to students not well served by traditional approaches.

- Teacher Development articles discuss important topics to help teachers develop their expertise in teaching students who have a range of needs, backgrounds, and experience.

Synopses of Articles

In the first article, "English Language Learners Learning from, and Contributing to, Mathematical Discussions," Luz A. Maldonado, Erin E. Turner, Higinio Domínguez, and Susan B. Empson use vignettes to illustrate their suggestions for best practices to support the involvement of English language learners (ELLs) with mathematical discussions. The discussions are rich with details about why and how the practices support the learning of ELLs.

The second article, "*Fíjense amorcitos, les voy a contar una historia*: The Power of Story to Support Solving and Discussing Mathematical Problems among Latino and Latina Kindergarten Students," by Erin Turner, Sylvia Celedón-Pattichis, Mary Marshall, and Alan Tennison, shares how two teachers used stories about students and class activities to organize problem-solving sessions for kindergarten students. The two teachers, Ms. Arenas and Ms. Fields, used stories in different ways to scaffold their students' learning, yet both teachers were able to develop students who are confident problem solvers and problem posers.

The third article, "Enhancing Mathematics Lessons to Support All Students"—by Kathryn B. Chval, Oscar Chavez, Sarah Pomerenke, and Kari Reams—chronicles the experiences of Ms. Reams, a first-grade teacher of students whose native languages include Chinese, Korean, Spanish, and English. This case follows Ms. Reams from the beginning of her search for ideas and resources to use in her classroom to the results of her teaching efforts. The article also provides suggestions for other teachers.

Article 4, Cheryl Roddick's "Conceptual Understanding of Fractions," furnishes a detailed description of activities, employing manipulatives, that students may use to explore the concept of fractions. She addresses common misconceptions that many students encounter when learning fractions and gives suggestions to guide students through these challenges.

The fifth article offers a challenge for many elementary school teachers—helping students learn their basic mathematics facts. In "Differentiating Practice to Help Students Master Basic Facts," authors Linda Forbringer and Allison Fahsl provide readers with a variety of games that teachers can adapt to differentiate practice in the classroom. They

We designed these articles to help teachers support high-quality mathematics learning for diverse student populations.

can redesign such classic games as bingo, Concentration, and Old Maid to build students' proficiency by grouping facts and gradually incorporating more of them into these motivating games and activities.

The importance of teaching mathematics with key developmental understandings (KDUs) is the focus of "In My Time—Learning to Think in Tens and Ones," the sixth article, by Susan N. Friel, Tery Gunter, and Catharina Ringer. The authors use the concept of place value to illustrate the crucial transitions that are essential for students' mathematical development. By analyzing students' work and thinking, they gradually move students to use more sophisticated strategies for solving problems.

Article 7, "Differentiating Mathematics by Using Task Difficulty," by Jill D. Cassone, expounds on the different aspects of differentiating mathematics by using task difficulty, including understanding content progression and students' readiness for skills and concepts, as well as targeted instruction. Cassone discusses the importance of all these aspects of differentiation and suggests an instructional strategy for delivering targeted instruction by using readiness.

In article 8, "Differentiating Instruction in First-Grade Geometry," Jennifer Taylor-Cox delineates the process of differentiating instruction by using forward- and back-mapping in a first-grade mathematics classroom. The case provides detailed steps of differentiation—including preassessments, grouping decisions, small-group work, independent tasks, and whole-class closure—to teach three groups of students. The author presents the ideas in a way that makes clear how to implement this strategy toward differentiation and presents its benefits in the teaching and learning of mathematics.

In article 9, Robert Q. Berry III provides a glimpse into an instructional model of coteaching, which teachers can use to teach a wide range of students. "Coteaching: Collaboration between an Elementary Mathematics Specialist and a Classroom Teacher" describes the process that two mathematics educators—Joanne, a fifth-grade teacher, and Susan, a mathematics specialist—used to plan, coteach, and assess how they met the individual needs of their students. The article offers the reader several models for coteaching.

Meeting the diverse mathematical needs of all students is a challenge for most teachers. In article 10, "Help One, Help All," authors Julie Sliva Spitzer, Dorothy Y. White, and Alfinio Flores describe instructional strategies that address the needs of specific students and actually support all students' learning of mathematics. The article highlights such strategies as the use of multiple representations and making connections to discuss the importance of teachers' creating learning environments that engage and support all types of learners.

Engaging parents in the mathematical learning of their children is a strategy used in "Mathematics beyond the School Walls Project: Exploring the Dynamic Role of Students' Lived Experiences" in article 11. Author Shonda Lemons-Smith shares the activities of a school-based family outreach project in which parents collected artifacts from their homes and communities to show how their children interacted with mathematics outside of school. The article describes sample artifacts and includes comments from teachers on how they analyzed and used the artifacts to enhance their mathematics teaching.

Article 12, "Dynamic Pedagogy in Diverse Elementary School Classrooms: Examining Teachers' Instructional Strategies"—by Erica N. Walker, Eleanor Armour-Thomas, and Edmund W. Gordon—compares the instructional strategies of two veteran third-grade teachers. The teachers were part of a professional development project to improve the mathematics performance of students in an ethnically and socioeconomically diverse school district. The article presents comparisons of the two teachers' interactions with students and their selection of instructional tasks to highlight strategies for actively engaging students in mathematics learning.

Every school district includes teachers who inspire students and help them learn mathematics. Authors Emily Peterek and Thomasenia Lott-Adams present Ms. Kay in article 13, "Meeting the Challenge of Engaging Students for Success in Mathematics by Using Culturally Responsive Methods." This article offers readers an overview of culturally responsive teaching and describes how Ms. Kay incorporates its tenets while she teaches her African American students.

Helping to frame the perspective driving this book series, which sees all students as able to do mathematics, article 14, "Moving from Deficiencies to Possibilities: Some Thoughts on Differentiation in the Mathematics Classroom," by Mark W. Ellis, raises questions about the traditional ways in which educators have labeled students as proficient or not proficient in school mathematics in the United States. In particular, Ellis asks readers to consider the intent behind such concepts as ability and differentiation and challenges readers to think about creating possibilities for all students to succeed in mathematics.

Daniel S. Battey and Meg Stark provide a powerful close to this book with a discussion about the importance of appropriately diagnosing mathematical misconceptions, specifically as they relate to how we view students' abilities. In article 15, "Inequitable Classroom Practices: Diagnosing Misconceptions as Inability in Mathematics," the authors posit that to better address issues of equity, we need to consider the broader educational and cultural contexts that structure the frames of mind of students and all individuals involved in the educational process.

— Carol E. Malloy
Series Editor

REFERENCES

Burke, Nancy. *Teachers Are Special.* New York: Random House, 1996.

Marquis, David M., and Robin Sachs. *I Am a Teacher: A Tribute to America's Teachers.* New York: Simon & Schuster, 1990.

McLeod, Douglas. "Research on Learning and Instruction in Mathematics: The Role of Affect." In *Integrating Research on Teaching and Learning Mathematics,* edited by Elizabeth Fennema, Thomas P. Carpenter, and Susan J. Lamon, pp. 55–82. Albany: State University of New York Press, 1991.

National Council of Teachers of Mathematics (NCTM). *Principles and Standards for School Mathematics.* Reston, Va.: NCTM, 2000.

English-Language Learners Learning from, and Contributing to, Mathematical Discussions

Luz A. Maldonado
Erin E. Turner
Higinio Dominguez
Susan B. Empson

IN A classroom that reflects a growing trend in elementary schools across the country, students engaged in a classroom discussion and shared their problem-solving strategies for folding a paper into six equal parts. After Ernesto, an English-language learner (ELL), had explained his strategy in Spanish, the teacher asked his classmates for feedback and questions. Corinne, a native English speaker, raised her hand to make a comment but first asked the teacher, "Does he understand English?" Corinne's question is a powerful testament to the complexities and issues that teachers in linguistically diverse classrooms face while they strive to teach meaningful mathematics to all students in their classrooms. Because 63 percent of all public schools include students who are limited English proficient (LEP) and whose native language is a language other than English (Strizek et al. 2006), Corinne's comment reminds us of the need for further research in these classrooms.

Research suggests that such discussion practices as explaining thinking, conjecturing, analyzing strategies, and justifying solutions constitute an indispensable element of learning and doing mathematics (Cobb, Wood, and Yackel 1993; NCTM 2000). Although many teachers realize the importance of discussion in helping students learn, even those in monolingual classrooms find that actually incorporating discussions is challenging (O'Connor 2001; Silver et al. 2005). In this article, we draw on our research on mathematics learning in elementary school classrooms to recommend a set of practices that teachers can adopt to support ELLs so that they can learn from, and contribute to, mathematical discussions.

Two Linguistically Diverse Classrooms

The research team designed a ten-week-long teaching experiment in a diverse urban elementary school in which 99 percent of the students participated in the free or reduced-price lunch program and 59 percent of the

> **After Ernesto, an English-language learner (ELL), had explained his strategy in Spanish, the teacher asked his classmates for feedback and questions. Corinne, a native English speaker, raised her hand to make a comment but first asked the teacher, "Does he understand English?"**

This research was supported in part by National Science Foundation Grant 01388877 to Susan Empson.

Although many teachers realize the importance of discussion in helping students learn, even those in monolingual classrooms find that actually incorporating discussions is challenging (O'Connor 2001; Silver et al. 2005).

students were classified as LEP. The researchers placed students into two linguistically diverse classes, with approximately seventeen fourth- and fifth-grade students in each class. The classes met twice a week after school for one and a half hours, and the research team videotaped them. Of the thirty-four students, twenty-two were ELLs. The school had a transitional Spanish-English bilingual program, in which ELLs spent the first three to four years of elementary school in bilingual classrooms that used both Spanish and English as the medium of instruction and then transitioned into English-only classrooms by fourth or fifth grade. Classroom teachers had recommended the students in this study for the after-school program for enrichment or additional help.

The teachers in the after-school program were two members of the research team. Both had experience teaching in various elementary school settings for more than five years, and one had been a bilingual teacher. Each class included fourth and fifth graders with a range of mathematics achievement levels, as well as a combination of monolingual English-speaking students and Spanish-English bilingual students with varying levels of English proficiency. The language of instruction was English in one classroom and a combination of English and Spanish in the other classroom. Consistent with the goal of engaging all students was the belief that all students, regardless of their level of English proficiency, were capable of participating in meaningful mathematics discussions. As a result, we make no claims about the validity of the type of bilingual education model that we adhered to in our teaching experiment and point out that of utmost importance was that students communicated their mathematical thinking in ways that made sense to them.

A Typical Day

The classes had a problem-solving focus. Students typically used their own strategies to solve two or three fraction and ratio problems each day. The research team drew on research of children's understanding of fractions and ratios as multiplicative structures in designing the problems (Empson and Turner 2006; Empson et al. 2006). Because solving and discussing problems were the focal points of the study, the researchers devoted much attention to allowing for multiple entry points into problems by carefully choosing the numerical relationships, selecting contexts that we believed were familiar to students, and selecting contexts that might lend themselves to different kinds of representations (e.g., discrete objects, such as pizzas and chocolate bars; and then less-discrete objects, such as lemonade). We provided problems (for example, see table 1.1) in English and in Spanish. We asked the students to paste the problems into their notebooks and to document their thinking in some form (e.g., writing, drawing, and making charts) while they solved the problems.

The teachers typically introduced new problems in a whole-group setting to maximize students' understanding. Then students dispersed to their small-group tables to work through the problems. The teachers traveled

---

1. All names are pseudonyms.

Table 1.1
Sample Problems Used in Teaching Experiment

Problem Type	Sample Problems
Paper-folding problems	Fold this piece of paper to make 24 equal parts. If you fold a piece of paper in halves, then in thirds, and then in fourths (without opening the paper between folds), how many equal parts will result?
Equal-sharing problems	At Patty's Pizza Hut, 6 children are sharing 26 minipizzas so that they each get the same amount. How much pizza does each child get? (To adjust mathematical difficulty, change the numbers to 4 and 18.) Twelve children want to share 9 pineapple cakes so that everyone gets the same amount. How much cake can each child have? (To adjust mathematical difficulty, change the numbers to 6 and 4.) — And if there were 24 children and 9 cakes, how much cake would each child get? — What if there were 24 children and 18 cakes? How much cake would each child get?
Ratio problems	Rose is making glasses of limeade for her friends. In the first glass, she puts 1 little cup of lime juice, and 4 little cups of water. In the second glass, she puts 3 little cups of lime juice. How many little cups of water does she need to add to this glass so that the limeade tastes the same as the limeade in the first glass?

around the room at this time, monitoring students' progress, asking for students' thinking, and adjusting the mathematical difficulty of problems as needed. After sufficient time, the students reconvened as a whole group to discuss various solutions for the problems. The teachers asked students with different strategies to share their ideas, or the students volunteered to share. The teachers expected students to use multiple strategies to solve the problems, share their questions and findings with their peers, and listen to other students' solutions. Students recreated their strategies by using oral explanations, reenactments, manipulatives, and drawings on poster paper.

An important component of the mathematics discussions in the classrooms was recognizing and valuing the role that participant structures in the classroom play in positioning students as mathematical thinkers (Goffman 1981). Thus, the teachers treated the students as competent problem solvers whose ideas and strategies were important to share with others.

The teachers treated the students as competent problem solvers whose ideas and strategies were important to share with others.

The teachers also modeled the types of questions that students should ask one another during small-group and whole-group discussions. In addition to asking students to share their thinking in a common space (that is, with the whole group), the teacher invited students into conversations with one another about the similarities or differences in their strategies or asked students to comment on, or ask questions about, a particular strategy.

Practices That Supported ELLs' Participation

The research team analyzed transcriptions of the videotapes to identify productive interactions among the teachers and the students in small- and whole-group discussions. The researchers created codes for the types of questions that teachers asked the students and the types of mathematics talk that the students used in discussing their strategies. An in-depth analysis of seven ELL students indicated that ELLs were participating in ways that were comparable with those of their monolingual peers. The researchers took a closer look at students who reported their thinking, commented on the thinking of other students, justified solutions, made claims and connections, and expanded on ideas introduced and discussed in whole-group settings. They also identified and described the teaching practices that enabled these various forms of participation by ELL students in mathematical discussions (see table 1.2).

Creating Opportunities for Students to Explain and Clarify Their Thinking in a Small Group

The research team noticed that students' substantial contributions to whole-group discussions almost always followed small-group conversations about the problem. These small-group conversations allowed ELLs to practice roles related to solving problems and sharing mathematical thinking.

The research team noticed that students' substantial contributions to whole-group discussions almost always followed small-group conversations about the problem. These small-group conversations allowed ELLs to practice roles related to solving problems and sharing mathematical thinking. For example, students had an opportunity to make sense of the tasks, clarify and prepare to share their ideas, and continue to build on mathematical strategies presented in previous whole-group discussions. These opportunities, in turn, allowed ELL students to practice the language that would enable them to best explain their mathematical thinking. In the small-group setting, ELL students often actively thought through problems and explained their thinking in Spanish. Of fundamental importance in these small-group conversations was the teacher's extending and supporting questions that helped students further refine their ideas. At the same time, these discussions gave students a sense of agency and confidence as problem solvers who were about to share their thinking in a whole-group discussion.

Accepting and Encouraging Students to Draw on Multiple Linguistic and Nonlinguistic Resources

Drawing on multiple linguistic and nonlinguistic resources to articulate their thinking enhanced the students' ability to communicate their reasoning (Dominguez 2005) and helped other students make sense of and comprehend their strategies. Students used an assortment of resources, including drawings, diagrams, gestures, objects, and interjections of English

Table 1.2
Best Practices That Support ELL Participation

Best Practice	How It Supports Participation of ELLs
Creating opportunities for students to explain and clarify their thinking in a small group	Practicing roles related to solving problems and sharing mathematical thinking in small groups enhanced ELLs' contributions to large-group discussions. Students benefit from small-group interactions that help them clarify and prepare to share their ideas. In addition, small groups afford opportunities to build on mathematical ideas generated in previous group discussions.
Accepting and encouraging students to draw on multiple linguistic and nonlinguistic resources	Drawing on multiple linguistic and nonlinguistic resources expands students' opportunities to articulate their thinking and increases the likelihood that those ideas will be understandable and that other students will adopt them. These resources can include drawings, diagrams, gestures, objects, and code switching between languages.
Teacher discourse moves: Clarifying and reenacting ideas in the public space	Teacher discourse moves highlighted and clarified the ideas and strategies of ELLs during whole-group discussions. Such strategies include pushing for details, making it more likely that other students can make sense of, or take up, the idea. In addition, the teacher can invite two students into a conversation with each other to compare their strategies and thinking.
Providing opportunities to solve related mathematics tasks	Opportunities to work on mathematically related tasks afford students opportunities to build on ideas and strategies that other students have shared in previous discussions.

into their Spanish oral description (or vice versa), to explain their thinking in discussions. The use of nonlinguistic resources supplemented an oral explanation, which might not have otherwise been as clear or understandable. This nonlinguistic aspect of whole-group discussions benefited all students, in that ELL students were able to understand strategies presented in their nondominant language and other students were able to understand strategies presented by ELLs.

Teacher Discourse Moves: Clarifying and Reenacting Ideas in the Public Space

Essential to ELLs' learning from, and contributing to, mathematics discussions were the teacher discourse moves that highlighted and clarified the strategies and thinking of ELLs during whole-group discussions.

Essential to ELLs' learning from, and contributing to, mathematics discussions were the teacher discourse moves that highlighted and clarified the strategies and thinking of ELLs during whole-group discussions.

11

Instead of simply asking students to share their thinking, teachers followed up with questions designed to help all students make sense of the ideas that students shared. For example, in one essential move that the researchers called *push for details,* the teacher asked questions or made remarks to help students more clearly explain their ideas or strategies when students might not have otherwise easily understood all the steps or thinking processes. One illustration of this move might entail the teacher's and students' working through a series of "how" or "why" questions to break down the strategy that the student used. The teacher then expected other students to comment on strategies just presented or to ask specific questions about why the presenter solved a problem in a specific manner.

Another important discourse move was inviting two or more students into a conversation about the strategies that they had just presented. The teachers conscientiously selected different students' strategies and invited students to make connections or claims about the thinking and reasoning of the authors of those strategies. For example, when students solved equal-sharing tasks, they often arrived at different answers that were actually equivalent fractions (the researchers carefully chose numbers to elicit multiple equivalent answers). The teachers posted these strategies side by side and asked students to compare the solutions and decide whether the answers were similar or different. Discourse moves such as these facilitated opportunities for students to make sense of strategies presented.

Providing Opportunities to Solve Related Mathematics Tasks

Finally, opportunities to work on related mathematical tasks afforded students the possibility of building on ideas and strategies that other students had shared in previous discussions. After practicing problem solving in the small group, presenting ideas and strategies by using multiple formats, and listening to ideas clarified and reenacted in whole-group settings, students benefited from solving tasks in which they could use ideas that they had just encountered. For example, from the second equal-sharing problem in table 1.1, a student may have solved the first two parts of the problem without realizing that a halving or doubling relationship existed between the quantities in the problem. After whole-group discussion and the opportunity to hear how other students solved this problem, students benefited from solving the third part of the problem, which extends the halving and doubling concept even further. In analyzing the strategies that ELL students tried after whole-group discussions, the researchers found that related tasks afforded an opportunity to continue to build on ideas presented in the public space.

A Profile of ELL Participation

Central to the researchers' philosophy of teaching was a view of ELL students as capable doers of mathematics. Throughout the ten-week-long teaching experiment, ELLs participated in, contributed to, and learned

Opportunities to work on related mathematical tasks afforded students the possibility of building on ideas and strategies that other students had shared in previous discussions.

from mathematical discussions; and other students used the ideas that ELL students presented. The following two vignettes illustrate the previously described instructional practices.

Vignette 1: Sixteen Children Sharing Twelve Pizzas

Alberto, a fifth grader classified as having medium English-language proficiency (on a scale of low, medium, and high English proficiency) and who had a history of low achievement in mathematics, worked on the following problem:

> Sixteen children want to share 12 pizzas so that they all receive the same amount. How much pizza will each child receive?

Alberto was working at his small-group table with a pile of Unifix cubes in front of him when his teacher, Mrs. J., came over to his side and asked, "What have you got?" Alberto shared his strategy, in which he paired two orange cubes (people) and distributed one "pizza," a green cube, to each pair. He described the sharing as "I slice it, so it's two." He continued to distribute one green cube to each pair until four pizzas remained. He then placed two orange pairs next to each other and distributed one leftover pizza to each group of four (see fig. 1.1). When Alberto finished, he had four groups of four orange cubes (people) sharing three green cubes (pizza).

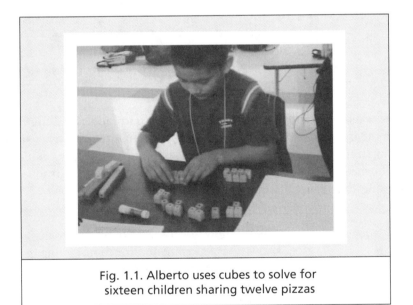

Fig. 1.1. Alberto uses cubes to solve for sixteen children sharing twelve pizzas

Mrs. J.:	OK, now, what does it mean when you have three pizzas for four people?
A:	I cut this one in half and give one to him. *(Alberto makes a slicing motion over the cube while he explains.)* And remember when I had one pizza and two people, each one gets a half.

Mrs. J.:   OK.

A: I cut this one, I take away one of these. I cut this one into *(pause)* in one-half. And give it to … *(pause)* I cut it in four.

Alberto continued to explain that he would give two of the four pieces to each pair in a group, essentially giving one-half and one-fourth to each person. His teacher then invited him to record his strategy on paper (see fig. 1.2).

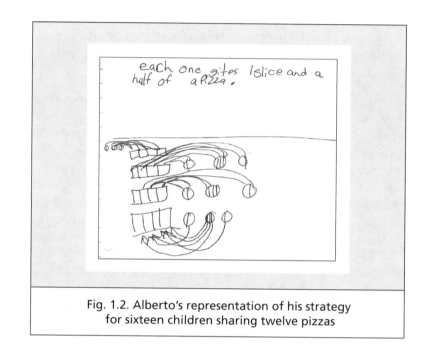

Fig. 1.2. Alberto's representation of his strategy for sixteen children sharing twelve pizzas

The teacher walked around to all the groups and then called the class back to the front of the room for whole-group discussion. The teacher sat in a chair at the front of the room, and the students sat on the carpet in front of her. After two students had shared their strategies, the teacher asked Alberto to share his strategy. She was holding his notebook.

Mrs. J.:   Alberto, how do you want to tell this? Oh, I know what I'm going to do. I'm just going to hold this picture up. *(To class)* OK, scoot up and come see his picture. *(The students move forward.)*

Mrs. J.:   I wanted to share this one of Alberto's. This one—I don't think I'm doing a good job on this discussion, because I'm doing too much talking. You all need to be asking these questions. This is Holly's Pizza Hut. Sixteen people are sharing twelve pizzas. Alberto, tell us how you got this answer. *(Alberto stands next to the teacher.)*

A: Um. I had sixteen—um. Wait. (*He looks at the notebook.*) I had twelve pizzas and sixteen kids. I put them in line. And then I put one of the cubes in front of two people. And then I put them all, and I had four left over.

Mrs. J.: OK, hold on. I'm going to draw a picture of what that looked like. I think I can have that. He did two; these were two people and one pizza. And he kept ...

A: I had four, four left over. (*He holds up four fingers. The teacher draws eight pairs of squares on the chalkboard. She draws a circle underneath each one to represent the pizzas.*) So now, so then, I had four left over. Four pizzas left over. (*The teacher draws the four pizzas.*) And I knew that I had groups, so I put them in fours.

Mrs. J.: OK, so you took this one and put it here.

A: I put these two together (*points to two pairs of cubes*), these two together, so I could make four. And I connected, um ... um ... I had four groups. (*The teacher draws lines between two pairs of cubes to represent a connection.*) And I connected, um, more pizza, another pizza to another group. So that would give me three. (*The teacher draws another pizza between two pairs of cubes, as shown in fig. 1.3.*) And I make this halves. And I would cut the third one into four pieces.

Fig. 1.3. During whole-group discussion, the teacher records Alberto's ratio strategy for sixteen children sharing twelve pizzas.

Mrs. J.: Yes, and his picture shows that. So he had four kids and three pizzas in his final ...

A:	I cut this in half, and then I cut this in three pieces.
Mrs. J.:	Three lines, but that made how many pieces?
A:	Four.
Mrs. J.:	OK. So you cut that in half *(points to the pizza between a pair of cubes)*, and then you made three lines on here. *(Teacher draws lines on third pizza for group of four cubes.)*
A:	Then I give this one to him, this one to him, and that one to him. And the last one to him. *(He points to the pizza slices and the respective cubes representing children.)*

The teacher helped Alberto refine his answer by quantifying the amount of pizza that each child received as one-half of a pizza and one-fourth of a pizza. She then asked the students, "Did anybody else get that?" A couple of students raised their hands; and one student, Ramón, said he got four-sixteenths instead of one-fourth. The discussion continued with Ramón describing his solution to the problem.

Best Practices for This Vignette

This vignette illustrates how one student, Alberto, participated in a whole-group discussion and shared his idea with other students. Alberto initially used only the Unifix cubes as a means to solve equal-sharing problems. The opportunities to solve and explain problems in the small group were instrumental to his successful explanation in a whole-group setting. The support and the questioning during small-group interaction helped him make sense of the problem and explain it in a way that made sense to him. An important point to note is that Alberto had difficulty naming the fractional pieces both in his small-group discussion and in the whole-group discussion. However, because he presented his strategy in multiple formats (with cubes, his drawing in the notebook, and the teacher's diagram on the chalkboard), and because the process of solving the problem was the focus of the conversation, not just the answer, other students were able to understand his answer.

The teacher played an important role in bringing Alberto's idea to the attention of the group and in clarifying his oral explanation with a reenactment by drawing on the chalkboard. In fact, the teacher was able to continue the discussion after Alberto shared his strategy to help students debate the connection between four-sixteenths and one-fourth. Moreover, other students appropriated Alberto's idea, made sense of it, and applied it to future problems. For example, the following day, the students were assigned a related problem that involved twelve penguins sharing nine pineapple cakes. During the small-group exploration time, the teacher noticed that Amalia had created a drawing in which she had divided the twelve penguins into three groups of four and had distributed three cakes to each group. When the teacher asked Amalia to share her thinking, she replied,

"It's because last week, somebody, like, did that.... I think it was Alberto.... I think he was dividing pizzas into groups. And that's how I put them into groups."

This vignette illustrates one way in which an ELL student can contribute to a discussion and other students can benefit from the ELL student's contributions. In the following vignette, an ELL student learned from a discussion by making sense of the strategies that other students had presented.

Vignette 2: Eliciting Relational Thinking

Half the students were sitting around two tables working on problems while the other half were completing another activity. The group sitting around the table was solving the following problem:

> Susana and Rose are out shopping for limes to make limeade. They agree to buy the same number of limes. Susana bought 6 bags of limes with 8 limes in each bag. Rose found bags with 4 limes in a bag. How many bags does she need to buy to have the same number of limes as Susana?

Bety, an English-language learner with medium proficiency, drew a picture of six squares as bags of eight limes and then drew two squares as bags of four limes (see fig. 1.4). She realized that a bag of four is half a bag of eight and that Rose would need to buy two bags of four for every one of Susana's bags of eight. The teacher asked Bety to explain her strategy.

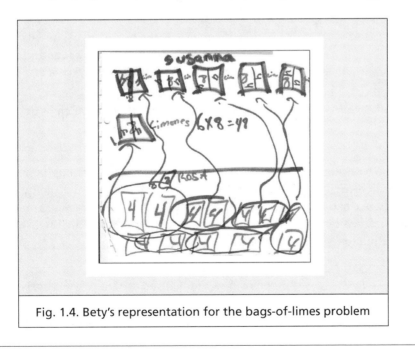

Fig. 1.4. Bety's representation for the bags-of-limes problem

B: So it would be … I know that if you count, to get, like this … *(circles two boxes of four).* This,

	it would be eight. It's like one box of eight *(draws small box above two boxes of four, writes the number 8; draws line connecting the two boxes of four with one box of eight).* It would be like one box of eight. And then this, it would be like another box. Like, another box.
Ms. T.:	Uh-huh.
B:	This one, it would be another box. And then this one, it would be another box. And then this one, it would be another box. And then this one would be the last box *(continues to circle boxes of four in groups of two and links each pair to a box of eight).* So I put twelve, and then … I put twelve, and then four in each one. *(See fig. 1.4.)*
Ms. T.:	Can we show everybody your picture? *(Bety nods.)* Look at how she figured out the number of boxes. *(Holds up Bety's picture for the group to see.)* I'm going to hold it up so they can see it, versus making you redraw this again. She figured out that there, there's eight *(points to boxes of eight).* The bags come with eight limes. So she said she'd need four and four, she'd need two of these *(points to two boxes of four)* to make a box *(points to box of eight).* And then these two would make another box.…
B:	It's like if you cut it [the box of eight] in half, and then you put a four and then a four and it will equal eight *(draws line to cut box of eight in half, writes four in each half).*
Ms. T.:	Ahhh! It's like if you cut that bag of eight in half.

The teacher asked other students how many bags Bety bought, and one student, Ernesto, offered an invalid interpretation of her strategy. He thought she had found her answer of twelve by adding eight plus four. The teacher asked Bety to clarify her strategy one more time. (The English translation for spoken Spanish follows each statement.)

Ms. T.:	Tell us how you figured out there were twelve of them then. How did you know?
B:	Because, because, can I say it in Spanish and English?
Ms. T.:	Yeah.
B:	Porque yo sabía que, si lo ponieramos [sic] en

um, en like *(traces a line, to divide box of eight limes in half)*. Por que cuatro más cuatro son ocho *(points to two boxes of four, below, and then to box of eight)*. So yo, puse … Pues yo lo estaba imaginando en mi mente, que poniéndolos así, a la mitad cada uno *(traces line over each box of eight, to show how she imagined cutting each in half)*.

(Because I knew that if we put it in, like … Because four plus four is eight. So I put … Well, I was imagining it in my mind, putting them like this, each one in half.)

Ms. T.:	Uh-huh.
B:	Después, cuatro más cuatro son ocho *(points to a box of eight divided in half with four in each half)*. Entonces yo agarré doce, porque si tú cuentas doce aqui, dos, cuatro, seis, ocho, diez, doce *(counts two in each box of eight)*.
	(Then four plus four is eight. And then I got twelve, because if you count two here, two, four, six, eight, ten, twelve.)
Ms. T.:	Who understands what Bety did? ¿Quién entiende lo que hizo Bety? *(Marco raises his hand.)*
Ms. T.:	Marco, what did she do?
M:	Cada ocho valía por dos *(holds up two fingers)*.
	(Each [bag of eight] was worth two.)
Ms. T.:	Every bag was worth two; very nice, Marco. (See fig. 1.5.)

Later, the teacher noted that Adán, another ELL student in the group, was using Bety's strategy to solve the problem. He had been using nonrelational thinking to solve the problem but finally used the method described in the whole-group discussion.

The next problem that the teacher gave the students was the following:

This time, Susana bought 16 bags of limes, with 12 limes in each bag. Rose needs to know how many bags of 6 limes to buy so that she has the same amount.

Students who had previously solved the problem correctly, but without using relational thinking, appropriated Bety's representation and used it to find that a bag of twelve limes is equivalent to two bags of six limes. In the whole-group discussion, the teacher asked Ernesto to explain his strategy

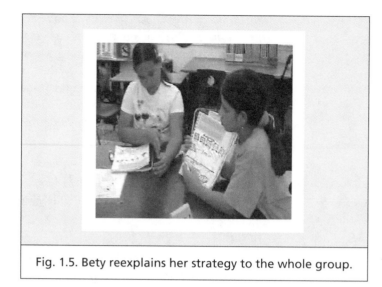

Fig. 1.5. Bety reexplains her strategy to the whole group.

(which was relational) and specifically asked him how he knew how many bags of six limes Susana would have to buy.

E:	Porque — seis por dos son doce. Y la mitad de doce son seis.
	(Because ... six times two is twelve. And half of twelve is six.)
Ms. T.:	Uh-huh.
E:	Por eso es lo doble.
	(That's why it's double.)
	(Adán chimes in.)
A:	Yes.
Ms. T.:	How do you know? Tell me.
A.:	Porque seis más seis es doce. Es como ... la mitad de, de doce.
	(Because six plus six is twelve. It's like ... half of twelve.)
A:	Como si es, seis times dos is doce.
	(It's like, six times two is twelve.)
Ms. T.:	Son doce. ¿Entonces cuántas bolsas tengo que comprar?
	(Then how many bags do I have to buy?)
E:	Treinta y dos, porque dieciséis por dos son treinta y dos. En el doce, van a ser dieciséis, dieciséis bolsas, las que van a comprar. Y aqui como lo doble también. Treinta y dos.
	(Thirty-two, because sixteen times two is thirty-two. With the twelve, it's going to be sixteen

bags that they're going to buy. And here it's like the double. Thirty-two.)

Best Practices for This Vignette

The students had an opportunity to work on the problems on their own while the teacher walked around the table asking them questions that extended and supported their thinking before the whole-group discussion. Most of the students had solved this problem by using multiplication and had not noticed the relationship between the numbers. Bety communicated her idea by using multiple resources, including drawings and diagrams; oral explanation accompanied by gestures and a reenactment of her strategy; and two languages (English and Spanish). In revoicing and emphasizing Bety's strategy and diagram, the teacher gave students access to another way of thinking about relational ideas. Revoicing serves not only to repeat or rephrase a student's idea but also to position an idea as worthy of consideration, and it can help make an unclear idea potentially more accessible to all students. Throughout the vignette, the teacher revoiced the students' ideas and asked them to explain their thinking and reasoning. In addition, she called on students to explain Bety's thinking and make connections between her drawing and her answers.

In calling attention to Bety's generative drawing, the teacher helped make Bety's thinking available so that other students could learn from it. Not only did Adán attempt to solve the problem in the same manner, but other ELL students solved similar tasks with a halving-doubling strategy in a subsequent session. Students were able to create their own strategies from the generative representation whose important features the teacher's questioning had highlighted. Ernesto further voiced his finding that half as many limes would require doubling the number of bags. In sum, this vignette illustrates how an ELL student participated in a whole-group discussion and how the best practices then helped other ELL students make sense of and then appropriate the ideas presented.

> Revoicing serves not only to repeat or rephrase a student's idea but also to position an idea as worthy of consideration, and it can help make an unclear idea potentially more accessible to all students.

Concluding Remarks

This article presents possible ways for teachers not only to improve discussions for all students but also to treat linguistic differences as a resource rather than as an impediment to teaching mathematics. The findings from this teaching experiment suggest that the practices of opportunities to work in a small group, using multiple linguistic and nonlinguistic resources to explain thinking, teacher discourse moves, and related mathematical tasks are some of the resources that can enhance ELLs' participation in whole-group discussion. Although the practices described do not encompass all the positive practices that teachers can implement in their classrooms, they provide a stepping-stone toward beginning to include ELL students in discussions in which they might otherwise not be heard. However, further research should explore the challenges and dilemmas that teachers face when they try to implement student-centered discussion in their linguistically diverse classrooms. As we continue to realize that much of what we understand about learning mathematics is inseparable from learning to participate in mathematical discussions, we continue to strive for classrooms in which ELLs are learning from, and contributing to, those discussions.

REFERENCES

Cobb, Paul, Terry Wood, and Erna Yackel. "Discourse, Mathematical Thinking, and Classroom Practice." In *Contexts for Learning: Sociocultural Dynamics in Children's Development,* edited by Ellice A. Forman, Norris Minick, and C. Addison Stone, pp. 91–119. New York: Oxford University Press, 1993.

Dominguez, Higinio. "Bilingual Students' Articulation and Gesticulation of Mathematical Knowledge during Problem Solving." *Bilingual Research Journal* 29 (Summer 2005): 269–93.

Empson, Susan B., Debra Junk, Higinio Dominguez, and Erin Turner. "Fractions as the Coordination of Multiplicatively Related Quantities: A Cross-Sectional Study of Children's Thinking." *Educational Studies in Mathematics* 63 (September 2006): 1–27.

Empson, Susan B., and Erin Turner. "The Emergence of Multiplicative Thinking in Children's Solutions to Paper Folding Tasks." *Journal of Mathematical Behavior* 25 (January 2006): 46–56.

Goffman, Erving. *Forms of Talk.* Philadelphia: University of Pennsylvania Press, 1981.

National Council of Teachers of Mathematics (NCTM). *Principles and Standards for School Mathematics.* Reston, Va.: NCTM, 2000.

O'Connor, Mary Catherine. "Can Any Fraction Be Turned into a Decimal? A Case Study of Mathematical Group Discussion." *Educational Studies in Mathematics* 46 (March 2001): 143–85.

Silver, Edward, Hala Ghousseini, Dana Gosen, Charalambos Charalambous, and Beatriz T. Font Strawhun. "Moving from Rhetoric to Praxis: Issues Faced by Teachers in Having Students Consider Multiple Solutions for Problems in the Mathematics Classroom." *Journal of Mathematical Behavior* 24 (January 2005): 287–301.

Strizek, Gregory A., Jayme L. Pittsonberger, Kate E. Riordan, Deanna M. Lyter, and Greg F. Oriofsky. *Characteristics of Schools, Districts, Teachers, Principals, and School Libraries in the United States: 2003–04 Schools and Staffing Survey.* No. NCES 2006-313 revised. Washington, D.C.: U.S. Government Printing Office, 2006.

2

"Fíjense amorcitos, les voy a contar una historia": The Power of Story to Support Solving and Discussing Mathematical Problems among Latino and Latina Kindergarten Students

Erin E. Turner
Sylvia Celedón-Pattichis
Mary Marshall
Alan Tennison

A CENTRAL tenet of *Principles and Standards for School Mathematics* (NCTM 2000) is that students at all levels, even young children, should participate in solving problems and explaining and justifying their mathematical thinking (NCTM [2000]; see also Cobb, Wood, and Yackel [1993]; Lampert [2001]). Previous research has demonstrated that children as young as kindergarten (Carpenter et al. 1993; Outhred and Sardelich 2005) and first grade (Secada 1991; Villaseñor and Kepner 1993) can solve a broad range of mathematical problems, often by modeling the quantities and relationships involved (see also Carpenter et al. [1999]). For example, a five-year-old might solve a simple multiplication problem, such as "Sara had three pockets. She put two pennies in each pocket. How many pennies does she have in all?" by drawing three pockets, placing two counters (pennies) in each of the pockets, and then counting all the counters to determine that she has six pennies altogether. Carpenter and his colleagues (1993) found that kindergarteners who had repeated opportunities to solve a variety of basic word problems demonstrated remarkable success on an end-of-the-year assessment. Almost half of the seventy students interviewed used valid strategies on all the word problems, which included multiplication, division, and multistep problems; and most students were successful on very basic problem types (e.g., subtraction).

Although we know that young children are capable of solving problems and engaging in mathematical reasoning (Tang and Ginsburg 1999), we know less about how early primary-grade teachers support problem solving and mathematical discussion, particularly in culturally and linguistically diverse classrooms, as well as in classrooms in which students have a wide range of prior mathematical experiences. Teachers may worry

> **Although we know that young children are capable of solving problems and engaging in mathematical reasoning (Tang and Ginsburg 1999), we know less about how early primary-grade teachers support problem solving and mathematical discussion, particularly in culturally and linguistically diverse classrooms.**

The research reported here was partially supported by NSF grant number ESI-0424983 to CEMELA, The Center for the Mathematics Education of Latinos. Any opinions, findings, and recommendations expressed here are those of the authors and do not necessarily reflect the views of the National Science Foundation.

that until young children have mastered certain basic skills (e.g., counting, recognizing numbers, and comparing sets), they may struggle to solve problems and explain their reasoning. Another concern is that if students are learning the language of instruction, as with many children who are English language learners (ELLs), such language-intensive activities as interpreting, solving, and discussing word problems in one's second language may be too challenging (Iddings 2005).

Overview of Classroom Study

The goals of this study were to document the development of problem solving among Latino and Latina kindergarten students and to identify specific instructional practices that teachers used to help students solve problems and communicate their mathematical thinking. Specifically, this article describes practices that draw on students' cultural and linguistic knowledge and experiences (e.g., González, Moll, and Amanti 2005). We focused on two kindergarten classrooms, both in schools with predominantly Latino and Latina student populations (87 percent and 72 percent), in which more than 90 percent of the students qualified for free or reduced-price lunch. In Ms. Arenas's[1] classroom, all students were native Spanish speakers with varying degrees of English language proficiency. Ms. Arenas, also a native Spanish speaker, followed a bilingual model of instruction. Each morning, students worked in their native language on reading, writing, and mathematics activities. During the afternoon, students participated in integrated projects and additional literacy-related tasks in English. Ms. Field, who had training in English as a second language (ESL) strategies, taught mathematics in English. Half of Ms. Field's students were ELLs, and the rest were native English speakers.

> **The goals of this study were to document the development of problem solving among Latino and Latina kindergarten students and to identify specific instructional practices that teachers used to help students solve problems and communicate their mathematical thinking.**

We selected these two classrooms because both teachers had participated in Cognitively Guided Instruction (CGI), a summer professional development workshop that focused on the development of young children's mathematical thinking about basic operations (see Carpenter et al. [1999]), and they were interested in implementing problem-solving lessons with their students. We visited each classroom biweekly to videotape lessons. At the beginning of the year, we selected sixteen students (eight from each class) who represented a range of achievement levels to participate in a problem-solving interview assessment (Ginsburg et al. 1983). This preassessment included both counting and problem-solving tasks (e.g., join, separate, multiplication, and division word problems). The researchers presented all problems orally, and students had access to multiple problem-solving tools (counters, cubes, paper, and pencils). At the end of the year, we administered a similar postassessment that included a broader range of problems. We asked students to explain their reasoning for each problem.

In the sections that follow, we present a brief overview of the preassessment results and then describe typical problem-solving mathematics lessons in each of the classrooms. We then present detailed classroom examples to illustrate specific instructional strategies that teachers used

---

1. All names are pseudonyms.

to help all students make sense of and solve problems and explain their mathematical reasoning. We conclude with a discussion of students' performance on the postassessment to demonstrate the impact of these instructional strategies on students' learning.

Beginning-of-the-Year Problem-Solving Assessments

As is typical of many kindergarten classrooms, the children began the school year with a range of mathematical experiences and proficiencies. Most of the students could count a small set of objects (three to eight items) and recognize some numerals from 1 to 10, as measured by a Kindergarten Developmental Progress Record that the district administered. However, at the beginning of the year, several students could not count past two or three and did not demonstrate one-to-one correspondence, even with numbers under five. As Ms. Arenas noted, "My students, some of them didn't recognize any of the numbers, higher than three they probably didn't know. Some of them counted, one, two, [and then] one hundred! They didn't know how to count, so I had to develop that little by little at the same time that I was doing [problem solving]." In problem solving, slightly less than half ($n = 7$) of the sixteen students who participated in the preassessment successfully solved a basic addition problem (six jelly beans plus three more), and slightly more than half ($n = 10$) solved a basic subtraction problem (five pennies take away two).

Other problems on the preassessment—such as the multiplication, division, and comparison problems—were significantly more difficult; only two or three of the sixteen children used valid solution strategies for these problems. As is typical of young children, students provided short and often vague descriptions of their thinking, using such phrases as "I just knew it" and "I counted" to justify their answers. We include this overview to establish that students reflected a typical range of understanding, and if anything, that some students began the year with less-developed counting skills than kindergarten teachers might expect.

Classroom Learning Context

Ms. Arenas and Ms. Field drew on a variety of instructional formats in their problem-solving lessons. Although the researchers did not provide Ms. Arenas and Ms. Field with specific guidelines for instruction, the researchers encouraged the teachers to use information about children's thinking and about basic problem structures (e.g., different types of addition and subtraction problems) to plan and adapt problem-solving tasks. Common to each of their lessons was that the teacher orally presented a word problem to students and then encouraged students to solve the problem in ways that made sense to them. Table 2.1 gives examples of problems that the teachers presented. The students often used such concrete materials as counters and cubes or drew pictures on small whiteboards to support their reasoning (fig. 2.1 and fig. 2.2). After most students had solved a problem, the teachers facilitated group discussion in which several students shared their strategies.

The teacher orally presented a word problem to students and then encouraged students to solve the problem in ways that made sense to them.

Table 2.1
Examples of "Mathematical Stories" That Ms. Arenas and Ms. Field Presented to Their Students

Problem Type		"Mathematical Story"
Join (result unknown)	a.	Ms. Arenas went to the market because she had to buy oranges. She got 4 oranges and put them in her basket, and then her son José got another 4 oranges, and he put those in the basket too. How many oranges did they have in the basket?
Join (change unknown)	b.	Marian goes to the store, and she wants to buy a bag of candies; but the bag of candies costs 8 dollars, and she only has 5 dollars. How many more dollars does she need?
Multiplication	c.	You and your two best friends are playing at recess, and you find some pennies outside on the playground. You each find 2 pennies and you each put the pennies in your pocket. How many pennies did you find altogether?
Separate (result unknown)	d.	Let's say that Alfredo had 9 marbles, and then he gave 4 marbles to Cesar. How many marbles does he have left?
Division (partitive)	e.	Ms. Arenas has 15 little puppies, and she wants to give them to Paolo, Daniel, and Mónica. What can she do so that they each get the same number? How many should she give to each of them?

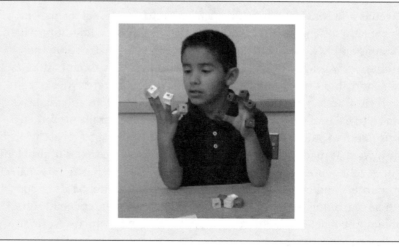

Fig. 2.1. Orlando uses cubes to solve a multiplication problem.

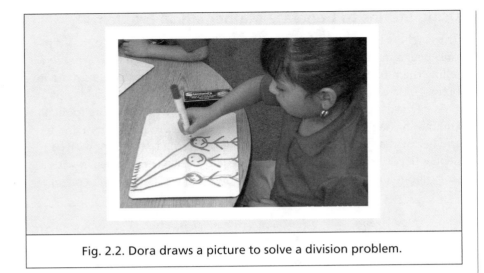

Fig. 2.2. Dora draws a picture to solve a division problem.

In some instances, particularly early in the year, the teachers worked on problem solving with one small group of students at a time while other students participated in center activities. Typically, the teachers grouped students heterogeneously, although sometimes the teacher grouped specific students because she believed that they would benefit from working collaboratively on a particular type of problem. On other occasions, the teachers presented the entire class with a problem, and students worked individually or with a partner to generate a solution. Both teachers also used center activities that involved building and counting sets to support students' number sense and counting skills. The teachers did not wait until students had mastered a set of basic skills to begin problem-solving lessons. Instead, they introduced problem solving at the very beginning of the year and used contextual problems "to strengthen students' counting ... numerical skills and reasoning" (interview with Ms. Arenas).

Powerful Instructional Strategy: The Use of Story

As the researchers analyzed lessons from each classroom, they identified a number of instructional strategies that the teachers used to support students' learning. Although a discussion of all strategies is beyond the scope of this article, the focus here is on a particular feature of the lessons that was especially generative: the use of story as a way to organize problem-solving sessions and scaffold kindergarten students' understanding while they solved and discussed basic word problems. Using children's stories to generate mathematical problems and to connect students' cultural knowledge and experiences with their mathematical activity has been documented in prior research (Lo Cicero, Fuson, and Allexsaht-Snider 1999; Lo Cicero, De La Cruz, and Fuson 1999). Our work extends previous research by contributing a detailed analysis of how the use of stories supports the learning of Latino and Latina kindergarten students, in particular, how it supports students while they learn to make sense of, represent, and explain their thinking about mathematical problems.

The teachers did not wait until students had mastered a set of basic skills to begin problem-solving lessons. Instead, they introduced problem solving at the very beginning of the year and used contextual problems "to strengthen students' counting ... numerical skills and reasoning."

Using children's stories to generate mathematical problems and to connect students' cultural knowledge and experiences with their mathematical activity has been documented in prior research (Lo Cicero, Fuson, and Allexsaht-Snider 1999; Lo Cicero, De La Cruz, and Fuson 1999).

Using Stories to Generate Mathematical Problems

The teachers in this study used stories in different ways. Ms. Arenas typically began mathematics lessons by gathering students on the carpet and telling them to listen carefully because she was about to share a story with them. Her stories drew on students' shared experiences (e.g., field trips and class parties), events and activities in the community (e.g., going to the fair and purchasing fruit at the local market; see table 2.1, problems a and b), and her own experiences outside school (e.g., going to the park with her nephew). For example, during a lesson early in the year, she began with a story about a woman who lived directly behind the school and her cats.

Ms. Arenas:	Fíjense, mis niños, fíjense que la señora, aquí atrás de la escuela, que vive aquí atrás. ...
	(Listen, my dear children, you know the woman, the woman here behind the school, that lives right here in the back [of the school].)
Students:	¡Sí! *(nodding heads, indicating that they know the woman to whom she is referring)*
Ms. Arenas:	La señora tenía tres gatos. *(The woman had three cats.)*
Students:	¿¡Tres gatos!? *(Three cats?)*
Ms. Arenas:	Sí, pero luego, su hija le regaló otros tres. Y luego, todos los gatos vienen a jugar aquí a la escuela. ¿Cuántos vendrán? ¿Cuántos gatos?
	(Yes, but then, her daughter gave her another three. And then, all the cats came here to play at the school. How many came? How many cats?)
Student:	Seis!
Ms. Arenas:	Escuchen, la señora tenía tres gatos, y luego su hija le regaló otros tres, ¿cuántos tendrá ahora? Piensen, y ahora me van a decir.
	(Listen, the woman had three cats, and then her daughter gave her another three; how many would she have? Think about it, and then you are going to tell me.)

Later in the same lesson, Ms. Arenas presented another story about going to the pet store and purchasing six puppies and then giving several of the puppies away. She included rich contextual information, including such details as what the puppies looked like or how her nephew played with the puppies at the park. Another distinctive feature of the stories that Ms. Arenas told was that she presented them in a very informal, conversational manner. That is, Ms. Arenas framed her talk as telling a story and not as presenting a mathematics problem. Students responded accordingly, making comments, adding their own details, and asking questions.

Ms. Field also told stories about students and class activities to frame mathematical problems. She used such events as children's finding pennies on the playground and a game of marbles between two students to structure multiplication and subtraction problems, respectively (table 2.1, problems c and d). In addition, Ms. Field used conversations about books as contexts for generating mathematical problems. For example, during a lesson in the spring, Ms. Field shared a book about honeybees with her students. She read small portions of the book, shared pictures of beehives, and even passed around a piece of honeycomb for students to examine. Ms. Field used the book to elicit a conversation about honeybees; and throughout the conversation, students shared their personal experiences and existing knowledge.

At one point, Bernardo noted that the bees' honeycomb was the same shape as the hexagon pattern block that students often used to create geometric designs (see fig. 2.3). This realization sparked a discussion of how many sides a hexagon has and ultimately, the multiplication problem "Then how many sides would three hexagons have?" Although Ms. Field may have anticipated this mathematical connection, the multiplication problem arose spontaneously as students talked, told stories, and asked questions about honeybees. Of significance is that in addition to using students' home and school experiences as contexts for mathematical problems, Ms. Field used a story and an informal conversation about honeybees to create a new, shared experience (i.e., examining the geometry of a honeycomb) that then generated a series of problems for students to solve.

Fig. 2.3. Bernardo makes a connection between
a honeycomb and hexagons.

The previous examples provide a sense of how Ms. Arenas and Ms. Field used stories to generate mathematical problems in their kindergarten classrooms. The following series of classroom episodes describe how this instructional practice supported students while they made sense of, represented, solved, and communicated their reasoning about a variety of problems.

Episode 1. Teachers Use Stories to Draw on Students' Funds of Knowledge—Familiar Ways of Talking, Cultural Experiences, and Activities

Ms. Arenas and Ms. Field shared mathematical stories with their students in an informal, conversational manner. At times, the teachers and the children coconstructed the stories while students made such decisions as how many children would share a box of twelve cookies or how much money a toy airplane should cost. For example, during a lesson in November, Ms. Arenas and her students constructed the following story about shopping at the local produce market.

Ms. Arenas:	El otro día, fui al mercado con mi hijo Eduardo, ¿Y qué creen que compramos?
	(The other day, I went to the market with my son Eduardo, and what do you think we bought?)
Student:	¡Naranjas! ¡Naranjas?
	(Oranges! Oranges!)
Ms. Arenas:	Muy bien. Yo agarré una bolsa y metí seis naranjas en la bolsa. Y luego, Eduardo fue por más naranjas. ¿Cuántas creen que él agarró?
	(OK, I got a bag and put six oranges in the bag. And then, Eduardo went to get more oranges. How many do you think he got?)
Students:	Seis! Cuatro! Metió seis más!
	(Six! Four! He put in six more!)
Ms. Arenas:	Muy bien, metió seis más. Asi que yo puse seis naranjas en la bolsa y luego Eduardo metió seis más. ¿Cuántas naranjas están en la bolsa?
	(OK, he put in six more. So I put six oranges in the bag, and Eduardo put in six more. How many oranges are in the bag?)

The fact that the teachers and students generated mathematical problems from authentic conversations is important, because the teachers drew on ways of talking and negotiating meaning that were familiar to children. That is, all children have experience telling and listening to stories and using stories to communicate meaning, a practice that is particularly prevalent in Latino families (Delgado-Gaitan 1987; Villenas and Moreno 2001). Teachers also drew on students' cultural knowledge and experiences by creating stories that reflected familiar situations. As Ms. Arenas noted,

> [Children] bring rich experiences in going to the market with their parents. ... The market experience, the open market

The fact that the teachers and students generated mathematical problems from authentic conversations is important, because the teachers drew on ways of talking and negotiating meaning that were familiar to children.

experience, [experiences] with money and how much do you pay for this or that. ... They have other cultural experiences, too. A lot of times they plant with their parents, and even counting the seeds or transferring the seeds is mathematics.

When teachers draw on language and ways of talking that are familiar to children and use relevant contexts to introduce new ideas (for example, using a story about planting seeds to frame a multiplication problem), this teaching practice supports students' understanding (Dalton 1998).

Episode 2. Teachers Use Stories to Help Students Represent Mathematical Relationships and Connect Multiple Representations

Teachers also used stories to support students while they learned to represent quantities and mathematical relationships in different ways (e.g., with objects, drawings, and symbols). The following episode from Ms. Field's classroom illustrates how the teacher continuously referred to the story to clarify the meaning of different representations.

Ms. Field:	OK, let's try a different one. You ready? OK, let's just say that Alberto had nine marbles, and he's playing marbles, and he gave four to Cesar. How many marbles does Alberto have left?

Students began to work on the problem, and Ms. Field talked with them about their strategies. Alberto held up nine fingers, and then lowered four, one at a time, to figure out how many marbles he had left. Iván drew nine circles on his whiteboard, crossed out four, and counted those that remained. After most students had solved the problem, Ms. Field asked Verónica to share her strategy.

Ms. Field:	Verónica?
Verónica:	Take four and it would be five.
Ms. Field:	Ah, draw that again, and show us. Let's look at Verónica's *(positions Verónica's whiteboard so that other students can see her work)*. So what did you draw first?
Verónica:	Nine *(points to nine circles that she has drawn)*.
Ms. Field:	And then what did you do?
Verónica:	Then I erased these ones *(points to four circles, and begins to erase them)*, and it would be five.
Ms. Field:	Go ahead, go ahead.
	(Verónica erases four of the nine circles that she has drawn on her whiteboard.)

31

Ms. Field:	(Ms. Field points to the circles that Verónica has erased.) So those are the ones that he gave to Cesar?
	(Verónica nods.)
Ms. Field:	And you have how many left?
Verónica:	Five.
Ms. Field:	And guess what, that's a takeaway, that's a minus (begins to write a number sentence on the whiteboard). It's nine, he started with nine marbles (writes the number 9, and then above the number draws nine circles). Then give away four marbles (she erases four of the circles), so I take away four (writes "– 4" next to the 9), that equals five. That's the number sentence! (She completes the number sentence by writing "= 5.")

In this example, we see how Ms. Field referred to the story both to clarify Verónica's pictorial representation (i.e., "So those [the circles she erased] are the ones that he gave to Cesar?") and to introduce a new representation, a number sentence, that students could use to model the problem. As she wrote the number sentence on the board, Ms. Field linked each element to a part of the story. For example, as she wrote "– 4" she reminded the students that Alberto gave away four marbles, which she also represented by erasing four of the nine circles that she had drawn (see fig. 2.4).

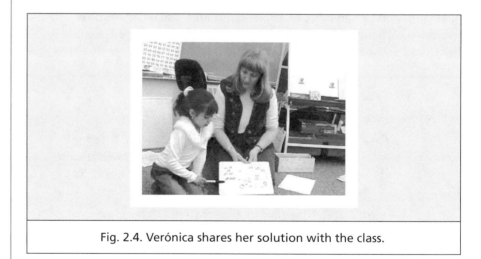

Fig. 2.4. Verónica shares her solution with the class.

The teachers used stories to help students make sense of different representations—those used by other students and those that the teacher introduced—and to connect multiple representations for a particular problem.

The teachers used stories to help students make sense of different representations—those used by other students and those that the teacher introduced—and to connect multiple representations for a particular problem. Consider the following example from a lesson in Ms. Arenas's classroom.

| *Ms. Arenas:* | OK, mis niños, ahora viene otra historia, fíjense. Oscar fue al parque, y vio cuatro gatos. Escuchen. Oscar fue al parque y vio cuatro gatos; ¿cuántas patas vio? Vio cuatro gatos! ¿Cuántas patas vio? Piensen. |
| | *(OK, dear children, here comes another story. Listen, Oscar went to the park, and he saw four cats. Listen. Oscar went to the park and he saw four cats; how many legs did he see? He saw four cats! How many legs did he see? Think about it.)* |

After students worked on the problem, Ms. Arenas asked several students to share their solutions with the group. Daniel came to the whiteboard first and drew four sets of four tally marks to show how he figured out that the four cats had sixteen legs (fig. 2.5). Ms. Arenas asked him about his drawing, and he explained that each group of four tally marks represented one cat. He then counted all the legs and said that there were sixteen legs altogether. Next Ms. Arenas invited other comments about the problem.

Fig. 2.5. Daniel uses tally marks to represent four cats with four legs each.

Ms. Arenas:	Muy bien. ¿Hay alguien que quisiera hacer algo más con este problema? ¿A ver Emilio?
	(Very good. Is there someone who would like to do something else with this problem? Let's see, Emilio?)
Emilio:	¡En números!
	(With numbers!)
Ms. Arenas:	¿Cómo lo vas a poner Emilio?
	(How are you going to put it, Emilio?)

Student:	Cuatro más cuatro más cuatro más cuatro!
	(Four plus four plus four plus four!)
	(Emilio goes up to the white board and writes 4 + 4 + ...)
Ms. Arenas:	Muy bien. Ahora, ¿cuántas patas hay ahí?
	(Very good. Now, how many legs are here?) *(points to the next group of four tally marks)*
	(Emilio continues writing + 4 + 4.)
Ms. Arenas:	Muy bien, ¿y ahora qué pones? ¿Es igual a cuántos? ¿Cuántos te habían dado?
	(Very good, and now what are you going to put, it's equal to how many? How many did you get?)
	(Emilio writes = 16.)
Ms. Arenas:	Mira como lo hizo Emilio, él puso cuatro patas de un gato *(points to four tallies, then to the number 4)*, más *(points to the plus sign)* cuatro patas del otro, más cuatro patas del otro, más cuatro patas del otro, son dieciséis *(continues to point back and forth between each group of four tallies and each number 4 in the number sentence)*. Muy bien, esto es lo que se llama una suma larga.
	(Look at how Emilio did it, he put four legs from one cat, plus four legs from another, plus four legs from another one, plus four legs from the other one, it's sixteen. Very good, this is what is called a long addition.)

In this episode, we see how Ms. Arenas repeatedly referred to the story context in an effort to help students connect Daniel's tally-mark representation with Emilio's number-sentence representation. She carefully pointed back and forth between a set of four tally marks and a 4 in the number sentence while she explained that each representation stood for the four legs on one cat and that the addition symbol indicated that they should add the legs from all four cats (fig. 2.6). Learning to represent quantities and mathematical relationships and to connect multiple representations of the same situation are important mathematical goals for young children (NCTM 2000). Access to multiple representations may be especially helpful for ELLs because each representation creates a new opportunity for students to make sense of the problem.

Episode 3. Teachers Use the Structure of Stories to Support Students While They Learn to Explain Their Thinking

Another way that the teachers used stories to support mathematical learning was by drawing on the structure of stories to scaffold students'

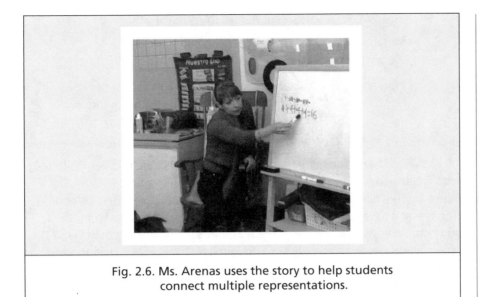

Fig. 2.6. Ms. Arenas uses the story to help students connect multiple representations.

language while students learned to explain their thinking. When students struggled to explain their ideas, the teachers often reminded them of the story context and then used the story as a framework to guide the students while they explained the steps that they took to solve the problem. For example, Ms. Field presented her class with the following story about a game of marbles between Sarita and Kyle:

> Sarita had eight marbles, and then Sarita gave some of those marbles to Kyle. She gave them away. And now she only has four left. So how many did she give to Kyle? Go ahead, try it.

She repeated the story several times, clarifying the quantities involved, and then allowed students time to work. After several minutes, Penny asked whether she could share her solution with the class.

Ms. Field:	Sure, come on up Penny. Everybody, eyes up here. Tell us what you did.
Penny:	First I started with four, and then I started with four more, then I counted then it made nine, and then I counted, and then … *(she pauses, seems uncertain, and looks up at Ms. Field).*
Ms. Field:	OK, Penny, wait a minute, let me tell you the problem one more time. We said that Sarita had eight marbles, and then she gave Kyle some, and she had four left. So how many did she give him?
Penny:	Four, four. *(Penny points to her picture. She has drawn a line of eight marbles, with four marbles on one side of her whiteboard and four marbles on the other.)*

Ms. Field:	So she gave him four marbles?
Penny:	Yes.
Ms. Field:	And then how many did she have?
Penny:	She gave [him] four and had four more left. Cause [it's] like four and four. Eight *(points to the two groups of four on her board).*

Ms. Field then restated Penny's solution, emphasizing that Sarita started with eight marbles and gave away four, and she then had four left and that Penny figured out that she gave away four because she knew that four and four is equal to eight. In this episode, Ms. Field drew Penny back into the story context ("Wait a minute…. We said that Sarita had eight marbles …") when Penny seemed unsure how to explain her strategy. Ms. Field then asked focused questions about various parts of the story ("So how many did she give him?") as a way of guiding Penny to draw on the story to help her explain her thinking. In the end, when Ms. Field restated Penny's ideas, she again offered Penny a model of how she might use the story to frame her explanation.

When we compared lessons from various points during the year, we noticed that although the teachers initially provided substantial guidance and used modeling to help students communicate their reasoning, many students began to contribute clearer and more complete explanations as the year progressed. Almost without exception, students grounded their explanations in the mathematical stories.

We suspect that repeated teacher-student interactions in which the teacher used the structure and events of stories to guide students' explanations, along with repeated opportunities to hear explanations from their peers, helped students learn to explain their thinking. For example, in the following episode from a lesson in the spring, two girls in Ms. Arenas's class presented their solutions to a multistep word problem: "Ms. Arenas had two boxes of little chocolate eggs. In each box, there were four eggs. Then Ms. Arenas ate two of the eggs. How many were left?" The first student to explain, Delia, was initially hesitant; and Ms. Arenas drew on the structure and the details of the story to help her begin.

Delia:	Primero Ms. Arenas se comió …
	(First Ms. Arenas ate …)
	(She pauses, not sure what to say next.)
Ms. Arenas:	Bueno. Primero, ¿cuántos tenía en cada cajita?
	(OK, first how many did I have in each box?)
Delia:	Cuatro.
	(Four.)
Ms. Arenas:	OK, muy bien, y pusiste cuatro en cada cajita. Y luego me comí dos …
	(OK, very good, and you put four in each box. And then I ate two …)

Delia:	Y le quedaron seis.
	(And there were six left.)
	(Delia points to the picture that she has drawn. It has two groups with four circles in each, and she has crossed out two of the circles.)
Ms. Arenas:	Y ¿como supiste?
	(And how did you know?)
Delia:	Porque los conté, conté cuántos huevitos quedaron.
	(Because I counted them, I counted how many eggs were left.)
	(Delia points to the six leftover eggs that she counted.)

Immediately after Delia's explanation, Yessenia volunteered to share her solution. Yessenia's contribution was significant both because she was a very shy student who rarely volunteered to share and because she presented a very articulate explanation describing how she solved the problem (see fig. 2.7). She grounded her explanation in the story's context, and her opportunities to hear peers, including Delia, explain their solutions may have supported her explanation.

Fig. 2.7. Yessenia explains her solution to a multistep problem.

Ms. Arenas:	A ver Yessenia, explícanos.
	(Let's see; Yessenia, tell us how you did it.)
Yessenia:	Ud, tenía dos cajitas, y tenía cuatro huevos en cada caja.
	(You had two boxes, and you had four eggs in each box.)

Ms. Arenas:	Y eran ocho, ¿verdad?
	(And it was eight, right?)
	(Ms. Arenas points to the number 8 that Yessenia has written on her whiteboard.)
Yessenia:	Eran ocho. Y después comió dos y puse una linea, y luego conté y quedaron seis. Comió dos y quedaron seis.
	(There were eight. And then you ate two and I put a line, and I counted and there were six left. You ate two, and there were six left.)
	(Yessenia points to drawing. She drew eight circles and then a line to separate two of the circles—the eggs that Ms. Arenas ate—from the rest of the set.)
Ms. Arenas:	Y aquí, ¿qué pusiste?
	(And here, what did you put here?)
	(Ms. Arenas points to number sentence that Yessenia has recorded, 8 – 2 = 6.)
Yessenia:	Ocho menos dos igual a seis.
	(Eight minus two equals six.)

The fact that children in kindergarten struggle to articulate their mathematical reasoning is not surprising. Even older students find challenging the need to clearly explain ideas that they are in the process of learning. Of significance here is how stories, which are familiar to children both in their form and—in the stories told by Ms. Field and Ms. Arenas—in their content, provided a structure that guided young children while they explained the steps that they took to solve a given problem.

Impact on Students' Learning: Posttest Results

The previous sections have described how two teachers used stories both to generate mathematical problems and to support students while they solved problems and discussed their thinking. To further document the effect of these instructional strategies on students' learning, we conclude with a brief overview of students' performance on an end-of-the-year problem-solving assessment that we administered to all students ($n = 32$) in both classrooms. The assessment consisted of ten word problems, including basic join and separate problems (table 2.2, problems a and b), as well as such more-complex problems as multistep problems and division problems with a remainder (problems c and d). The teacher presented all problems orally in the students' dominant language, and students had access to various tools to support their reasoning.

Much like the students in the study by Carpenter and others (1993), the students in the classes of Ms. Field and Ms. Arenas demonstrated remarkable capabilities on the end-of-the-year assessment. Most of the

Table 2.2
Sample Postassessment Items

Problem Type		Problem
Join (result unknown)	a.	Julio had 6 cookies, and then his sister gave him 6 more cookies. How many cookies does Julio have now?
Separate (result unknown)	b.	Paola had 13 candies, and then she ate 5 of them. How many candies does she have left?
Multistep	c.	Javier had 2 bags of marbles. There were 4 marbles in each bag. Then he gave away 3 of his marbles. How many marbles does he have left?
Division with remainder	d.	Fifteen children want to paint. They are going to sit at tables, but only 4 children can fit at each table. How many tables are they going to need so that all the children can paint?

students successfully solved the most basic join and separate problems (80 percent and 75 percent, respectively); 60 percent of the students correctly solved the multiplication problem (3×6), 50 percent solved the division problem ($15 \div 3$), and 50 percent solved the multistep problem. The most difficult problem for students was the division problem that involved a remainder; and even so, one-third of the students solved it accurately.

When we analyzed the performance of individual students, we found that twenty-one of the thirty-two students (65.6 percent) successfully solved at least half the items on the posttest and that nine students (28 percent) solved all, or all but one or two, of the ten items correctly. Moreover, whereas students' explanations at the beginning of the year were often vague and incomplete, most students produced clear and more mathematical explanations on the posttest. Considering that many students began the year with limited counting and problem-solving skills and that some students lacked such basic skills as one-to-one correspondence and rote counting, these results are significant and indicate the power of teachers' use of "story" as a way to organize problem-solving sessions and support Latino and Latina kindergarten students as they make sense of, represent, and communicate their reasoning about basic word problems.

Conclusion

We conclude with a final episode from Ms. Field's classroom. At the end of one problem-solving session, Verónica (an ELL student) stopped Ms. Field as she was about to transition to the next activity and announced to the group, "Ms. Field, wait, let's try another one! Let's try this one. One girl have [sic] ten rings and then one [other] girl take[s] three. So how many is left?" Ms. Field quickly changed her plans and engaged students in solving and discussing Verónica's problem. Verónica's spontaneous problem posing generated a burst of activity because other students also wanted to pose mathematical stories for the class to solve. We end with this example because we believe that it captures the generative power of framing problem solving as "telling mathematical stories" for this diverse group of kindergarten students. Not only did the teachers' use of stories help students bridge home and family experiences with more formal school-based mathematics and help students learn to communicate their mathematical thinking while they also developed problem-solving and basic number skills, but the familiar narrative tone of "telling math stories" coupled with opportunities to coconstruct mathematical stories as a class created an entry point for students to pose their own mathematical problems. In short, framing, telling, and investigating mathematical stories created opportunities for all students to develop important problem-solving skills. Students ended the year not only as competent and more confident problem solvers but also as problem posers, which is no small feat for children in kindergarten.

The familiar narrative tone of "telling math stories" coupled with opportunities to coconstruct mathematical stories as a class created an entry point for students to pose their own mathematical problems.

REFERENCES

Carpenter, Thomas P., Ellen Ansell, Megan P. Franke, Elizabeth Fennema, and Linda Weisbeck. "Models of Problem Solving: A Study of Kindergarten Children's Problem-Solving Processes." *Journal for Research in Mathematics Education* 24, no. 5 (November 1993): 428–41.

Carpenter, Thomas P., Elizabeth Fennema, Megan Loef Franke, Linda Levi, and Susan B. Empson. *Children's Mathematics: Cognitively Guided Instruction.* Portsmouth, N.H.: Heinemann, 1999.

Cobb, Paul, Terry Wood, and Erna Yackel. "Discourse, Mathematical Thinking, and Classroom Practice." In *Contexts for Learning: Sociocultural Dynamics in Children's Development,* edited by Ellice A. Forman, Norris Minick, and C. Addison Stone, pp. 91–119. New York: Oxford University Press, 1993.

Dalton, Stephanie S. *Pedagogy Matters: Standards for Effective Teaching Practice.* Santa Cruz, Calif.: Center for Research on Education, Diversity, and Excellence, University of California, Santa Cruz, 1998.

Delgado-Gaitan, Concha. "Traditions and Transitions in the Learning Process of Mexican Children: An Ethnographic View." In *Interpretive Ethnography of Education: At Home and Abroad,* edited by George Spindler and Louise Spindler, pp. 333–59. Hillsdale, N.J.: Lawrence Erlbaum Associates, 1987.

Ginsburg, Herbert P., Nancy Kossan, Robert Schwartz, and David Swanson. "Protocol Methods in Research on Mathematical Thinking." In *The Development of Mathematical Thinking,* edited by Herbert P. Ginsburg, pp. 7–47. New York: Academic Press, 1983.

González, Norma, Luis Moll, and Cathy Amanti. *Funds of Knowledge: Theorizing Practices in Households, Communities, and Classrooms.* Mahwah, N.J.: Lawrence Erlbaum Associates, 2005.

Iddings, DaSilva. "Linguistic Access and Participation: English Language Learners in an English-Dominant Community of Practice." *Bilingual Research Journal* 29 (Spring 2005): 165–83.

Lampert, Magdalene. *Teaching Problems and the Problems of Teaching.* New Haven, Conn.: Yale University Press, 2001.

Lo Cicero, Ana Maria, Yolanda De La Cruz, and Karen C. Fuson. "Teaching and Learning Creatively: Using Children's Narratives." *Teaching Children Mathematics* 5, no. 9 (May 1999): 544–47.

Lo Cicero, Ana Maria, Karen C. Fuson, and Martha Allexsaht-Snider. "Mathematizing Children's Stories, Helping Children Solve Word Problems, and Supporting Parental Involvement." In *Changing the Faces of Mathematics: Perspectives on Latinos,* edited by Luis Ortiz-Franco, Norma G. Gonzalez, and Yolanda De La Cruz, pp. 59–70. Reston, Va.: National Council of Teachers of Mathematics, 1999.

National Council of Teachers of Mathematics (NCTM). *Principles and Standards for School Mathematics.* Reston, Va: NCTM, 2000.

Outhred, Lynne, and Sarah Sardelich. "A Problem Is Something You Don't Want to Have: Problem Solving by Kindergarteners." *Teaching Children Mathematics* 12, no. 3 (October 2005): 146–54.

Secada, Walter G. "Degree of Bilingualism and Arithmetic Problem Solving in Hispanic First Graders." *Elementary School Journal* 92, no. 2 (November 1991): 213–31.

Tang, Eileen P., and Herbert P. Ginsburg. "Young Children's Mathematical Reasoning: A Psychological View." In *Developing Mathematical Reasoning in Grades K–12,* 1999 Yearbook, edited by Lee V. Stiff, pp. 45–61. Reston, Va.: National Council of Teachers of Mathematics, 1999.

Villaseñor, Albert, Jr., and Henry S. Kepner, Jr. "Arithmetic from a Problem-Solving Perspective: An Urban Implementation." *Journal for Research in Mathematics Education* 24, no. 1 (January 1993): 6–69.

Villenas, Sofia, and Melissa Moreno. "To Valerse por Si Misma: Between Race, Capitalism, and Patriarchy: Latina Mother-Daughter Pedagogies in North Carolina." *International Journal of Qualitative Studies in Education* 14, no. 5 (September 2001): 671–87.

Enhancing Mathematics Lessons to Support All Students

Kathryn B. Chval
Oscar Chavez
Sarah Pomerenke
Kari Reams

AFTER Ms. Reams had taught kindergarten for two years, the principal assigned her to teach first grade. While she was preparing for her third year of teaching, she learned that seven of her twenty-two students were English language learners (ELLs) whose native languages were Chinese, Korean, and Spanish. She realized that her immediate challenges in preparing to teach at a new grade level included familiarizing herself with the first-grade Investigations in Number, Data, and Space mathematics curriculum (TERC 1998), as well as the curriculum for the other subject areas, and learning how to meet the needs of all her students, including the ELL students.

Ms. Reams acknowledged that her teacher-preparation experiences had not prepared her to teach ELL students effectively, and she had not had opportunities to participate in professional development related to teaching ELL students. She knew that the students would spend two hours a week in an English as a Second Language (ESL) support classroom, but she wanted to know how she could best support the students while they participated in her lessons.

Ms. Reams Is Not Alone

The example of Ms. Reams is not unique. Every classroom for students in kindergarten through second grade—even monolingual English-speaking classrooms—includes children who have a wide range of English language proficiencies. Moreover, many classrooms also have students who are learning English as a second or third language. Some of these classrooms have a single ELL student, whereas others have many ELL students with different native languages. The recent growth of the ELL population in the United States has challenged school administrators and teachers to identify effective strategies for meeting the needs of ELL students and their families. According to the National Center for Education Statistics (Wirt et al. 2005), the number of children from five to seventeen years old who spoke a language other than English at home grew from 3.8 million (9 percent of that population) in 1979 to 9.9 million (19 percent) in 2003.

Every classroom for students in kindergarten through second grade—even monolingual English-speaking classrooms—includes children who have a wide range of English language proficiencies. Moreover, many classrooms also have students who are learning English as a second or third language.

Even though teachers and administrators want to identify appropriate support and resources for ELL students, teachers are typically unfamiliar with effective strategies for supporting ELL students, especially in the elementary mathematics classroom (Gándara, Maxwell-Jolly, and Driscoll 2005), and teachers are not participating in professional development related to teaching ELL students (Wenglinsky 2002). Teachers obviously need access to professional development opportunities, as well as practical, effective strategies that they can apply in classrooms. Ms. Reams's situation provides an example for other teachers of children in kindergarten through second grade who desire effective approaches so that they can meet the needs of all their students.

Ms. Reams Begins Her Search

To strengthen her professional knowledge and teaching practices related to teaching ELL students, Ms. Reams decided to design an action research project focused on teaching her ELL students in the mathematics classroom. At the same time, she teamed with two local researchers (two of the authors) who were interested in studying the participation of ELL students in the mathematics classroom. The researchers provided Ms. Reams with research articles that could help strengthen her knowledge about teaching ELL students more effectively. Additionally, the researchers offered specific ideas about connecting the research with the Investigations curriculum and her teaching. In turn, Ms. Reams invited the researchers to observe and videotape twelve of her mathematics lessons during the school year. After they had videotaped a few lessons, Ms. Reams also met with the researchers to watch and discuss the videotapes so that she could obtain an added perspective on meeting the needs of her students. Throughout this collaboration, Ms. Reams asked questions about effectively teaching all her students. She also opened her classroom for others to observe, videotape, and discuss her teaching, thereby demonstrating her dedication and commitment to meeting her students' needs.

Throughout this process, Ms. Reams learned a great deal about herself and her students. This article therefore presents an example that describes how Ms. Reams used the research to enhance one lesson from the Investigations curriculum to meet the needs of all her students who were developing their mathematical thinking, problem-solving, and communication skills. The article concludes with a discussion of the results from Ms. Reams's efforts, as well as suggestions that other teachers of children in kindergarten through second grade can consider for enhancing K–2 mathematics lessons for ELL students in ways that support all students.

Ms. Reams Investigates the Research

Ms. Reams considered ideas from research while she began to think about and plan her mathematics instruction differently so that she could better meet the needs of all her students, including the ELL students. As the National Council of Teachers of Mathematics recommends in *Principles and Standards for School Mathematics* (NCTM 2000), "Students who are not native speakers of English, for instance, may need special attention to allow them to participate fully in classroom discussions" (p. 13). The following list of research-based strategies used by Ms. Reams highlights the types of special attention that ELL students need so that they can fully participate in mathematics classrooms:

- Connect mathematics with students' life experiences and existing knowledge (Anstrom 1997; Barwell 2003; Secada and De La Cruz 1996).

- Promote active student participation in classroom discussions regarding mathematics (Brenner 1998; Brown et al. 1993).

- Create classroom environments that are rich in language and mathematics content (Anstrom 1997).

- Emphasize meaning—students may need to communicate meaning through using gestures or drawings while they develop command of the English language (Moll 1988, 1989; Morales, Khisty, and Chval 2003).

- Rephrase and emphasize important mathematical ideas and concepts (Khisty and Chval 2002).

- Connect language with such visual aids as pictures, tables, and graphs (Khisty and Chval 2002).

- Use concrete materials, illustrations, and demonstrations to enhance mathematical learning (Raborn 1995).

- Write essential ideas, concepts, and words on the board—use as much board space as possible so that you do not have to erase during the lesson and so that students can refer back to your writing throughout the lesson (Stigler, Fernandez, and Yoshida 1996).

- Make writing a public process. Discuss examples of students' writing (Chval and Khisty 2001).

All these ideas suggest that educators should not view supporting ELL students as a separate activity. Ms. Reams could have worked with her ELL students in isolation, simplified the mathematics or the language, or reduced expectations; however, she wanted them to participate fully in mathematical activities with all their peers while she maintained mathematical integrity and high expectations. Furthermore, all the preceding suggestions supported the academic growth of all students in the mathematics classroom because all the first-grade students engaged in learning mathematics and English. The following section demonstrates how Ms. Reams used the preceding research ideas to enhance one lesson from the Investigations curriculum.

Ms. Reams's Lesson

Before teaching the Investigations lesson, Ms. Reams read pages 90–94 in the *Survey Questions and Secret Rules Teachers' Guide* (Wright and Mokros 1998) to prepare for teaching a lesson related to collecting and representing attendance data, both real and fictitious. In the lesson,

Ms. Reams could have worked with her ELL students in isolation, simplified the mathematics or the language, or reduced expectations; however, she wanted them to participate fully in mathematical activities with all their peers while she maintained mathematical integrity and high expectations.

students collect their attendance data for the day and create a graph by using colored paper. They also listen to a story about an unusual day during which most of the students are absent because of extraordinary events that occur on the way to school. For example, some students climb into the nest of a giant bird and never arrive at school. After listening to the story, the students represent the attendance data from the fictitious story. The teacher materials for the lesson include the following words related to teaching ELL students (Wright and Mokros 1998, p. 92):

> **Tips for Linguistically Diverse Students.** There are a variety of ways to aid comprehension of this story. Plan to simplify the story to its most basic elements as needed. Sketch drawings on the board to represent each "unusual situation" that keeps the students out of school (an enormous dark puddle, a tree with a giant nest, a shiny coin). Students might also use props and act out described events as they occur.

After reading the *Teachers' Guide,* Ms. Reams decided to use the tip in the *Teachers Guide* about sketching pictures on the board. In addition, she made decisions about ways to enhance the proposed mathematical activities on the basis of suggestions from the research on meeting the needs of ELL students, as described in the following paragraphs. The researchers videotaped the resulting lesson with three digital video cameras.

To begin the lesson, Ms. Reams wrote the following on the whiteboard: "Today in math, we will collect attendance information." Ms. Reams then explained that the children would make an attendance chart to show who was at school and who was not. To help the children build meaning for the terms *attendance* and *collect information,* Ms. Reams made a connection back to a daily routine that she had used earlier in the school year, in which the children used connecting cubes to represent and count the number of children who were present each day, as described on pages 100–101 in the *Teachers' Guide.* The children then came to the whiteboard one-by-one to create a graph by using stick-on notes, as shown in figure 3.1. Ms. Reams followed the suggestions in the *Teachers' Guide* and used yellow stick-on notes to represent children who were present and pink stick-on notes to represent children who were absent. Ms. Reams then asked a volunteer to read the sentence on the whiteboard, "Today in math, we will collect attendance information." She then began a conversation by asking, "What does that mean?" As the students responded, Ms. Reams was able to further clarify and support the children's understanding related to *collect* and *attendance.* She tied the discussion to previous experiences in the classroom, the graph that the children created during the lesson, and the words that she had written on the whiteboard to support all her students.

In the next part of the lesson, Ms. Reams used a story from the Investigations *Teachers' Guide* to introduce some fictitious attendance data. Ms. Reams used the suggestion from the *Teachers' Guide* to draw pictures of some of the obstacles that inhibited the attendance of the students in the story. In addition, she enhanced this part of the lesson by using other strategies identified in the research on teaching ELL students. For example, instead of beginning the story with "Once upon a time…," she connected the story with students' life experiences by saying, "Last night, I had a very unusual dream." She also emphasized the meaning of *unusual* so that the children could fully participate in the conversation. The following transcript demonstrates how she began the conversation:

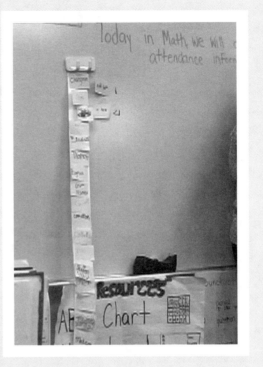

Fig. 3.1. Ms. Reams begins to use the whiteboard space.

Ms. Reams:	Who has ever heard of the word *unusual?* What does that mean, *unusual?*
Ms. Reams:	Who has ever had an unusual dream? Something that's just kind of weird? I think of the word *weird* when I think [of] "unusual." Has anyone ever had a weird dream that's not something that happens every day? Hannah, you have? OK. Thomas have you had an unusual dream? You have. Catherine, have you? You've had an unusual dream.
Ms. Reams:	Last night, I had a very unusual dream. It had to do with you.
Students:	Tell us it! Tell us it!
Ms. Reams:	Are you sure? I'm not sure.
Students:	Yes!
Ms. Reams:	Are you ready to be listeners?
Students:	Yes!
Ms. Reams:	Let me see [that you are ready to be listeners], because we're going to laugh some but you have to listen, too. OK? I'm going to tell the story and be writing stuff as I tell it, and I'm going to call it "The Unusual Day." (*Ms. Reams writes "The Unusual Day" on the whiteboard.*)
Student:	You mean night or dream?
Ms. Reams:	[It was] my dream—I had it. But it was about an unusual day here [at school]. "The Unusual Day." And then if I say your name in this dream, I want you to come put it up and I'll tell you where to put it up, OK? But you're going to put your magnet up on the side that it belongs, OK? So, these are the people that came to school on the unusual day. They were here. These are the people that didn't come to school on the unusual day. They were not here.

As the last segment of the transcript explains, Ms. Reams used magnetic name tags with the children's names to help illustrate the story. She also used the whiteboard to capture the entire story line. When she mentioned each child in the story, he or she walked to the whiteboard to add his or her picture, thereby enhancing the students' participation level beyond just listening. For example, when Ms. Reams read that Mary, James, and John investigated the bird's nest and did not go to school, those three children walked to the whiteboard and placed their pictures next to the picture of the bird's nest that Ms. Reams had drawn. Throughout the lesson, Ms. Reams did not erase the whiteboard, so that the children could refer to the board during the story as well as during the assessment that followed. As illustrated in the preceding paragraphs, Ms. Reams used the research-based strategies listed previously in this article to facilitate the participation and engagement of ELL students, thereby helping them learn. Figure 3.2 displays the final product with all the students' names.

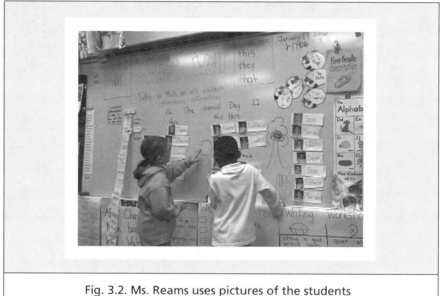

Fig. 3.2. Ms. Reams uses pictures of the students
and the whiteboard to tell the story.

The representations and concrete materials shown in figure 3.2 helped all the children build meaning for the mathematics. While the children worked in pairs independently to create a representation of the fictitious data, a number of the students walked up to the whiteboard so that they could put their fingers on the names and faces while they counted. Ms. Reams also circulated in the classroom to assess her students' understanding and provide additional support to students by asking questions. For example, Ms. Reams posed a question about the data on the whiteboard to one ELL student and his partner.

After Ms. Reams had allowed sufficient time for the students to create representations of the data presented in the story, she brought the whole class together to display and discuss the students' work (see fig. 3.3), another effective strategy for all students, but especially for the ELL students.

While the children worked in pairs independently to create a representation of the fictitious data, a number of the students walked up to the whiteboard so that they could put their fingers on the names and faces while they counted.

During this discussion, she summarized the important mathematical ideas and language. She also made students' writing a public process so that students could gain insights into additional mathematical representations and ideas that their classmates used.

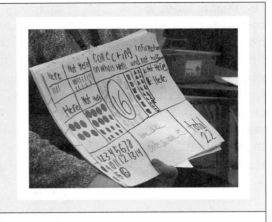

Fig. 3.3. Ms. Reams leads a discussion of student work.

The Results of Ms. Reams's Efforts

While Ms. Reams worked to improve her mathematics instruction for all the students in her classroom, she identified ways to facilitate the participation of her ELL students and attempted to ensure that she did not isolate them. Moreover, she did not want to lower expectations for the ELL students, because she wanted all students to achieve. Therefore, she maintained the mathematical integrity of the Investigations curriculum while using the previously identified research-based strategies. As a result, her ELL students were participants in, rather than spectators of, the mathematical discourse in the classroom. Their ability to communicate their mathematical ideas improved during the year, and their confidence grew as a result of their successful participation. In observing her students' growth while enhancing her mathematics lessons for ELL students, Ms. Reams also realized that her own mathematics teaching improved and her confidence in working with ELL students in mathematics classrooms became stronger.

Suggestions for Other Teachers of Grades K–2

In recent years, curriculum developers and textbook companies have invested great effort to create mathematical tasks and suggestions for meeting the needs of ELLs for their student and teacher materials. The example presented in this article involved a lesson from a curriculum that was based on NCTM's *Principles and Standards for School Mathematics* (2000) and research about teaching and learning mathematics. As a result, enhancing the lesson was easier. Some mathematics curricula take more effort to enhance. No matter which mathematics curriculum educators use, enhancing lessons helps ELL students participate more actively. As the NCTM's *Principles and Standards for School Mathematics* (2000) states,

> Students whose primary language is not English may need some additional support in order to benefit from communication-rich mathematics classes, but they can participate fully if classroom activities are appropriately structured (Silver, Smith, and Nelson 1995, p. 60).

Ms. Reams's lesson demonstrates how one teacher enhanced one mathematics lesson and appropriately structured the environment to facilitate the participation and learning of her ELL students. Ms. Reams made

Ms. Reams made a commitment and invested additional time to think about how she could effectively use the research-based strategies and her mathematics curriculum to support her ELL students.

a commitment and invested additional time to think about how she could effectively use the research-based strategies and her mathematics curriculum to support her ELL students. This example can furnish ideas for other teachers of grades K–2 who wish to enhance their own mathematics lessons. For example, teachers need to provide opportunities for ELL students to participate in purposeful and contextual conversations with others to support both language and conceptual development (Moschkovich 1999). The following questions can help guide teachers while they think about creating these opportunities:

- How can I best use the classroom's board and writing space during the lesson?

- How can I connect the mathematics with students' life experiences and with their existing knowledge?

- How can I help children build meaning for the mathematical language involved in the lesson?

- How can I encourage students to use gestures or drawings to communicate their mathematical thinking?

- What are the important mathematical ideas and concepts that I need to emphasize during the lesson?

- What representations would help the children build meaning for these important mathematical ideas and concepts?

- How can I convey and help students make connections among the concepts with such visual aids as pictures, tables, and graphs?

- How can I use concrete materials, illustrations, and demonstrations to enhance mathematical learning?

- What words, pictures, or representations are important to write on the board to develop a mathematical story line for the entire lesson?

- What am I going to ask students to write during the lesson? Which examples of students' work should the class discuss?

Ms. Reams knew that she did not have time to consider all these questions for every lesson. However, she did begin a process of thinking about some of them for a few lessons. She realizes that with more time and experience, her lessons will continue to improve and meet the needs of all her students, especially her ELL students.

REFERENCES

Anstrom, Kris. *Academic Achievement for Secondary Language Minority Students: Standards, Measures, and Promising Practices.* Washington, D.C.: National Clearinghouse for Bilingual Education, 1997. Available at www.ncela.gwu.edu/pubs/reports/acadach.htm (accessed July 1, 2005) .

Barwell, Richard. "Patterns of Attention in the Interaction of a Primary School Mathematics Student with English as an Additional Language." *Educational Studies in Mathematics* 53, no. 1 (May 2003): 35–59.

Brenner, Mary. "Development of Mathematical Communication in Problem Solving Groups by Language Minority Students." *Bilingual Research Journal* 22, nos. 2–4 (Spring/Summer/Fall 1998): 103–28.

Brown, Ann L., Doris Ash, Martha Rutherford, Kathryn Nakagawa, Ann Gordon, and Joseph C. Campione. "Distributed Expertise in the Classroom." In *Distributed Cognitions: Psychological and Educational Considerations,* edited by Gavriel Salomon, pp. 188–228. New York: Cambridge University Press, 1993.

Chval, Kathryn B., and Lena L. Khisty. "Writing in Mathematics with Latino Fifth-Grade Students." Paper presented at the annual meeting of the American Educational Research Association, Seattle, Wash., April 2001.

Gándara, Patricia, Julie Maxwell-Jolly, and Anne Driscoll. *Listening to Teachers of English Language Learners: A Survey of California Teachers: Challenges, Experiences, and Professional Development Needs.* Santa Cruz, Calif.: The Center for the Future of Teaching and Learning, 2005.

Khisty, Lena L., and Kathryn Chval. "Pedagogic Discourse and Equity in Mathematics: When Teachers' Talk Matters." *Mathematics Education Research Journal* 14, no. 3 (December 2002): 154–68.

Moll, Luis. "Key Issues in Teaching Latino Students." *Language Arts* 65, no. 5 (September 1988): 465–72.

———. "Teaching Second-Language Students: A Vygotskian Perspective." In *Richness in Writing: Empowering ESL Students,* edited by Donna M. Johnson and Duane H. Roen, pp. 55–69. New York: Longman, 1989.

Morales, Hector, Lena L. Khisty, and Kathryn B. Chval. "Beyond Discourse: A Multimodal Perspective of Learning Mathematics in a Multilingual Context." In *Proceedings of the 2003 Joint Meeting of PME and PMENA,* edited by Neil A. Pateman, Barbara J. Dougherty, and Joseph Zilliox, vol. 3, pp. 133–40. Honolulu, Hawaii: Center for Research and Development Group, University of Hawaii, 2003.

Moschkovich, Judit N. "Understanding the Needs of Latino Students in Reform-Oriented Mathematics Classrooms." In *Changing the Faces of Mathematics: Perspectives on Latinos,* edited by Walter G. Secada, Luis Ortiz-Franco, Norma G. Hernandez, and Yolanda De La Cruz, pp. 5–12. Reston, Va.: National Council of Teachers of Mathematics, 1999.

National Council of Teachers of Mathematics (NCTM). *Principles and Standards for School Mathematics.* Reston, Va.: NCTM, 2000.

Raborn, Diane T. "Mathematics for Students with Learning Disabilities from Language-Minority Backgrounds: Recommendations for Teaching." *New York State Association for Bilingual Education Journal* 10 (Summer 1995): 25–33.

Secada, Walter G., and Yolanda De La Cruz. "Teaching Mathematics for Understanding to Bilingual Students." In *Children of la Frontera,* edited by Judith LeBlanc Flores, pp. 285–308. Charleston, W.Va.: ERIC Clearinghouse on Rural Education and Small Schools, 1996.

Silver, Edward A., Margaret Schwan Smith, and Barbara Scott Nelson. "The QUASAR Project: Equity Concerns Meet Mathematics Education Reform in the Middle School." In *New Directions for Equity in Mathematics Education,* edited by Walter G. Secada, Elizabeth Fennema, and Lisa Byrd Adajian, pp. 9–56. New York: Cambridge University Press, 1995.

Stigler, James W., Clea Fernandez, and Makoto Yoshida. "Traditions of School Mathematics in Japanese and American Elementary Classrooms." In *Theories of Mathematical Learning,* edited by Leslie P. Steffe, Pearla Nesher, Paul Cobb, Gerald A. Goldin, and Brian Greer, pp. 149–75. Mahwah, N.J.: Lawrence Erlbaum Associates, 1996.

TERC. *Investigations in Number, Data, and Space.* Palo Alto, Calif.: Dale Seymour Publications, 1998.

Wenglinsky, Harold. "How Schools Matter: The Link between Teacher Classroom Practices and Student Academic Performance." *Education Policy Analysis Archive* 10, no. 12 (February 2002).

Wirt, John, Patrick Rooney, Bill Hussar, Susan Choy, Stephen Provasnik, and Gillian Hampden-Thompson. The Condition of Education. Washington, D.C.: U.S. Government Printing Office, U.S. Department of Education, National Center for Education Statistics, 2005. Available at nces.ed.gov/pubsearch/search.asp?PubSectionID=1&searchstring=The+Condition+of+Education&searchcat=title&searchtype=AND&searchmonth=8&searchyear=2004&datetype=%3E%3D&surveyname (accessed July 3, 2006).

Wright, Tracey, and Jan Mokros. *Survey Questions and Secret Rules: Collecting and Sorting Data.* Palo Alto, Calif.: Dale Seymour Publications, 1998.

Conceptual Understanding of Fractions

Cheryl D. Roddick

CLASSROOMS across the country are becoming increasingly diverse. Although educators have made efforts toward more-differentiated instruction, far too many elementary school classrooms remain dependent on lecture, with a focus on hand computations using memorized algorithms that make little sense to the child. When approaching a diverse audience, the teacher needs to consider the various ways that learning occurs. NCTM (2000) advocates that learning should be equitable and that educators should have high expectations and provide strong support for all students so that they can learn high-quality mathematics. NCTM (2000) also emphasizes that students should build on their prior experiences and knowledge and actively learn mathematics with understanding.

In particular, understanding fractions continues to be a stumbling block for many students. Steffe and Olive (2002) suggest that students' difficulties stem from learning fractions by using rote memorization of procedures without a connection with informal ways of solving problems involving fractions. This article presents two activities , created by Roddick and Silvas-Centeno (2007), designed to capitalize on students' informal ways of sense making by using manipulatives to explore the concepts of fractions. Teachers have used draft versions of the activities with children in third, fifth, and sixth grade in schools serving students of low to middle socioeconomic status from diverse cultural backgrounds and racial origins. This article discusses the activities with reference to common misunderstandings that students have when learning fractions.

The activities address the diverse needs that students have when learning mathematics and focus on the development of conceptual understanding while considering the following ideas:

- The activities use a hands-on approach. Pattern blocks are the foundation for understanding all aspects of fraction concepts, as well as computations with fractions. Students experience what a fractional piece is by manipulating the pattern blocks and making "fair trades." They then use this understanding of fair trades to create equivalent fractions and to add, subtract, multiply, and divide fractions.

- The instruction progresses through three distinct phases of learning and understanding fractions by using visual representation, number sense, and computation:
  — Visual representation: Using pattern blocks helps develop understanding of different fractional sizes.

The teacher assigns students word problems that involve fractions and asks them to make sense of the problems by using pattern blocks and models that they have created.

Although teachers often introduce fractions by using pictures or some sort of manipulatives, they frequently give students too few opportunities to develop deep conceptual understandings before they move on to pencil-and-paper computations that have little meaning to the students (National Research Council 2001).

— Number sense: Using pattern blocks helps students make links between the visual and the symbolic representations of fractions. Students learn to compare and order fractions before they learn how to find common denominators and convert fractions to decimals. This process gives them an opportunity to observe patterns between the manipulatives and the relative size of the fractions, thereby encouraging them to develop number sense related to fractions and independent of the visual representation. This step is crucial in paving the way to teaching fraction computations in a meaningful manner.

— Computation: Using pattern blocks and pictures, as well as using fair trades to determine equivalent fractions, gives meaning to the algorithms for addition, subtraction, multiplication, and division of fractions.

• Real-life problems add a context to the operations. The teacher assigns students word problems that involve fractions and asks them to make sense of the problems by using pattern blocks and models that they have created.

Although teachers often introduce fractions by using pictures or some sort of manipulatives, they frequently give students too few opportunities to develop deep conceptual understandings before they move on to pencil-and-paper computations that have little meaning to the students (National Research Council 2001). Students often have poorly developed number sense as a result of spending too much time drilling on the algorithms. This underdeveloped number sense can lead to weak understanding and poor connections, especially in a classroom in which the students have diverse needs. By focusing mainly on computations, teachers fail to provide a rich environment for learning mathematics from multiple perspectives. Van de Walle and Lovin (2006), who advocate a student-centered approach to teaching, were a source of inspiration during the development of these activities.

Issues in the Teaching and Learning of Fractions

When students participated in the fraction activities, they obviously did not have a strong foundational understanding of fractions. More specifically, students exhibited the following problems:

• The students lacked an understanding of the relative size of fractions, and this lack of understanding resulted in difficulties when they ordered fractions. For example, they did not seem to understand that a larger denominator represents a smaller fractional piece.

• The students did not understand that the denominator represents the number of groups of equal size. Siebert and Gaskin (2006) found that the terminology that students and teachers used may not indicate the necessity of equal-sized pieces. When students and teachers refer to one-third as "one out of three," students may have the impression that they need one of those three pieces but that the pieces do not necessarily have to be equal.

- Students viewed the denominator as the number of equal pieces instead of the number of equal groups. They demonstrated this misconception by being able to solve such problems as "find 1/5 of 5" while being unable to solve such problems as "find 1/5 of 20." Steffe and Olive (2002) refer to prefractional concepts, one of those being the belief that one-fifth refers to "five single elements in a collection or to five parts of a continuous whole" (p. 129) rather than "five composite units of indefinite numerosity" (p. 129).

- Although students were able to determine an equivalent fraction procedurally, they were often unable to give a meaningful explanation describing why two fractions were equivalent.

This article revisits these common misconceptions during the discussion of the following two activities.

"Finding the Fractional Part"

The goals of the activity "Finding the Fractional Part" (see fig 4.1) are for students to find fractional parts given the whole, to develop an understanding of the relative size of fractions (with different representations of 1), to introduce equivalent fractions, and to introduce the comparison of fractions. The pattern blocks used are the yellow hexagons, red trapezoids, blue rhombuses, and green triangles. A few techniques emerged from this activity. First, when students receive a particular shape made up of pattern blocks, they can rearrange the pattern-block pieces as necessary. They can stack other pieces on top to show equivalence and make fair trades. These three techniques naturally arise during the course of this activity.

In problem 1, students first use pattern blocks to find one-fourth of the flower. Because the flower has exactly four equal pieces, this task should pose few problems. In part (b), students might demonstrate finding one-half of the flower by stacking two of the blue rhombuses on top of the other two blue rhombuses to show two equal groups. In part (d), students find one-eighth of the flower. Because the flower has only four pieces, students must make a fair trade. They can trade each blue rhombus for two green triangles so that they have eight pieces. This first problem is a gentle introduction to the process for solving the remaining problems.

Problem 2, which depicts a bat, calls into play concepts of equivalence as well as the multiplicative relationship of fractions with the same denominator. Students can observe that two-sixths and one-third are represented by pattern blocks that are fair trades for each other (i.e., two green triangles are a fair trade for one blue rhombus; see fig 4.2). They may also begin to realize that two-sixths is twice as large as one-sixth and that two-thirds is twice as large as one-third. Class discussion may take this idea further by having students determine three-sixths, four-sixths, five-sixths, and six-sixths by using their answers for one-sixth and two-sixths.

In problem 3, the king's crown, students find one-half of the shape.

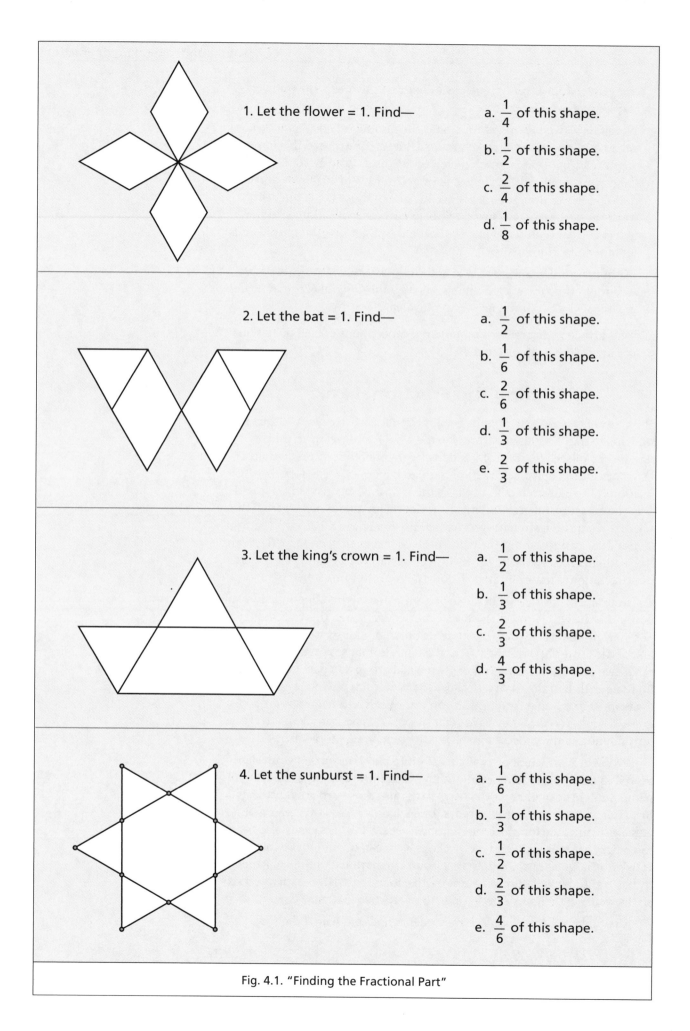

1. Let the flower = 1. Find—

    a. $\frac{1}{4}$ of this shape.

    b. $\frac{1}{2}$ of this shape.

    c. $\frac{2}{4}$ of this shape.

    d. $\frac{1}{8}$ of this shape.

2. Let the bat = 1. Find—

    a. $\frac{1}{2}$ of this shape.

    b. $\frac{1}{6}$ of this shape.

    c. $\frac{2}{6}$ of this shape.

    d. $\frac{1}{3}$ of this shape.

    e. $\frac{2}{3}$ of this shape.

3. Let the king's crown = 1. Find—

    a. $\frac{1}{2}$ of this shape.

    b. $\frac{1}{3}$ of this shape.

    c. $\frac{2}{3}$ of this shape.

    d. $\frac{4}{3}$ of this shape.

4. Let the sunburst = 1. Find—

    a. $\frac{1}{6}$ of this shape.

    b. $\frac{1}{3}$ of this shape.

    c. $\frac{1}{2}$ of this shape.

    d. $\frac{2}{3}$ of this shape.

    e. $\frac{4}{6}$ of this shape.

Fig. 4.1. "Finding the Fractional Part"

Optional

5. Put all the fractions from the flower in order from least to greatest. Identify any that are the same. Explain your ordering, and use pattern-block pieces in your explanation.

6. Put all the fractions from the bat in order from least to greatest. Identify any that are the same. Explain your ordering, and use pattern-block pieces in your explanation.

7. Put all the fractions from the king's crown in order from least to greatest. Identify any that are the same. Explain your ordering, and use pattern-block pieces in your explanation.

8. Put all the fractions from the sunburst in order from least to greatest. Identify any that are the same. Explain your ordering, and use pattern block pieces in your explanation.

Fig. 4.1. "Finding the Fractional Part"—*Continued*

However, they begin with one red trapezoid and three green triangles, and they cannot take half of either of those pieces. Yet when they make a fair trade—and more than one type of fair trade is possible—they can more easily see what one-half is. Students who use a different approach and re-arrange the blocks may quickly see that they can arrange the king's crown to form a yellow hexagon, which is a fair trade for two red trapezoids. Problem 4 is actually two king's crowns, so students can find some answers by doubling the answers from problem 3.

Students need to explore the many different fair trades and rearrangements to develop their understanding of fraction equivalence. Although students can actually solve all the problems in this activity quickly by trading each piece for triangles, the teacher should not point out this fact to students. Many students will arrive at this conclusion on their own as they gain experience with the pattern blocks and fair trades.

The unit, or whole, in these problems is not constant. Students begin to develop flexibility in finding fractional parts by using different representations of a whole. For example, in problems 2 and 3 one red trapezoid represents one-half. Yet in problem 4, one yellow hexagon represents one-half because the whole is twice as large as in problems 2 and 3. The relationship between the pattern blocks remains the same, however. For example, the green triangle is always one-third of the red trapezoid.

Using This Activity to Address Fraction Misconceptions

"Finding the Fractional Part" is an activity that helps students develop conceptual understanding of fractions and helps them reduce common misconceptions associated with fractions. This article next revisits issues presented previously, with reference to specific elements of the activity.

1. As previously mentioned, students had difficulty ordering fractions because of their misconceptions about the relative size of

Fig. 4.2. Third graders working on problem 2

fractions. The use of actual manipulatives to solve the problems in this activity furnishes a visual reminder of the size of the fraction. During the discussion of the activity, the teacher asked students what they noticed about their answers. In particular, the teacher asked them to comment on the size of the answers 1/2, 1/6, and 1/3 from the bat problem. Several third graders noticed that the smaller fraction pieces had larger denominators (see fig. 4.3). A sixth-grade student explained why one-sixth is the smallest of the three fractions: "The denominator is bigger, but that gives you a smaller piece." The visual representations provided by the pattern blocks assisted students in making these observations.

This visual representation of the fractions also helps students order fractions from least to greatest. In this activity, the teacher had not taught students to use common denominators to compare fractions. This goal of this part of the activity was to encourage students to think about the relative sizes of the fractions in comparison with the whole figure. The idea is that students can compare the fractions by the size of the pieces and begin to develop some sense of which fractions are larger than others. When students compare the two fractions one-half and two-thirds, for example, they can use the yellow hexagon to represent one whole and then show that one red trapezoid represents one-half and that two blue rhombuses represent two-thirds. Students can trade one red trapezoid for three green triangles, and they can trade two blue rhombuses for four green triangles. Four green triangles are greater than three green triangles; therefore, two-thirds is greater than one-half. In fact, students who represent each fraction with green triangles are actually finding a common denominator: 1/2 = 3/6 and 2/3 = 4/6. The teacher can subsequently make this concept explicit when students begin to observe the patterns in their block manipulations.

2. Students did not understand that the denominator represents the number of groups of equal size. Although this situation is not inherent in the activity as written, discussing the following question as a class can shed light on this issue for all students:

    Can you find one-fifth of the king's crown? Use fair trades and pattern blocks to show that your answer is correct.

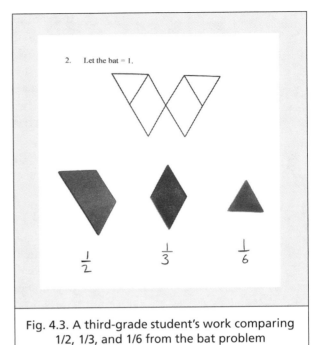

Fig. 4.3. A third-grade student's work comparing 1/2, 1/3, and 1/6 from the bat problem

The teacher posed this question to fifth and sixth graders, who met it with confusion and frustration. One student wanted to trade the shape for three blue rhombuses and "add two more." Another student traded the shape for six green triangles. Since he needed five pieces, he decided to trade two of the green triangles for one blue rhombus. He then had four green triangles and one blue rhombus. Although the pieces were not equal, he believed he had found one-fifth of the king's crown because he now had five pieces. This student experienced no cognitive dissonance between his answer and his concept of fractional parts because his understanding of fractions did not yet require the parts to be equal. When this student attempted the second part of this question, that is, using fair trades with pattern blocks to "prove" that his answer was correct, he encountered a situation that made him reflect on his understanding of fractions. Students were often unable to prove their answers, and they had to reconsider what they had done.

3. Students viewed the denominator as the number of equal pieces instead of as the number of equal groups. The teacher gave students with this misconception problems that encouraged them to broaden their schema of fractions to reflect a certain number of equal parts rather than maintain the limited view of a fraction as a certain number of equal pieces, with the number of pieces equal to the denominator (i.e., sometimes the equal parts consisted of more than one piece). In "Finding the Fractional Part," students found unit fractions when the denominator was equal to the number of same-color pattern blocks that composed the whole. For example, in the first problem, students found one-fourth of the flower. The flower consists of four blue rhombuses, so students needed only to select one of the four equal pieces to get the answer. In this activity, they also encountered situations in which their groups consisted of more than one pattern block. To determine one-half of the flower, they needed to create two groups—not two pieces—and each group consisted of two blue rhombuses. In problem 4,

the sunburst, students also had to create groups of equal size, with more than one piece in each group. Part (b) asked students to find one-third of the shape. No fair trade can be made that creates the sunburst with only three pieces. However, students can respond with an answer of four green triangles (four-twelfths) by trading the hexagon for six triangles and creating three equal groups of four triangles. Another correct answer is two blue rhombuses (two-sixths), which students can find by trading the sunburst for six blue rhombuses and creating three equal groups of two blue rhombuses.

4. Students who were able to determine an equivalent fraction procedurally were often unable to explain why the two fractions were equivalent. Further discussion of the sunburst problem can explore the reasons that four-twelfths, two-sixths, and one-third are all equivalent fractions. Students can demonstrate this equivalence by using pattern blocks, making fair trades, and stacking their answers on top of one another to show equality.

When students manipulate numbers according to algorithms that the teacher has given them, the misunderstandings that are evident usually relate to the procedures. However, when students use pattern blocks in their learning, they can continuously demonstrate understanding of the concepts. Students working on this activity initially expressed frustration at their obvious weaknesses. Over time, however, these students made great strides in their abilities to communicate their understanding. For example, after students had finished the sunburst problem, classroom discussion involved an explanation of why 2/3 = 4/6. A normal response from students who have not used manipulatives and the idea of fair trade might be the following: "you multiply the top and bottom by two and you get four-sixths." When the teacher asked sixth-grade students this question, they were likely to give the same answer; however, many of them were also able to respond with a more conceptual answer, such as, "When you trade thirds for sixths, the pieces are half the size, so you need twice as many."

One of the essential understandings related to fractions is that of equivalent fractions. Students need an understanding of equivalent fractions when developing the concept of a fraction and comparing fractions, as well as when solving real-world problems involving fractions. One might say that understanding equivalent fractions is the fundamental concept and leads to either success or frustration with the study of fractions. The next activity, "Brownies for Everyone," builds on the understanding of equivalent fractions that students practiced in "Finding the Fractional Part."

"Brownies for Everyone"

The importance of equivalent fractions is obvious when using algorithms for adding or subtracting two or more fractions. Yet the algorithms for multiplying and dividing fractions do not require common denominators or any facility with equivalent fractions. However, students who use manipulatives to solve word problems involving the multiplication or division

Students need an understanding of equivalent fractions when developing the concept of a fraction and comparing fractions, as well as when solving real-world problems involving fractions.

of fractions actually make liberal use of equivalent fractions. The activity "Brownies for Everyone" illustrates this process (see fig. 4.4). Consider the first problem in this activity:

> Selena's mom made a batch of brownies. Selena takes 1/3 of the entire pan of brownies and goes next door to her friend Janie's house. Her friend asks for 1/2 of the brownies that Selena has. What fraction of the whole pan does Janie get?

Brownies for Everyone

Selena's mom made a batch of brownies. They are still cooling in the pan, and she has not yet cut them up. Her mom tells her that she can take a portion of the pan of brownies to share with her friends.

Use pattern blocks to represent and solve the different possible scenarios below. Draw and label all your steps.

1. Scenario 1: Selena takes $\frac{1}{3}$ of the entire pan of brownies and goes next door to her friend Janie's house. Her friend asks for $\frac{1}{2}$ of the brownies that Selena has. What fraction of the whole pan of brownies does Janie get?

2. Scenario 2: Selena takes $\frac{1}{2}$ of the entire pan of brownies and heads for her friend Jamal's house. He asks for $\frac{2}{3}$ of what Selena has. What fraction of the whole pan of brownies does Jamal get?

3. Scenario 3: Selena takes $\frac{2}{3}$ of the entire pan of brownies and heads for her friend Jon's house. He asks for $\frac{3}{4}$ of what Selena has. What fraction of the whole pan of brownies does Jon get?

4. What mathematics problem are you solving in each of the scenarios above?

Fig. 4.4. "Brownies for Everyone"

This scenario is a natural extension of the first activity, which involves finding a fractional part of a picture, where the picture consists of a group of objects. When students find one-third of the bat and have traded the bat for six triangles, they have actually found one-third of six objects. One conceptual interpretation of this multiplication problem is that finding "one of the three groups that make up six" is necessary. The brownie problem is also a multiplication problem, which students can solve by finding the answer to $1/2 \times 1/3$. Students who do not know the algorithm for multiplying fractions can approach this problem by modeling it with pattern blocks. A conceptual approach to the problem $1/2 \times 1/3$ is to use one yellow hexagon to represent one, or the entire pan of brownies. Then one blue rhombus equals one-third, the amount of brownies that Selena brought to Janie's house. To take one-half of one-third, students need to find one of the two equal parts that make up one-third. They can accomplish this task by trading the blue rhombus for two green triangles. The answer then becomes one green triangle, which is one-sixth of the whole, so the answer is one-sixth.

The Mathematics behind the Blocks

The fair trade has altered the original problem, $1/2 \times 1/3$. When students trade one blue rhombus for two green triangles, they create two-sixths as a fraction that is equivalent to one-third. Thus, using equivalent fractions orchestrated by the fair trade makes the problem $1/2 \times 2/6$. Taking one of the two equal parts of two-sixths (two green triangles) is now a straightforward task, and the answer is one green triangle, or one-sixth. Observing patterns can help students understand that this answer is the same one that they obtained when applying the algorithm, and the method involving equivalent fractions connects better with their informal ways of operating.

Students build on the concept of equivalent fractions to solve a multiplication problem by creating equivalent fractions so that the denominator of the first fraction is equal to the numerator of the second fraction. In fact, the easiest problems to solve are those that are already in this form. For example, in problem 2, Selena takes one-half of the pan of brownies and gives her friend two-thirds of what she has. If the teacher turns this problem around so that Selena gives her friend one-half of the two-thirds of the pan that she has, then students can easily solve this problem by finding one of the two groups that make up two-thirds. Because two-thirds is already in two equal parts, the answer is obviously one of those two pieces, each of which is a third, resulting in an answer of one-third. In contrast with simply applying the algorithm, this process helps students develop a conceptual idea of what multiplying fractions means.

Fifth-grade students who completed this activity were able to find the answers to the word problems solely by manipulating the pattern blocks, making fair trades, and creating equivalent fractions. These students had not yet learned the algorithm for multiplying fractions, yet they demonstrated an ability to make sense of the fraction problems using informal methods, in a manner suggested by Steffe and Olive (2002).

Summary

The two activities discussed in this article promote a conceptual understanding of fractions. Although the methods target students who need more than just lecture and paper-and-pencil manipulation to be successful in mathematics, the activities increased understanding among all students. The teacher can address many common misconceptions related to the understanding of fractions with the tasks presented in this study; these tasks encouraged students to further refine and adapt their conceptions of fractions. The use of pattern blocks and the concept of fair trade help students attach meaning to the formerly abstract procedures related to fractions.

REFERENCES

National Council of Teachers of Mathematics (NCTM). *Principles and Standards for School Mathematics*. Reston, Va.: NCTM, 2000.

National Research Council. *Adding It Up: Helping Children Learn Mathematics*, edited by Jeremy Kilpatrick, Jane Swafford, and Bradford Findell. Washington, D.C.: National Academies Press, Mathematics Learning Study Committee, Center for Education, Division of Behavioral and Social Sciences and Education, 2001.

Roddick, Cheryl, and Christina Silvas-Centeno. "Developing Understanding of Fractions through Pattern Blocks and Fair Trade." *Teaching Children Mathematics* 14, no. 3 (October 2007): 140–45.

Siebert, Daniel, and Nicole Gaskin. "Creating, Naming, and Justifying Fractions." *Teaching Children Mathematics* 12, no. 8 (April 2006): 394–400.

Steffe, Leslie P., and John Olive. "The Problem of Fractions in the Elementary School." In *Putting Research into Practice in the Elementary Grades: Readings from Journals of the National Council of Teachers of Mathematics*, edited by Donald L. Chambers, pp. 128–32. Reston, Va.: National Council of Teachers of Mathematics, 2002.

Van de Walle, John A., and LouAnn H. Lovin. *Teaching Student-Centered Mathematics, Grades 5–8*. Boston, Mass.: Pearson Education, 2006.

Differentiating Practice
to Help Students Master Basic Facts

Linda Forbringer
Allison J. Fahsl

How can I help all my students become fluent with basic mathematics facts? Some students seem to master them effortlessly, whereas others struggle. How can I meet the diverse needs of all students in my classroom?

THE PRECEDING questions trouble both new and experienced teachers. All students should learn to compute fluently (NCTM 2000), and students must be able to solve mathematics facts accurately and efficiently to attain this fluency. Basic addition facts consist of all combinations of single-digit addends, and basic subtraction facts are the inverse of the addition facts. Basic multiplication facts consist of all combinations of single-digit factors, and division facts are the inverse of the multiplication facts (Hudson and Miller 2006). Students who master basic facts can direct their cognitive energy to more-complicated tasks. Those students who continue to struggle with basic facts often fail to develop an understanding of higher mathematical concepts. When these students encounter more-complex problems, their working memory is consumed with the basic computation and they have little cognitive energy available to focus on conceptual understanding (Bos and Vaughn 2006; Friend and Bursuck 2002).

Within a single classroom, however, students often differ widely in the rate at which they master basic computation. Although all students begin the process of developing computational fluency at the concrete level and gradually develop the conceptual understanding that is fundamental to mathematical reasoning (Baroody 2006), learners differ in the amount of time and support that they need to develop number sense. Some students seem to move quickly beyond understanding to automaticity, whereas others may struggle. An instructional pace appropriate for most of the class often leaves these students confused and overwhelmed.

One way to support struggling learners is to offer extended opportunities for them to explore mathematics at the concrete level. Miller and Mercer (1993) determined that students may need as many as seven lessons using manipulatives and pictures before they can transfer their understanding to such abstract representations as mathematics problems presented in algorithmic form. Students with learning disabilities, mental retardation,

Some students seem to quickly move beyond understanding to automaticity, whereas others may struggle. An instructional pace appropriate for most of the class often leaves these students confused and overwhelmed.

and other disabilities may require extra practice to reach mastery (Choate 2004; Erlauer 2003; Friend and Bursuck 2002; Tucker, Singleton, and Weaver 2005), whereas gifted students typically learn quickly and require less practice (Davis and Rimm 1998). In a mixed-ability classroom, students are often at different points in their progression from concrete to abstract representation. Some students may benefit from using the manipulatives for a long time, whereas others will be able to progress to abstract representation more quickly. By creating an atmosphere in which both approaches are acceptable, the teacher can provide differentiated support that meets the needs of all students in the class.

Another powerful way to address diverse students' needs is to differentiate the amount of content that students practice at one time. In the 1950s, research studies of cognitive capacity revealed that the average adult can hold seven items, plus or minus two, in working memory (Miller 1994). Subsequent studies have shown that capacity increases with age. Although Miller reported that adults can remember five to nine items, Pascual-Leon (1970) found that the average seven-year-old can recall only three items, plus or minus two, and the average nine-year-old can recall four items, plus or minus two.

Grouping facts into meaningful clusters can relieve cognitive load and aid memory. For example, students who understand the commutative property are able to learn all the multiplication facts by practicing only half of them (Baroody 2006). A student who understands that multiplying by zero always results in an answer of zero also has fewer discrete facts to remember. Since zero is a factor in nineteen multiplication facts, the student can master nineteen facts by understanding just one important relationship (Tucker, Singleton, and Weaver 2005). Although many students intuitively discern these concepts, students with learning problems often need additional instructional time, more examples, and more discussion of strategies before they develop the same understanding.

Textbooks and instructional materials often overlook cognitive research. Many commercial games and materials have students practice too many facts at once, and they often do not cluster those facts in any meaningful way. For example, until students have mastered a large portion of the facts, using flashcards or playing a game with all the addition facts—or all the multiplication facts—violates research regarding the short-term memory capacity of most children in elementary school. Teachers can make such materials more effective by limiting the number of facts practiced and by grouping the facts into more-meaningful clusters. Because capacity differs among learners, the number of items that some students in the class should be practicing at any one time may be as few as one, whereas other students in the same class may successfully work with as many as six new items at a time.

Additionally, research has documented the importance of allowing sufficient time for consolidation. Attempting to teach something new too soon, without allowing sufficient time for previous learning to consolidate, can actually disrupt the learning process (Wolfe 2001). Overloading working memory is especially problematic for students with disabilities, who frequently have problems with short-term memory (Bos and Vaughn 2006; Freund and Rich 2005; Haager and Klingner 2005). These students learn more easily when they have sufficient time to master one group of facts before they have to focus on the next (Choate 2004; Erlauer 2003; Friend and Bursuck 2002; Tucker, Singleton, and Weaver 2005). In contrast, gifted students typically have exceptional memory skills, learn quickly, and need less practice. Since most classrooms include a variety of students who differ in their short-term memory capacity, teachers must be able to differentiate the number of facts presented, as well as the amount of time spent in practice, to match the diverse needs of students in the classroom.

Differentiating instruction begins with assessment. On the basis of assessment results, the teacher identifies a small number of appropriately challenging facts for each child to practice. When students gain proficiency, they are able to tackle additional facts or groups of related facts. For example, a student may begin working on four or five related facts that he or she did not know at the time of the initial assessment. When the student gains fluency with those facts, the teacher can add additional facts or groups of facts. Monitoring students' progress allows the teacher to make appropriate adaptations so that each child continues to experience both challenge and success.

The activities that follow include a variety of games that the teacher can easily adapt to differentiate practice within a classroom. Games furnish motivating opportunities for students to practice mathematics facts. Research indicates that games increase student involvement, encourage communication, and facilitate social interaction, all of which are positively related to increased academic achievement (Desforges 2001; Gough 1999; Kamii and Anderson 2003; Lewis 2005; O'Doherty 2000). When used as part of a comprehensive program, games can help students develop computational fluency. Students also need opportunities to discuss strategies, to connect mathematics facts with other mathematical activities, and to use those facts while they engage in mathematical reasoning and problem-solving activities.

The authors selected the activities for this article because they are engaging, promote peer interaction, and can easily be differentiated to meet students' needs. Teachers are sometimes reluctant to differentiate instruction because they are concerned about the social repercussions of giving students assignments that look different. With these games, all students can be engaged in the same activity, but the number and type of facts that each individual practices can vary. All students can therefore experience appropriately challenging activities that can help each one develop automaticity with basic mathematics facts.

Students also need opportunities to discuss strategies, to connect mathematics facts with other mathematical activities, and to use those facts while they engage in mathematical reasoning and problem-solving activities.

Activities That the Teacher Can Adapt to Differentiate Students' Practice

Game Boards

Game boards are an enjoyable and easy way to differentiate instruction. Many classrooms already have game boards available for practicing basic facts. If teachers make slight modifications to the games, all students in the class can enjoy the same games while engaging in practice that appropriately meets each student's individual needs. The teacher can use two common ways of modifying the level of difficulty when using game boards. Some games require the student to draw a card and answer a question to advance. The teacher can modify the level of difficulty of this type of game simply by changing the cards in the draw pile to match the readiness level of the students playing. Some students may benefit from focused practice with a small number of facts, whereas others can play the same game but use more facts or more-difficult combinations. A variation of this method is to use multiple draw piles that differ in level of difficulty. Each student can then choose a card of the appropriate level on her or his turn.

Another way to differentiate board games is to use laminated game boards with blank spaces. The teacher can use erasable markers to write questions or mathematics facts at the appropriate level of complexity on the game board. The teacher can change the questions according to the skill level of the children playing the game. Either way, all students can play the same board game while they each practice facts at the appropriate level of complexity.

Self-Checking Puzzle Pieces

The teacher can make self-checking puzzle pieces for any mathematics facts. Templates are available for die-cutting machines, or educators can purchase blank puzzle pieces from teacher supply stores. Teachers can also make puzzle pieces from construction paper, cardstock, or foam. They can write a problem on one puzzle piece and the answer on the corresponding piece (see fig. 5.1). The teacher then gives students puzzle pieces containing the facts that they need to practice. Self-checking puzzle pieces provide another easy way to allow all children to work on the same type of task while differentiating the level of difficulty of the problems.

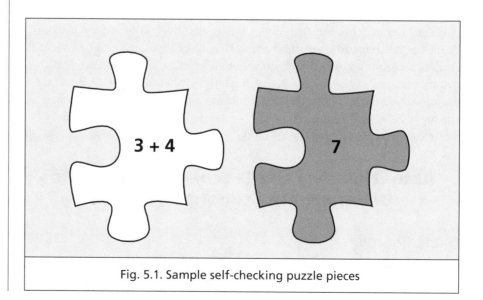

Fig. 5.1. Sample self-checking puzzle pieces

Old Dog

Two to four children who need to practice the same mathematics facts can play this variation of the popular children's card game of Old Maid. The teacher creates a deck containing twenty-four pairs of cards (mathematics facts and answers) and one card with a picture of a dog (or other picture of his or her choice), which is the "old dog" card. The object of the game is to avoid being the player left holding the old-dog card when someone runs out of cards. The dealer first shuffles the cards and then deals the entire deck. The number of cards that each child receives varies depending on the number of children playing the game. All players do not need to receive the same number of cards (i.e., some players may receive one more card than the others). Players form pairs by matching any facts and corresponding answers in their hands and place these pairs faceup on the table. Then, beginning with the player on the dealer's left, each player in turn offers his or her hand (facedown) to the player on the left, who draws one card. If that card creates a pair with a card in the hand of the player on the left, the player places it faceup on the table. The game ends when someone runs out of cards. The player left with the old-dog card is the old dog.

Versions of this game are available for purchase. Unfortunately, most commercially available decks of cards include too many facts to furnish the focused practice necessary for efficient learning. By making multiple decks of the game so that each deck contains a limited number of facts, teachers can provide differentiated practice. Groups of students can use the deck that matches their readiness level. All students can participate in the same activity, but each can focus on learning an appropriately limited number of facts.

Concentration

One student—or a pair of students who need to practice the same mathematics facts—can play this old-fashioned card game. The teacher creates eight, ten, or twelve pairs of cards with the mathematics fact written on one card and the answer on the other (similar to the cards used in old dog). The objective of the game is to form pairs of matching cards. A match consists of two cards that represent equivalent amounts (see fig. 5.2). To play the game, players shuffle the cards, then arrange all the cards facedown on the playing surface. When two students play, they take turns turning over two cards. If the cards match, the player who turned them over receives the cards and takes another turn. If the cards do not match, the player turns them back over to their original position and the next player's turn begins. After the students have matched all cards, the player with the most cards is the winner. When students play the solitaire version of the game, the procedure is similar, but the objective is to collect all the pairs as quickly as possible.

Again, teachers can purchase concentration card games. As with the other card games, most of the commercially available decks of cards include too many facts. Creating multiple decks and limiting the number and type of facts included in each deck allow the teacher to give each student practice that is appropriately differentiated to match his or her ability level.

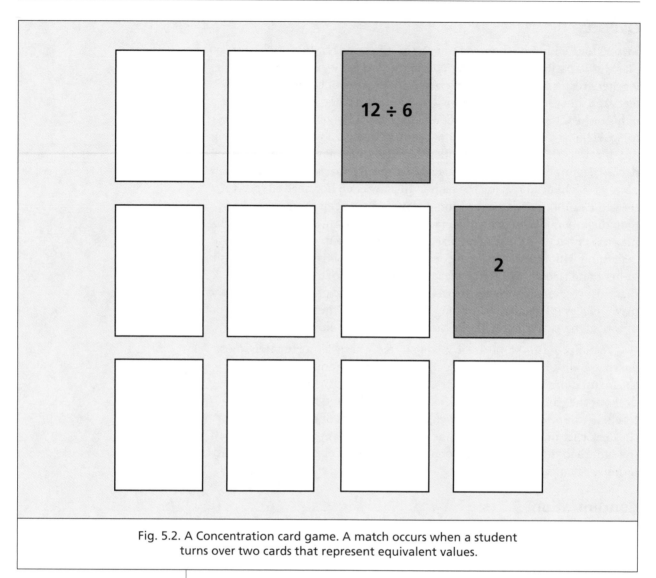

Fig. 5.2. A Concentration card game. A match occurs when a student turns over two cards that represent equivalent values.

Bingo

Teachers commonly use the game of Bingo to review a variety of concepts in the classroom. They can purchase Bingo boards for teaching mathematics facts, or they can print them from the Internet. Unfortunately, most commercially available boards contain too many facts to provide the focused practice that students need for efficient learning. However, teachers can easily adapt Bingo. Since every player receives a different Bingo board, the teacher can easily differentiate practice by giving each student a board that focuses on the specific facts that the child needs to practice. The teacher can easily and unobtrusively distribute different boards to different students. When the class plays the game, the teacher draws answers from a pool of cards that includes all possible answers. If the teacher draws answers randomly, all students should have an equal chance to win. All students can participate in the same activity, but each can focus on an appropriately limited number of facts.

Roundtable and Roundrobin

Roundtable and roundrobin are cooperative learning structures developed by Spencer Kagan (1994). Students work in small groups to brainstorm examples of a concept, ways to approach a problem, and so on. In roundtable, the students pass a piece of paper clockwise around the group, and each student in turn writes one new idea on the paper. Roundrobin is similar, except that students respond verbally rather than in writing. Either approach works well for practicing mathematics facts. The teacher can ask the students to brainstorm all the ways of forming a particular number, such as twelve; brainstorm all the facts in a related facts family; or create a list of multiples of nine. In a variation of roundtable, students can pass around a hundreds chart and take turns coloring in multiples of three, multiples of four, and so on (Andrini 1991).

Typically, when teachers use roundtable or roundrobin, the students work in small groups, but all students in the class brainstorm the same concept. However, either structure can easily become a differentiated activity if the teacher asks each group to brainstorm facts that fit the particular needs of the members in the group. For example, the teacher can ask one group to brainstorm all the ways to form twelve while another group lists ways to form seven and a group of students needing more challenge brainstorms ways to form a total of twenty. For students who still require concrete representation, the teacher can provide blocks or other manipulatives. This variation offers yet another way to differentiate instruction to meet the unique needs of students in the classroom.

Dominoes

Dominoes provide another way to differentiate instruction on the basis of a student's level of readiness or ability. When students play dominoes, the teacher can involve all students in the same engaging activity while they experience differentiated practice that focuses on their individual needs. Teachers can obtain dominoes that contain mathematics problems by purchasing them, printing them from the Internet, or making them by hand. Again, teachers must exercise caution because many commercially available sets of dominoes contain problems that vary greatly in their level of difficulty. Whether the teacher makes her or his own dominoes or reorganizes purchased sets, students will learn facts faster if the teacher gives them sets of dominoes that allow them repeated practice of a smaller range of items.

Each domino is a rectangular tile with a line down the center and a mathematics problem or answer written on each end. A set of dominoes usually contains twenty-eight tiles, although teachers may choose to alter this number. The teacher can create sets of dominoes that focus on specific facts, fact families, or concepts. Two to four students play the game. Before the game begins, the students place all dominoes face-down on the table and shuffle them. Each player then takes six dominoes and arranges them so that the other players cannot see them. Play begins with the youngest player (or play can go in alphabetical order or reverse alphabetical order). The first player lays one domino right-side-up on the table. Play progresses clockwise. The second player tries to place on the table a domino that matches one side of the domino already played. For example, if the first domino played contained 24 ÷ 8 on one side and 5 on the other, the second player could use a domino containing the solution to 24 ÷ 8 (i.e., 3) or a domino containing a problem whose answer is 5, such as 10 ÷ 2 or 15 ÷ 3.

Play usually involves joining dominoes lengthwise, end to end, so that a problem matches its corresponding answer. If a domino contains doubles (i.e., both halves of the tile are identical), the player should play it crosswise, across the line of play. After a student plays a double, the player adding the next tile again plays it lengthwise. If a player does not have a domino that matches any of the open facts on the table, the player picks a domino from the pile and skips that turn. Play continues clockwise around the table, with each player adding a tile or drawing a domino and skipping a turn. The winner is the first person to dispose of all his or her dominoes. If no one disposes of all his or her tiles, then the person with the fewest dominoes left is the winner.

Conclusion

The Equity Principle "demands that reasonable and appropriate accommodations be made as needed to promote access and attainment for all students" (NCTM 2000, p. 12). Some students benefit from multisensory formats, and others need extra practice time or additional challenges. In any classroom, students differ in their learning styles, readiness levels, and practice time needed for mastery. As specified in *Principles and Standards for School Mathematics*, "Equity does not mean that every student should receive identical instruction.... All students should have access to an excellent and equitable mathematics program that furnishes solid support for their learning and is responsive to their prior knowledge, intellectual strengths, and personal interests" (NCTM 2000, pp. 12–13). Differentiating instruction allows teachers to meet the diverse needs of learners in today's classrooms. The use of mathematics games gives students an interesting and engaging way to practice basic facts in a manner that is highly motivating and promotes active participation and social interaction. When teachers modify practice activities in response to learner differences, all students can increase fluency with basic mathematics facts.

When teachers modify practice activities in response to learner differences, all students can increase fluency with basic mathematics facts.

REFERENCES

Andrini, Beth. *Cooperative Learning and Mathematics.* San Juan Capistrano, Calif.: Resources for Teachers, 1991.

Baroody, Arthur J. "Why Children Have Difficulties Mastering the Basic Number Combinations and How to Help Them." *Teaching Children Mathematics* 13, no. 1 (August 2006): 22–31.

Bos, Candace S., and Sharon Vaughn. *Strategies for Teaching Students with Learning and Behavior Problems.* 6th ed. Boston: Pearson, 2006.

Choate, Joyce S. *Successful Inclusive Teaching: Proven Ways to Detect and Correct Special Needs.* Boston: Allyn & Bacon, 2004.

Davis, Gary A., and Sylvia B. Rimm. *Education of the Gifted and Talented.* 4th ed. Boston: Allyn & Bacon, 1998.

Desforges, Anne. "Can I Still Play When I Am Seven?" *Mathematics Teaching* no. 175 (June 2001): 16–19.

Erlauer, Laura. *The Brain-Compatible Classroom: Using What We Know about Learning to Improve Teaching.* Alexandria, Va.: Association for Supervision and Curriculum Development, 2003. Freund, Lisa, and Rebecca Rich. *Teaching Students with Learning Problems in the Inclusive Classroom.* Upper Saddle River, N.J.: Pearson, 2005.

Friend, Marilyn, and William Bursuck. *Including Students with Special Needs: A Practical Guide for Classroom Teachers.* Boston: Pearson, 2002.

Gough, John. "Arithmetic Games—Very Equable?" *Australian Primary Mathematics Classroom* 4, no. 3 (September 1999): 12–17.

Haager, Diane, and Janette K. Klingner. *Differentiating Instruction in Inclusive Classrooms.* Boston: Pearson, 2005.

Hudson, Pamela, and Susan P. Miller. *Developing and Implementing Mathematics Instruction for Students with Diverse Learning Needs.* Boston: Pearson, 2006.

Kagan, Spencer. *Cooperative Learning.* San Clemente, Calif.: Resources for Teachers, 1994.

Kamii, Constance, and Catherine Anderson. "Multiplication Games: How We Made and Used Them." *Teaching Children Mathematics* 10, no. 3 (November 2003): 135–41.

Lewis, Tom. "Facts + Fun = Fluency." *Teaching Children Mathematics* 12, no. 1 (August 2005): 8.

Miller, George A. "The Magical Number Seven, Plus or Minus Two: Some Limits on Our Capacity for Processing Information." *Psychological Review Journal* 101, no. 2 (April 1994): 343–52.

Miller, Susan P., and Cecil D. Mercer. "Using Data to Learn about Concrete-Semiconcrete-Abstract Instruction for Students with Math Disabilities." *Learning Disabilities Research and Practice* 8, no. 2 (Spring 1993): 89–96.

National Council of Teachers of Mathematics (NCTM). *Principles and Standards for School Mathematics.* Reston, Va.: NCTM, 2000.

O'Doherty, Cassandra. "Let's Play Mathematics." *Australian Primary Mathematics Classroom* 5, no. 1 (March 2000): 28–31.

Pascual-Leon, Juan. "A Mathematical Model for the Transition Rule in Piaget's Developmental Stages." *Acta Psychologica Journal* 32 (Spring 1970): 301–45.

Tucker, Benny F., Ann H. Singleton, and Terry L. Weaver. *Teaching Mathematics to All Children.* 2nd ed. Upper Saddle River, N.J.: Prentice Hall, 2005.

Wolfe, Patricia. *Brain Matters: Translating Research into Classroom Practice.* Alexandria, Va.: Association for Supervision and Curriculum Development, 2001.

6

In My Time—Learning to Think in Tens and Ones

Susan N. Friel
Tery Gunter
Catharina Ringer

Try putting yourself in *their* shoes. Imagine yourself as a child encountering the "school" world of mathematics. You come to school knowing something about quantity and how to operate on quantities when you encounter their use in a variety of contexts. You are able to operate with quantities mentally by using a variety of strategies. You do not see any connection with a "school need" to learn a notational system and a set of written procedures to solve mathematics problems. However, your teachers need to build a bridge so that you can move in that direction, that is, to on-paper work, with the eventual goal of reducing the mental demands as you increase your ability to do your thinking by using paper-and-pencil procedures. Teachers need to think carefully and purposefully about how to help students construct and travel across that bridge. Traditional ways seldom help students do so. Rather, traditional paths appear to highlight mathematics as a disconnected, fragmented, abstract domain that students may come to view as somewhat arbitrary and inaccessible.

Variability and diversity in knowledge and preparation for school are to be anticipated. Many of you who work with 4–8 year olds do realize that—

- there are significant differences in numerical knowledge of children when they begin school;
- some 4-year-olds have attained a level of number knowledge that others will not attain until they are 7 years old.

However, did you also know that—

- children who are low-attaining in the early years tend to remain so throughout their schooling?
- the knowledge gap between low-attaining children and average or able children tends to increase over the course of their years at school (from a difference of 3 years initially to a difference of 7 years after ten years of schooling)?

(Wright, Martland, and Stafford 2006, p. 2)

How is it possible that some children face such daunting odds coming to this place called *school*—a place intended to provide comparable opportunities for all children to grow and develop mathematically?

> **How is it possible that some children face such daunting odds coming to this place called *school*—a place intended to provide comparable opportunities for all children to grow and develop mathematically?**

Simon (2006) highlights the need to pay attention to "key developmental understandings" (KDUs) that are foundational. KDUs mark crucial transitions that are essential for the mathematical development of students.

What do we need to know about learning mathematics that may help us address these daunting odds? Simon (2006) highlights the need to pay attention to "key developmental understandings" (KDUs) that are foundational. KDUs mark crucial transitions that are essential for the mathematical development of students. Simon identifies such transitions with qualitative shifts in students' abilities to think about and perceive particular mathematical relationships. Simon states,

> I am not referring to a missing piece of information that affects students' performance; rather, I am emphasizing that *without completing a developmental process* [italics added for emphasis], the students lack a particular mathematical ability. (p. 364)

Further, "students without the knowledge do not tend to acquire it as a result of an explanation or demonstration" (p. 362). We might ask what understandings are essential to the development of particular mathematical ideas and can help us account for differences between those learners who show evidence of more sophisticated conceptions and those who exhibit less sophisticated conceptions.

In early number work, cardinality, composite units, and conservation of number are examples of such understandings that "significantly affect children's abilities to conceive of and work with numbers" (Simon 2006, p. 367). Knowledge of composite units includes the ability to think in tens and ones. This knowledge—of composite units and tens and ones—provides the basis for the development of a rich and robust conceptual understanding of place value.

Children can and do develop initial place-value knowledge through their work with problems that engage them in adding and subtracting multidigit numbers. Such work involves developing not only sound knowledge of the tens and ones structure of the teen numbers but also the tens and ones structure of numbers from 20 to 100 (Carpenter et al. 1999; Wright, Stanger, Stafford, and Martland 2006). Table 6.1 shows three kinds of tasks related to place-value understanding by showing the contrasting responses of two children to these tasks; one of the children has little or no knowledge of the tens and ones structure of teen numbers, and the other one does have this knowledge (Wright, Stanger, et al. 2006, p. 26).

One way that we can help students develop their understanding of this kind of place-value knowledge is through their work with addition and subtraction of multidigit numbers, specifically by posing word problems about situations that have different problem structures. For example, consider the following two problems:

> There are 24 people on the bus. Some people get off. Now there are 19 people on the bus. How many people got off the bus?

> Twenty-four children are playing soccer. Nineteen are girls, and the rest are boys. How many boys are playing soccer?

Table 6.1
Contrasting Students' Responses—Understanding Tens and Ones

Task	Response from Child with Sound Knowledge of Tens and Ones Structure	Response from Child Who Lacks Sound Knowledge of Tens and Ones Structure
1. Here is a bundle of ten sticks. Here are six more sticks. How many sticks are there in all?	Spontaneously answers "sixteen."	Counts on from ten to sixteen while looking at each of the six sticks in turn, or attempts to count all the sticks from one
2. Here are four sticks (cover with a screen), and here are ten more sticks (put out a pile of ten sticks); how many sticks are there in all?	Spontaneously answers "fourteen."	Counts on from four to fourteen while looking at each stick in the pile of ten, or counts from one to four while looking at the screen, and then continues to count each of the ten sticks in the pile
3. Put out a numeral card for 18. Point to the numeral 1 in the 18, and ask the child what it stands for?	Answers "ten."	Answers "one."

Students can express both situations with the same number sentence: $24 - \square = 19$. The first problem involves a separate, or "take away," interpretation, whereas the second problem involves a "comparison" interpretation. The contexts help generate students' use of different solution strategies. Evidence suggests "that the general meaning of a problem [i.e., the problem structure] rather than specific words or phrases determines both the difficulty of the problem and the processes students use to solve it" (Chapin and Johnson 2006, p. 56).

Educators can classify problem structures for addition and subtraction problems by using four broad categories: join, separate, part-part-whole, and compare problems (Carpenter et al. 1999). Within the four broad categories are eleven problem types (see examples in table 6.2); in typical school settings, however, students use only one or two types of problems regularly. A far more powerful instructional approach exposes students to all eleven of the problem types.

In addition to the importance of problem types, the numbers used in problems also affect difficulty. A general rule of thumb about number choices is to use numbers that students know in composing problems, that is, students should not be learning the meanings of the numbers at the same time that they are considering the use of these numbers in problem contexts. Early number work focuses on structuring the numbers 1 to 10. Students move to structuring numbers 1 to 20 by first grade (i.e., including teen numbers) and by second grade, to structuring numbers 1 to 100 and larger (i.e., working with multidigit numbers and place-value concepts).

Table 6.2 furnishes sample problems that teachers can use to provoke students' knowledge development in working with tens and ones (multidigit numbers).

Table 6.2
Problem Types Using Tens and Ones

JOIN	Result unknown	Change unknown	Start unknown
	A total of 28 girls and 35 boys were on the playground at recess. How many children were on the playground at recess?	Maria made 9 snowballs. How many more snowballs would she need to make so that she would have a total of 21 snowballs?	Larry has some M&M's. His friend gave him 11 more M&M's. Now Larry has 22 M&M's. How many M&M's did he start with?
SEPARATE	**Result unknown**	**Change unknown**	**Start unknown**
	There were 51 geese in the farmer's field. Then 28 of the geese flew away. How many geese were left in the field?	Derek picked 30 flowers. He gave some to his teacher. Now he has 19 flowers. How many flowers did he give to his teacher?	Rene had some erasers. She lost 15 of the erasers. Then she had 16 left. How many erasers did Rene start with?
PART-PART-WHOLE	**Whole unknown**	**Part unknown**	
	Shawna has 39 red trucks and 52 blue trucks. How many trucks does Shawna have?	Carol has 38 tennis balls. Nineteen of them are green, and the rest are yellow. How many yellow tennis balls does Carol have?	
COMPARE	**Difference unknown**	**Larger quantity unknown**	**Smaller quantity unknown**
	Melissa has 17 books. George has 24 books. How many more books does George have than Melissa?	Emily has saved 38 cans for recycling. Matthew has saved 23 more cans than Emily. How many cans has Matthew saved?	Susan has 34 rocks in her collection. She has 15 more rocks than her brother. How many rocks does her brother have?

The number size can vary, as can the theme or context of the problems; however, the basic structure involving actions and relationships remains the same. Join and Separate problems involve actions.... Part-Part-Whole problems involve the relationship between a set and its two subsets. Compare problems involve comparisons between two disjoint sets. (Carpenter et al. 1999[1], p. 7)

We[2] worked with second-grade students and used these types of problems regularly throughout an entire school year. These second graders represented a wide range of abilities and backgrounds. They included students who were developmentally delayed, were deaf, had attention deficit hyperactivity disorder, were academically and intellectually gifted, and had specific learning disabilities. They represented various socioeconomic groups, with about one-third receiving free or reduced-price lunch, and various

---

1. *Children's Mathematics: Cognitively Guided Instruction* (Carpenter et al. 1999) is a comprehensive resource that provides detailed information about the use of word problems to encourage mathematics learning.
2. Gunter currently teaches second grade, and Ringer recently left her second-grade classroom to pursue graduate work. Friel, Gunter, and Ringer have been working together to explore ways to help second-grade students understand place-value concepts and work with multidigit numbers. They are committed to finding ways to help all the students in these classes be successful.

racial and ethnic groups, including students who were African American, Hispanic/Latino, White, Asian, and American Indian.

During the fall, the focus was primarily on solving join and separate problems, specifically the following: join result unknown, join change unknown, separate result unknown, and separate change unknown. Students typically encounter join and separate result-unknown problems in most school mathematics; they typically do not encounter change-unknown problem types. Join and separate problems involve actions that increase or decrease quantities, respectively; in these problems, the actions of adding or subtracting are explicit. Students moved fluidly between whole-class discussions, strategic partnerships, and small-group arrangements to facilitate deeper understanding and to enable the teacher to differentiate instruction on the basis of students' needs.

Early on, we began to work with "structuring the mathematics" that the students were reporting when they described their mental strategies. *Structuring the mathematics* means making explicit the mathematics that surfaced when students described their mental strategies. A fundamental component in this structuring was providing explicit notation for students' verbal mental processes, initially as a way of creating a record for the rest of the class to see. As learning progressed and students described their thinking in writing, many students adopted forms of notation that mirrored those that the teachers had already introduced; students typically wrote a description—after the fact—of what they had already done. Eventually, the notation became a tool for thinking, and students solved problems by working through the notation, connecting their mental work with paper-and-pencil recording, and thereby laying the groundwork for identifying more-systematic and more-consistent ways of solving problems.

We wanted to help students move to the use of written notation and eventually to strategies that would permit them to "think on paper" rather than mentally. Keeping this goal in mind, and being influenced by the work of Robert Wright and others (Wright, Martland, and Stafford 2006; Wright, Martland, Stafford, and Stanger 2006; Wright, Stanger, et al. 2006), we purposefully introduced specific written notations as a way of recording reported mental strategies; we intended the notations to mirror the students' mental strategies. From their first experiences with word problems, we asked students to also provide some written record of their thinking. Initially, many students were likely to document their work by drawing pictures. When they worked with multidigit numbers, we encouraged them to use tens-cube towers and ones to model their solutions.

The following paragraphs and charts give examples of mental strategies and their translation to written notation. This kind of thinking and working developed gradually. We intend to show the relation between mental work and written work and therefore do not highlight the development to this stage that occurs over time. The student-generated number sentences in these examples are situational equations as opposed to solution equations, that is, the number sentence reflects the problem structure but may not reflect the way that students solved the problem.

> Early on, we began to work with "structuring the mathematics" that the students were reporting when they described their mental strategies.
>
> A fundamental component in this structuring was providing explicit notation for students' verbal mental processes, initially as a way of creating a record for the rest of the class to see.

Examples

Example 1

Tom has 28 pennies in his bank. He collected 39 more pennies. How many pennies does Tom have in his bank now? (Carpenter et al. 1999)

The following chart describes the mental strategy that students might use and how the student might structure the written record of the mental strategy.

Mental Strategy	Structuring Written Record of Solution Strategy
Students use Unifix cubes arranged in tens-sticks, structured in two colors (five of each), intended to encourage thinking and counting in groups of fives. A student takes two tens (tens-sticks) and eight ones (cubes). Then the student takes three tens (tens-sticks) and nine ones (cubes) 	The teacher encourages students to record their number sentences first: $28 + 39 = \underline{\ \ \ }$ The student records the same actions that she used with tens-sticks and individual cubes. The student may do the actions with the cubes and then record the pictures, or she may have moved to a point in her development in which she completes actions through drawing pictures only, typically in the following way:
The student counts as follows: 10, 20, 30, 40, 50, 51, 52, 53, 54, 55, 56, 57, 58, 59, 60, 61, 62, 63, 64, 65, 66, 67. She writes a number sentence: $28 + 39 = 67$	The student still counts as follows: 10, 20, 30, 40, 50, 51, 52, 53, 54, 55, 56, 57, 58, 59, 60, 61, 62, 63, 64, 65, 66, 67. Then the student records an answer in equation form.

Not all students directly model problems. Some students demonstrate more advanced thinking with tens and ones through their use of counting strategies. For example, some students reported their mental work as described here; the notation that eventually evolved is the *jump strategy* (Wright, Stanger, et al. 2006).

Example 2

Max had 46 comic books. For his birthday, his father gave him 37 more comic books. How many comic books does Max have now? (Carpenter et al. 1999)

Mental Strategy	Structuring Written Record of Solution Strategy
A student reads the problem. He writes 46 and 37 on paper to remember the numbers. The student says, "46" and then counts on, saying, "56, 66, 76, 77, 78, 79, 80, 81, 82, 83." There are 83 comic books.	A student writes the number sentence: $$46 + 37 = \_\_\_$$ In mirroring this counting-on strategy in written form, the student can use an empty number line. Jumps of tens followed by jumps of ones reflect the mental strategy. This jump strategy introduces some "conventions," for example, recording the size of the jump above the jump. The student records his answer of 83 in the equation.

Some students used a strategy that involved decomposing numbers into tens and ones, using only numbers; it is a *split strategy* (Wright, Stanger, et al. 2006).

Example 3

Max had 44 comic books. For his birthday, his dad gave him 19 more comic books. How many comic books does Max have all together? (Carpenter et al. 1999)

Mental Strategy	Structuring Written Record of Solution Strategy
A student reads the problem and writes the number sentence: $$44 + 19 = \square$$ The student verbally describes the following solution path: I know that forty plus ten equals fifty. And four plus nine equals thirteen. Thirteen is three more than ten, so I knew I would have sixty-three.	A student writes the number sentence: $$44 + 19 = \_\_\_\_\_$$ Written notation for this strategy, which is called a *split strategy*, looks like the following: $$40 + 10 = 50$$ $$4 + 9 = 13$$ $$50 + 13 = 63$$

By January or February, some students moved to more formal recording of the jump strategy and used numerical representations instead of an empty number line. We actually modeled this method of solving problems by January to encourage this kind of next-steps thinking.

Example 4

Kevin had 84 gumdrops. During one week, he ate 29 gumdrops. How many gumdrops does he have left? (Carpenter et al. 1999)

Mental Strategy	Structuring Written Record of Solution Strategy
A student reads the problem, then writes the following: $$84 - 29 =$$ As he thinks out loud, we hear— "If I had eighty-four gumdrops … and I ate twenty …, I would have sixty-four gumdrops because it was eighty-four minus twenty, so that would sixty-four. I take away four more and that would be sixty, but I knew I had to take away five more, and so that would be fifty-five."	The student writes the number sentence: $$84 - 29 = \_\_\_$$ A possible translation to a jump strategy that does not use the number line looks like the following: $$84 - 20 = 64$$ $$64 - 4 = 60$$ $$60 - 5 = 55$$ At this level of thinking, students talk about subtracting to find "helpful tens," that is, getting to sixty as a helpful ten or a friendly number.

Students' work in devising and making explicit their strategies for solving problems develops over time. Our attempts to structure the mathematics of mental strategies by introducing notation that highlighted the use of tens and ones and at the same time honored the students' strategies helped move students to greater formalization of the mathematics of adding and subtracting multidigit numbers.

However, during this time, several different abilities related to the KDU of understanding tens and ones surfaced. Initially, we checked to verify that students did think of ten as a composite unit that they could count. One quick way to assess this understanding involved putting out a pile of thirty-three cubes and asking a student to make groups of tens. Assuming that the student was able to make groups of tens[3], the important question when the cubes were arranged in three tens and three ones was "Can you tell me how many cubes there are in all?" Some students pushed the cubes together and began to count by ones. Other students realized that counting by tens and ones was possible. The latter students were ready to move forward to develop the previously described strategies when solving multidigit word problems.

Those students who were not yet able to use tens and ones to count needed additional experiences to build this knowledge; the teacher could not simply tell them that they could do it. Such experiences as building and comparing numbers with cubes, counting by tens on and off the decade,

---

3. One of the authors worked with a second-grade student, who, when requested to make groups of tens, pulled out bunches of cubes but did not count to make sure that each group had ten. Observing this behavior certainly provided important information.

and using carefully selected numbers within problems all helped students construct this understanding.

However, students were not comfortable with all strategies described. By January, we were typically seeing three primary strategies in use: a *modeling strategy* that involved drawing pictures of tens and ones and counting, first by tens and then by ones; the *split strategy;* and the *jump strategy,* primarily by using an empty number line. Figure 6.1 shows samples of students' work that demonstrate these three strategies.

In January, we decided that students should move toward using a counting-on strategy, that is, should be able to count on from a number by tens and ones. At that point, we discovered that the students who preferred using a modeling strategy were not able to count off the decade by tens—another component of understanding and being able to think with tens and ones (Wright, Stanger, et al. 2006). Available assessments help identify this roadblock. Figure 6.2 shows one part of a possible assessment (Wright, Martland, and Stafford 2006).

The steps of this assessment are as follows:

a. Put out one strip of ten (have student determine that it is ten), and follow with a second strip of ten. Can the student count 10, 20? Follow with additional tens-strips for a count to 90.

b. Put out a strip of four and then a tens-strip. Can the student count 4, 14? Follow with additional tens-strips for a count to 94.

When students who used the modeling strategy were given part (b) of the task, they were unable to identify 14 by first identifying 4 and counting on by 10 to 14. Instead, they reverted to counting on by ones: 5, 6, 7, 8, 9, 10, 11, 12, 13, 14. Adults may have difficulty imagining that students who demonstrated apparent success by using tens and ones with the modeling strategy actually were stumped by an understanding that should have been

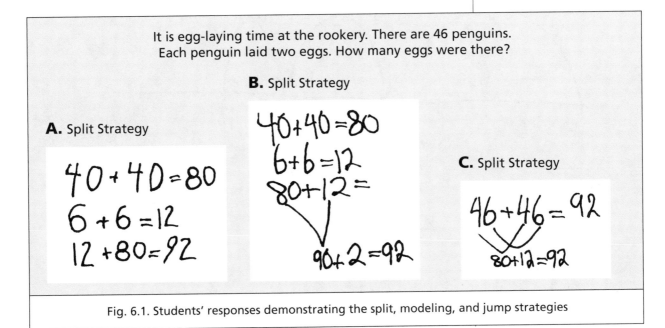

Fig. 6.1. Students' responses demonstrating the split, modeling, and jump strategies

The emperor penguin is 48 inches tall. The yellow-eyed penguin is 30 inches tall. How much taller is the emperor penguin than the yellow-eyed penguin?

D. Modeling strategy

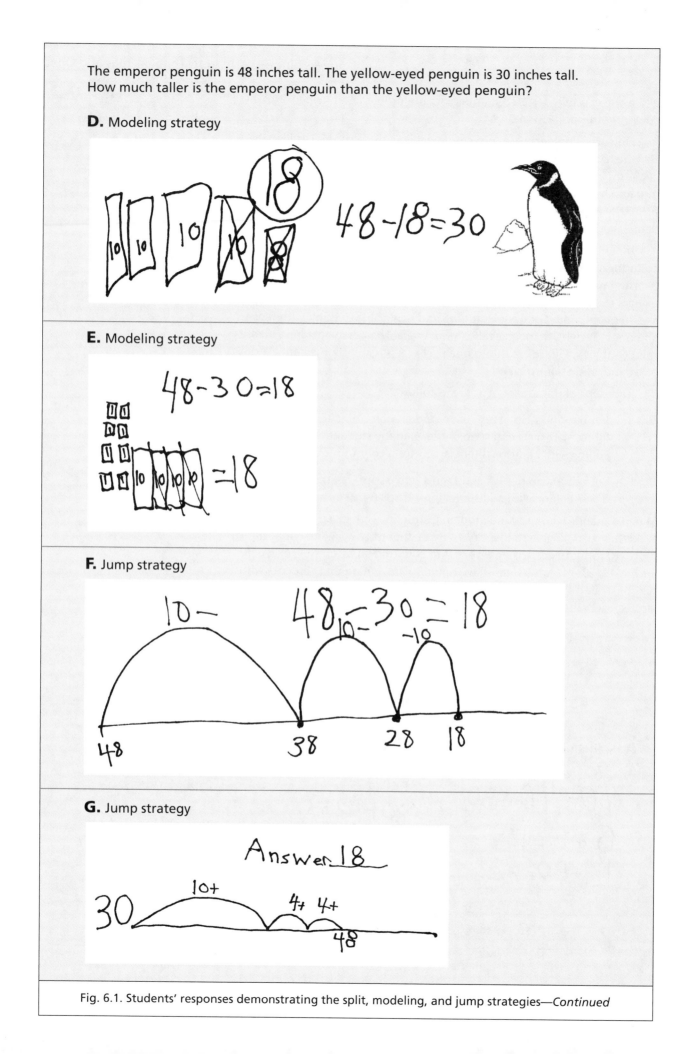

$48 - 18 = 30$

E. Modeling strategy

$48 - 30 = 18$

$= 18$

F. Jump strategy

$48 - 30 = 18$

10− −10 −10

48   38   28   18

G. Jump strategy

Answer 18

30   10+   4+ 4+

48

Fig. 6.1. Students' responses demonstrating the split, modeling, and jump strategies—*Continued*

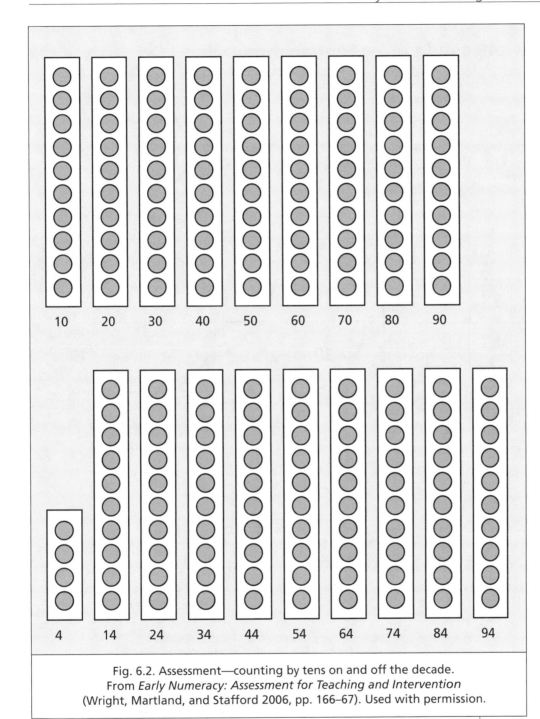

Fig. 6.2. Assessment—counting by tens on and off the decade.
From *Early Numeracy: Assessment for Teaching and Intervention*
(Wright, Martland, and Stafford 2006, pp. 166–67). Used with permission.

obvious, but they were. Again, as with any KDU, teachers could not tell students how to think; rather, a number of different instructional activities (Wright, Stanger, et al. 2006) helped them develop this understanding. Figure 6.3 shows one such task.

Did we manage to support the development of this understanding? Figure 6.4 shows several samples of students' work that they completed about a month after we first identified the need to support learning to

ACTIVITY IA8.4: Add to, or Subtract from, 49

Intended learning: To solve two-digit addition and subtraction problems with addends and subtrahends that are multiples of ten.

Description: Use the Add or Subtract from 49 game board to generate addition and subtraction problems that involve making jumps that are multiples of ten. The object is to cover three squares in a row with counters. Player A spins to determine the amount to add or subtract to 49. This player states the number sentence and places the counter on the answer. Player B repeats this process. Players take turns until one player has three counters in a row horizontally, vertically or diagonally.

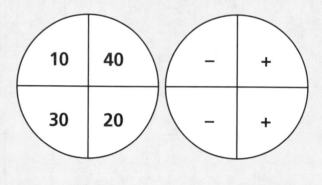

29	19	9	79	89
69	59	29	19	79
9	69	89	9	39
39	29	9	79	89
39	59	69	19	9

Spinner 1: 10, 40, 30, 20
Spinner 2: −, +, −, +

Figure 8.8 Add to, or subtract from, 49

Notes:
- This activity is suitable for a whole class, small groups, pairs, or individuals.
- A hundred chart and empty number line may be used to support learning.
- As a variation, use the Add or Subtract from 89 game board to bridge 100.

Materials: Add or Subtract from 49 game board and spinners, two kinds of counters or markers, paper clips and pencils for spinners, hundred chart (optional). (See Figure 8.8 above.)

Fig. 6.3. An activity that promotes counting by tens off the decade.
From *Teaching Number in the Classroom with 4–8 Year Olds*
(Wright, Stanger, et al. 2006, p. 138). Used with permission.

count off the decade by tens. As their work shows, students were more flexible in their written (and related mental) strategies at this time.

This article portrays a path of understanding that supports students' learning to think in tens and ones. The task is far more complex than many of us might have imagined. Along the way, the KDU of thinking with composite units and using tens and ones was foundational even in the students' initial work. The use of word problems both supported and encouraged students' development of mental strategies that used their knowledge of tens and ones. Over time, we were able to help students move from mental strategies to written descriptions to—finally, for many students—using

Yesterday my mom bought 67 valentines. Today I bought 45. How many did we have?

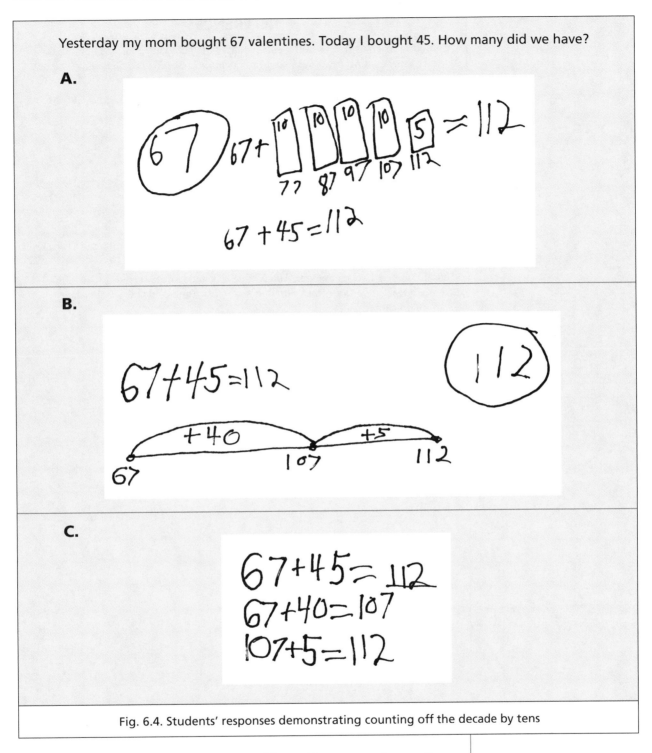

Fig. 6.4. Students' responses demonstrating counting off the decade by tens

written work to find solutions to these problems. However, understanding the structure and use of tens and ones involves more than just counting by tens. A subtle understanding that we might have missed involved the students' being able to count off the decade by tens. Teachers can miss such an understanding unless they pay careful attention to students' thinking and also purposefully seek to promote the use of more-sophisticated strategies (e.g., the jump strategy) for solving problems.

REFERENCES

Carpenter, Thomas P., Elizabeth Fennema, Megan Loef Franke, Linda Levi, and Susan B. Empson. *Children's Mathematics: Cognitively Guided Instruction.* Portsmouth, N.H.: Heinemann, 1999.

Chapin, Suzanne M., and Art Johnson. *Math Matters.* 2nd ed. Sausalito, Calif.: Math Solutions, 2006.

Simon, Martin A. "Key Developmental Understandings in Mathematics: A Direction for Investigating and Establishing Learning Goals." *Mathematical Thinking and Learning* 8, no. 4 (January 2006): 359–71.

Wright, Robert J., James Martland, and Ann K. Stafford. *Early Numeracy: Assessment for Teaching and Intervention.* 2nd ed. Thousand Oaks, Calif.: Sage Publications, 2006.

Wright, Robert J., James Martland, Ann K. Stafford, and Gary Stanger. *Teaching Number: Advancing Children's Skills and Strategies.* 2nd ed. Thousand Oaks, Calif.: Sage Publications, 2006.

Wright, Robert J., Gary Stanger, Ann K. Stafford, and James Martland. *Teaching Number in the Classroom with 4–8 Year Olds.* Thousand Oaks, Calif.: Sage Publications, 2006.

Differentiating Mathematics by Using Task Difficulty

Jill D. Cassone

EDUCATORS today face many challenges. Perhaps the most difficult of these challenges is meeting the needs of all their students despite the many differences that exist academically, socially, and developmentally. The teacher's goal is to move students along the learning continuum regardless of their starting point. Almost every elementary school classroom includes struggling students, students performing above grade-level expectations, and those who are between the two extremes. Each child presents with different existing knowledge, interests, and modes of learning. Any given class typically contains a heterogeneous mix of students of different ability levels and educational needs. The work of Tomlinson (1995, 1999), Gregory and Chapman (2002), and Keefe and Jenkins (2002) supports the belief that instruction must be assessment-driven and differentiated so that it can meet the needs of all learners. This article describes differentiated instruction and the role of students' readiness and suggests an instructional strategy for delivering targeted instruction by using readiness.

Meeting the Needs of All Learners

Meeting the needs of all learners in mathematics is like playing the game of Tetris. The game involves a pseudorandom sequence of tetrominoes (shapes composed of four blocks), which fall down into a playing field of varying backgrounds. The objective of the game is similar to that of teaching. The player manipulates the shapes in different ways by transposing them; the goal is to create horizontal lines of blocks without any gaps. When all the shapes line up perfectly, the player can clear lines. With practice, the player can use specific techniques to ensure success. What happens when a player cannot line up all the shapes so that no gaps occur? Eventually, the playing field fills up with shapes, and the game ends.

Unfortunately teaching mathematics is not a game; and more often than not, teachers do not have the luxury of a do-over. Every day, mathematics teachers must teach specific skills and concepts from their state and district curriculum with the hope of reaching every student while leaving no gaps. Like the shapes in the Tetris game, teachers can use specific strategies that manipulate certain elements of the instruction to ensure the success of all students. With practice, dedication, and tools, teachers can target instruction to reach all learners wherever they may be in their mathematical thinking. To *target instruction* means to focus instruction at

> Almost every elementary school classroom includes struggling students, students performing above grade-level expectations, and those who are between the two extremes. Each child presents with different existing knowledge, interests, and modes of learning.

> Every day, mathematics teachers must teach specific skills and concepts from their state and district curriculum with the hope of reaching every student while leaving no gaps.

a specific location along the mathematics continuum to achieve success. The vehicle for delivering this targeted instruction is differentiation.

Differentiation and Individualization

People often misunderstand the word *differentiation*. Although those who embrace differentiation believe that it is a way of thinking, learning, and teaching, they would also agree that time is needed to link assessment with instruction in a way that is meaningful. For many teachers, just the mention of differentiation conjures up visions of additional time, frustration, and chaos in the classroom, probably for many reasons. However, the greatest misconception regarding differentiated instruction is the belief that differentiated instruction is individualized instruction. Differentiation is not individualization. Differentiation does not involve the delivery of thirty different lessons in one class period.

Individualization or individualized teaching, by contrast, is a specific path of learning for one student that is based on the strengths and weaknesses of that student. Individualization now commonly occurs in cross-categorical classrooms that consist of students with varying identifications and special needs. Individualization might also occur in the regular classroom and involve a pull-out or push-in situation that considers a student's individual education plan (IEP), which has been drafted by educators to meet the needs of that specific learner. Individualized instruction is instruction that has the sole purpose of following a specific path of learning for a specific student and usually attempts to help that student meet grade-level expectations.

Differentiation does not assume that each learner requires a separate level of learning. Instead, differentiated instruction suggests that educators look at flexible, ever-changing groups or clusters of students. These clusters are formed so as to teach a specific concept or skill in mathematics and may change each time that the teacher introduces a new skill or concept or the class practices those skills and concepts. These clusters are like zones in that on any particular day, depending on the students and their needs, targeted instruction meets the needs of learners through two or three learning paths rather than through thirty individual ones.

Differentiation in the Elementary School Classroom

In the elementary school classroom, the primary elements of differentiating instruction include differentiating the content, the process, and the product. *Content* usually refers to the state mathematics teaching standards, that is, what the student needs to learn. *Process* refers to the activities, methods, or tasks in which the student engages to make meaning of the content. *Product* refers to the application of the learning or the way in which the student demonstrates his or her understanding (Tomlinson 1995).

Teachers can differentiate content in the elementary school classroom in many ways. These might include—

> **Differentiation does not assume that each learner requires a separate level of learning. Instead, differentiated instruction suggests that educators look at flexible, ever-changing groups or clusters of students.**

- using varying resources (such as different textbooks or teaching materials) to teach the concept or skill;

- providing mathematics vocabulary words to students on the basis of their readiness for the topic;

- using nonverbal examples and nonexamples of big concepts to allow discovery; or

- using a teacher-directed group to reteach a concept or provide foundations for a new concept or skill.

Examples of differentiated process include (a) learning centers that focus on skills that are a part of its knowledge cluster, (b) tiered lessons, (c) curriculum compacting, (d) manipulatives and hands-on materials that engage students in discovering a concept or skill, and (e) small groups that offer support while other students work as a larger group on related content in another content strand of mathematics. In the elementary school classroom, examples of differentiating product might include the following:

- Different modes of delivery: use of technology, differing materials or presentation mode, and so on.

- Engaging students to work as a part of a group, alone, or with partners, as well as changing where they work.

The Role of Students' Readiness

A differentiated lesson meets the range of needs for all students. Differentiating instruction requires that teachers determine the modifications that are best for students on the basis of one of the following three criteria: students' readiness level, students' interest, and students' learning mode or profile. Of those three, students' interest and students' learning mode are probably the most familiar ways that teachers connect with their students every day. Any teacher who has established rapport with his or her class understands which students are more visual than others, which students like sports, and so on. Teachers use many tools—ranging from daily conversation to students' inventories and observation—to gain this insight. Using this information to increase student motivation and comprehension during daily instruction does not require training in differentiation. Students' readiness, in contrast, is different.

Assessing students' readiness in mathematics presents many challenges. If differentiation involves flexible grouping that is based on a student's readiness for a specific skill, how does a teacher match this readiness with task difficulty? How does a teacher plan instruction for a class of students with varying levels of existing knowledge when that knowledge changes from day to day depending on the skill or concept being introduced? How does a teacher plan with readiness in mind if she or he cannot tell how difficult a task may be for each student? How does she or he group students for every lesson when the groups change?

Those tasks have never been easy ones, especially in mathematics. Teachers have used preassessments, unit tests, inventories, observation,

> **Differentiating instruction requires that teachers determine the modifications that are best for students on the basis of one of the following three criteria: students' readiness level, students' interest, and students' learning mode or profile.**

and even computer software to accomplish these tasks. However, the missing link for most teachers is that they cannot predict whether a student is really ready for a skill or concept because no tool places the student's mathematical achievement or understanding and the teaching standards on the same scale. The basic needs of teachers are twofold in this area: (1) to be able to predict the difficulty of a particular skill or concept in mathematics as compared with other skills and concepts that they must teach, and (2) to know what specific skills and concepts are precursory to, or supportive of, the one that they have focused on teaching. These two areas are essential in addressing students' readiness because they provide the underlying foundational concepts necessary for pinpointing students' needs as well as for matching the mathematical understanding or achievement of a student to a set skill or concept.

One way to accomplish that goal is the Quantile Framework for Mathematics, shareware developed by MetaMetrics of Durham, North Carolina, and freely available on the World Wide Web at www.quantiles .com. The framework is a developmental scale that helps teachers determine their students' readiness to make progress in mathematics. It enables educators to match students with resources and engage them in instruction that the students have a 50 percent likelihood of understanding. A student with a particular Quantile measure is ready for skills at that same measure. As a student's skill level grows, educators can match him or her with more-demanding concepts and skills. As the concepts and skills become more demanding or more challenging, the student grows.

A growing number of states have linked the Quantile Framework for Mathematics with their own state end-of-year assessments. When a state has done so, each student receives a Quantile measure, a number ending in a Q, on her or his end-of-year test report. However, even when a Quantile measure for the student is not available, the other component of the Quantile Framework—an empirically derived task-difficulty component— is available to all educators through the Quantiles.com Web site with no log-in or charge. MetaMetrics has made its scale and its taxonomy of skills and concepts available to educators across the nation with the hope of changing mathematics instruction to meet the needs of all learners.

By using a Quantile measure, MetaMetrics has located on this scale the difficulty level of each skill and concept typically taught between kindergarten and precalculus. This information is available to anyone who searches the online database. Although using the students' measure in conjunction with the measure for the skill or concept is ideal, it is not necessary. Teachers can still forecast students' understanding, predict readiness, target instruction, and match students with teaching resources at their level by using the tools that MetaMetrics has made available.

Further, the tools on the Quantile Framework for Mathematics Web site outline an instructional approach to differentiation without additional testing. The Quantile Framework serves as a strategy for differentiating instruction. This strategy creates opportunities for students to explore ideas at a level that builds on their existing knowledge and readiness to ensure continued growth.

A Model of Differentiation Using the Quantile Framework for Mathematics

Teachers must be masters of differentiating the curriculum to meet the needs of all students, to remediate or accelerate instruction, and to provide all students with the opportunity to learn and grow. The sample class shown in figure 7.1 demonstrates the range of students' readiness in mathematics in a typical fifth-grade classroom. Quantile measures have confirmed what educators have known for some time: the range of mathematics ability within each classroom is large.

The conclusion that not all students are alike is easy to draw. The following section outlines how teachers can use the Quantile Framework for Mathematics to provide targeted instruction with a seamless approach to differentiation.

Delivering Targeted Instruction

The Quantile Framework for Mathematics suggests a process for differentiating that is anchored by student readiness. The following three precepts are the basis of this process:

- Teaching standards, not the mathematics textbook, are the basis for instruction. The mathematics textbook, along with any other teaching material, is a resource that serves as a vehicle for delivering the mathematics curriculum.

- Regardless of the differing ability levels of students, teachers should expose every student to the full curriculum. Each lesson should begin and end with a whole-class activity and discussion that are anchored by standards and student communication.

- All groupings of students, regardless of the topic or lesson, are flexible. Students can move in and out of learning groups during one lesson, throughout the week, or throughout the unit.

Before a teacher uses the strategy for differentiation, she or he should familiarize herself or himself with the students by using student inventories and class discussions and by reading cumulative records. In addition, if she

Grade	Name	Quantile Measure
5	Caroline	410
5	Blake	425
5	Je Ree	465
5	Kyanna	475
5	Orinthius	490
5	Aliyah	490
5	Tony	500
5	Diana	520
5	Clifford	520
5	Carlos	540
5	Portia	550
5	Taquashia	575
5	Crystal	600
5	Juan	600
5	Shakur	615
5	Dustin	650
5	Victoria	725
5	Jacob	770
5	Cody	775
5	Infiniti	775
5	Destiny	790
5	Kaleb	800
5	Brandon	825
5	Holly	830
5	Henry	850
5	Ellen	925
5	Lee	975
5	Ashleigh	1030
5	Lauryn	1090
5	Corey	1100

Fig. 7.1. The range of mathematical readiness in a typical fifth-grade classroom is large.

The process for differentiating by using Quantile measures is a three-step process known as *AMP.*

This acronym refers to the three steps in developing a differentiated lesson that targets instruction on the basis of student readiness.

or he has access to students' Quantile measures from the students' end-of-grade test reports, the teacher should place that information on a class roster for analysis. Further, teachers should understand the progression of the mathematics content that they will deliver. In that way, teachers can engage in such planning activities as curriculum mapping and pacing before taking on differentiation. Teachers can then plan instruction that is standards-based, paced according to the needs of the class, and mapped to connect with other areas of the general curriculum across other subject matter.

The process for differentiating by using Quantile measures is a three-step process known as *AMP*, where A stands for *analyze*, M stands for *make connections*, and P stands for *plan*. This acronym refers to the three steps in developing a differentiated lesson that targets instruction on the basis of students' readiness. Educators who have no access to Quantile measures can easily adapt the process by focusing on task difficulty. This three-step process is available at the MetaMetrics Web site, www.quantiles.com, where a suite of free online tools is available. One of those tools, called the *lesson plan builder*, guides teachers through building a differentiated lesson by using this three-step process. Figure 7.2 demonstrates the three-step process.

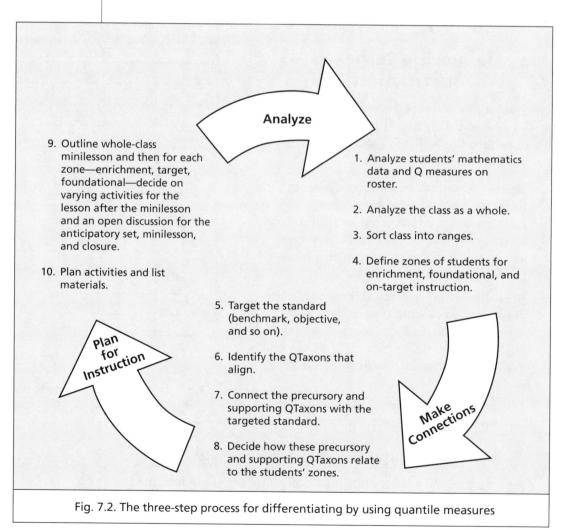

Analyze

1. Analyze students' mathematics data and Q measures on roster.

2. Analyze the class as a whole.

3. Sort class into ranges.

4. Define zones of students for enrichment, foundational, and on-target instruction.

5. Target the standard (benchmark, objective, and so on).

6. Identify the QTaxons that align.

7. Connect the precursory and supporting QTaxons with the targeted standard.

8. Decide how these precursory and supporting QTaxons relate to the students' zones.

9. Outline whole-class minilesson and then for each zone—enrichment, target, foundational—decide on varying activities for the lesson after the minilesson and an open discussion for the anticipatory set, minilesson, and closure.

10. Plan activities and list materials.

Plan for Instruction

Make Connections

Fig. 7.2. The three-step process for differentiating by using quantile measures

Analyze

In differentiating instruction, the most important step of the process is analyzing the readiness of the class. A teacher commonly does this type of analysis each time that she or he plans a lesson. Because the Quantile Framework for Mathematics provides a measure of the difficulty of each skill or concept, teachers can compare it with the range of Quantile measures for the class and with the Quantile for individual students. If no Quantile measures are available for the teacher, MetaMetrics has other resources on its Web site to help teachers estimate student readiness. In addition, the teacher can use a benchmark test or other type of diagnostic assessment that is anchored to state standards to identify the skills or concepts with which the student is likely to have difficulty. The teacher can then compare these skills and concepts with the Quantile measures in the taxonomy to gauge the students' readiness along the mathematics continuum. The teacher can accomplish this task seamlessly because the entire database of mathematics skills and concepts within the Quantile taxonomy align with each state's mathematics standards.

The Quantile measures of the fifth graders shown in figure 7.1 range from 410Q to 1100Q. The teacher derives this range by using reported measures for students. However, without Quantile measures, a teacher can use a teacher-generated or districtwide assessment to identify the skills with the greatest levels of difficulty. The teacher can then infer the students' Quantile measure from the skills that the student tackled easily or those with which the student had great difficulty. Either way, after finding the class range, the teacher can begin his or her analysis. For instance, if the targeted standard is to focus on identifying angles in the environment and this particular skill has a Quantile measure, or difficulty level, of 530Q (according to theQuantile Framework), some students need a great deal of scaffolding and modeling of precursory or related skills to understand the lesson, whereas others already have a good command of the content of the planned lesson. Armed with this knowledge, the teacher can, for this particular lesson, group students into three groups, which represent three entry points to the lesson content.

The teacher creates the three zones on the basis of the measure or task difficulty of the targeted standard. For a lesson on angles, since the class range is from 410 to 1100, the teacher should first identify the students who are ready for the lesson as presented in the standards that she or he needs to cover. These students are the ones who fall close to the measure of the focus lesson. In the sample class from figure 7.1, those students have measures from 500Q to 800Q, and constitute the on-target group, since they are exactly on target for receiving the lesson's focus as presented in the standards. Their readiness, indicated by their Quantile measures, predicts their success with the lesson's introductory instruction. They need different materials and different ways to express knowledge of the lesson concepts than their peers do.

The students who require more guidance and modeling to understand the focus of the lesson are those whose scores range from 410Q to 500Q. These students need a different entry point to the lesson's focus. They require more foundations for learning the targeted standard. They may also need different materials and different ways to express knowledge of the lesson's concepts, as well. The students for this lesson fall into a group identified as the foundational group.

The enrichment group is the last group. This group of students, with Quantile measures ranging from 825Q to 1100Q, needs extensions and opportunities to enhance the skills that the teacher is introducing. These students are the enrichment group because they need varying entry points to the lesson but are more likely to work on skills that relate to, connect with, or support the targeted standard or those that provide greater depth or understanding of it.

The Quantile Framework for Mathematics—in addition to providing for student, skill, and concept measures—also furnishes a knowledge cluster for each skill and concept. Like the knowledge cluster shown subsequently, it consists of the precursory and supporting skills connected with the targeted skill. This tool is powerful in the hands of a teacher who chooses to differentiate, because she or he can match related supporting skills and precursory skills with a lesson's focus to help provide greater meaning and challenge for the diverse learners in her or his classroom.

Make Connections

During the step of making connections, teachers connect the focus of the lesson with the other interconnected skills and concepts across content strands (geometry with data analysis, for example). After a teacher has compared the students and the lesson's focus and forecast readiness, she or he can plan activities and lesson components that provide targeted instruction for all students. Teachers flexibly connect skills across the content strands for different groups of students. The student groups (on-target, foundational, and enrichment) are flexible depending on the difficulty of the skill being presented that day.

Plan

Plan stands for plan the instruction. This step involves a minilesson, an activity period, and a closure. During the minilesson, the teacher exposes all students to the targeted standard (see fig. 7.3 for a specific description of the sample lesson). The purpose of the minilesson is to provide introductory instruction that serves as a basis for all students. It also ties the class together and helps students see the class as a learning community that allows flexible learning and that serves the students in it. By using Quantile measures, the teacher for the first time can begin a lesson with the full knowledge of who in the class will have difficulty engaging in the lesson, participating fully, adding to discussions, and so on. The teacher can tie in literature, visuals, music, and games to help furnish the motivation necessary for the foundational and enrichment students, since these students will need extra support to remain engaged for this lesson.

After the minilesson, for the remainder of the class period, except for the closure, during which the class is again together to make meaning of the lesson's focus, the class completes specific task-based activities at dif-

Main Lesson Focus—Minilesson—Whole Class:
QTaxon* Details

QMeasure: 530Q
Strand: Geometry
Description: Identify angles (acute, right, obtuse, and straight); identify them in the environment.

Knowledge Cluster

Precursory Taxons

QTaxon ID	QMeasure	Description
QT-G-176	400Q	Identify intersecting, parallel, and perpendicular lines and line segments and the midpoints of line segments; identify them in the environment.

Supportive Taxons

QTaxon ID	QMeasure	Description
QT-G-174	450Q	Use manipulatives, pictorial representations, and appropriate vocabulary (e.g., polygon, side, angle, vertex, diameter) to identify and compare properties of plane figures; identify in the environment.
QT-M-217	990Q	Use a protractor to draw and measure angles (acute, right, and obtuse).

* QTaxons are the skills and concepts located on the Quantile Scale.

Fig. 7.3. Using quantile measures to plan the minilesson

fering levels to meet the needs of all learners. In a traditional classroom, the students use this time for practice and drill or guided class activities in which everyone completes the same problems in the same time.

The Quantile Framework's knowledge cluster provides actionable information. The foundational group, for example, can engage in activities that focus on the precursory skill with a Quantile measure of 400Q, as shown in figure 7.3. The enrichment group can explore the use of a tool, without the pressure of mastery, by focusing on the supporting skill with a Quantile measure of 990Q (see fig. 7.3). The on-target group can focus on the skill at hand, with an approach of varying the expression mode (product) in their demonstration of mastery of the targeted skill or concept.

For a lesson on identifying angles, the teacher can prepare one lesson for each group that focuses on the state standard that she or he must cover, without doing additional work to meet the needs of her or his learners. The teacher can plan the base activity for this lesson. The base activity is one that the on-target group can do independently to practice the skill after the teacher has introduced it. With small modifications in the directions, the teacher can reuse the base activity for the other two groups of students, without needing additional planning or work on materials or preparation. For the lesson on identifying angles, the teacher can have the directions for the base activity state, "Cut and paste eight pictures of everyday objects found in a magazine onto your paper. Draw in the angles. Then use what you learned about acute, right, and obtuse angles to label them." The enrichment group's directions can state the same thing, except for the following small addition: "Afterward, explore with a protractor to estimate the angle measure and mark it next to the picture." The foundational group's directions can give the same directions, with the following clause at the beginning of the instructions: "Using the corners of an index card as a guide of what is smaller than a right angle and larger than a right angle,...." When armed with information, teachers can differentiate mathematics instruction without doing any more planning than they would do to plan a lesson for the entire class.

In conclusion, the Quantile Framework for Mathematics targets instruction, forecasts understanding, and improves mathematics instruction and achievement by placing the mathematics curriculum, the materials to teach mathematics, and the students themselves on the same scale. Differentiated instruction requires teachers to understand content progression, determine students' readiness for skills and concepts, and link students with appropriate instruction at their level. With the skills-and-concepts taxonomy, along with the knowledge clusters of the Quantile Framework, teachers can locate skills and use task difficulty to understand how the skills that they must teach fall into the full mathematics continuum. Additionally, by knowing each student's mathematical ability and readiness for a skill or concept, teachers can predict readiness, forecast success, and easily match the lesson to their students.

Differentiated instruction requires teachers to understand content progression, determine students' readiness for skills and concepts, and link students with appropriate instruction at their level.

REFERENCES

Gregory, Gayle H., and Carolyn Chapman. *Differentiated Instructional Strategies: One Size Doesn't Fit All.* Thousand Oaks, Calif.: Corwin Press, 2002.

"Quantile Framework for Mathematics." 2007. www.quantiles.com.

Keefe, James W., and John M. Jenkins. "Two Schools: Two Approaches to Personalized Learning." *Phi Delta Kappan* 83, no. 6 (February 2002): 449–56.

Tomlinson, Carol Ann. *How to Differentiate Instruction in Mixed-Ability Classrooms.* 2nd ed. Alexandria, Va.: Association for Supervision and Curriculum Development, 1995.

———. *The Differentiated Classroom: Responding to the Needs of All Learners.* Alexandria, Va. Association for Supervision and Curriculum Development, 1999.

Differentiating Instruction in First-Grade Geometry

Jennifer Taylor-Cox

ONE OF the most effective ways to teach mathematics is to differentiate instruction to meet the academic needs of all students. This example highlights how a first-grade teacher, Ms. Campbell, targeted geometry instruction for her students. The instructional goals for the unit included teaching students how to "analyze characteristics and properties of two- and three-dimensional geometric shapes and develop mathematical arguments about geometric relationships" (NCTM 2000, p. 96). NCTM also indicates that all students in prekindergarten though grade 2 should "recognize, name, build, draw, compare, and sort two- and three-dimensional shapes" (2000, p. 96). Although the geometry standard and expectations were the same for all students, Ms. Campbell targeted instruction at the level of her students. To do so, she used forward-mapping, which involves moving ahead to concepts that offer appropriate challenges, and back-mapping, which involves moving back to discuss or reteach earlier concepts so as to offer appropriate support and build stronger foundations. This case study begins with a preassessment, which precedes a detailed description of the process of differentiation for this first-grade class.

Preassessment

Ms. Campbell differentiated mathematics instruction for her first-grade students on a regular basis. Ongoing assessments and small-group work were common practice in her classroom. The students were comfortable with preassessments offered in a variety of forms. Often the students would answer index questions (Taylor-Cox 2008) to show what they knew about a mathematics concept before they received instruction on that concept. The index question served as an informal assessment of each student's specific, current knowledge (Taylor-Cox 2008). The teacher asked index questions throughout the learning process. Ms. Campbell usually asked the students to answer index questions at the end of the day so that she could use the information for the next day's instruction.

The class was starting a new unit in geometry, so Ms. Campbell wanted to determine her students' knowledge of three-dimensional shapes. She showed the students a rectangular prism and asked them the following index questions: What is this shape? How do you know? She wanted to find out whether the students could identify the shape and whether they could use characteristics and properties of the shape to support their answers.

> Although the geometry standard and expectations were the same for all students, Ms. Campbell targeted instruction at the level of her students. To do so, she used forward-mapping and back-mapping.

The students took less than five minutes to write their answers to the questions on index cards.

Forming the Groups

At the end of the day, Ms. Campbell took a few minutes to sort the index cards. She grouped the students according to what the responses indicated that they knew and what they needed to learn next. Because Ms. Campbell planned to differentiate instruction by using homogeneous groupings, she grouped the students by similar levels of understanding. She did not want any students to feel inferior—or superior, for that matter—so she never publicly labeled the groups with such terms as medium, high, and low. Instead, she used arbitrary group names (e.g., colors, shapes, foods, or sports). The following is a list of the students' responses that Ms. Campbell organized into three groups for targeted, differentiated instruction (note that students' spelling has been corrected):

Blue Group

Tymond:	Rectangle. I know because of the corners.
Afra:	The shape is a rectangle because it has straight sides.
Mannie:	It is a rectangle. I just know this is true.
Dionysus:	Rectangle. I know it in my brain.
Carl:	Rectangle with some other rectangles.
Mariellen:	It is a rectangle. I know because I think a lot.
Thomas:	It is a rectangle. It has four sides.
Marty:	Rectangle because it looks like a rectangle.
Portia:	It is a rectangle. I knew this when I was a baby.

Green Group

Joshua:	It is a rectangular prism because it is made of rectangles.
Effie:	The shape is a rectangular prism. It has six rectangle faces. I know my shapes.
Brittnee:	Rectangular prism. It has two big rectangles and four skinny rectangles.
Rihana:	That is a rectangle prism. I know because it has rectangle faces.
Oliver:	All the sides are rectangles. So it is a rectangular prism.

| Thedrick: | It is called a rectangle prism because it is not flat. |
| Kendre: | I think it is called a rectangular prism. It has all rectangles. |

Yellow Group

Daisy:	Triangle.
Jefferson:	I don't know.
Dermontt:	I think it is a rec-triangle. I see three sides.
Tiara:	It is a shape. I know because I saw it before.
Billy:	Triangle. I don't know why.
Suzie:	Shape. I know it.
Richmound:	I think it is a square. It looks like it.
Lamberto:	It is a spear. It can roll.

Thinking about the Academic Needs of Each Group

On the basis of the students' answers to, and comments about, the pre-assessment index questions, Ms. Campbell assessed how best to work with the students. Students in the blue group appeared to know about rectangles but not about rectangular prisms. All the students in that group used the word *rectangle* to describe the shape. They applied their previous knowledge of two-dimensional shapes to describe the rectangular prism. Ms. Campbell had not yet taught the students about rectangular prisms. She was pleased that the students in this group were able to use some mathematical language in their descriptions, even though the concept was new. Because the students in this group were ready to learn about rectangular prisms, Ms. Campbell decided to focus their small-group instruction on the grade-level concepts of identifying and describing the properties and characteristics of rectangular prisms and other three-dimensional shapes.

The students in the green group appeared to know some of the properties and characteristics of rectangular prisms. They already knew how to identify rectangular prisms; all the students accurately named the shape, although two students did call it a *rectangle prism* rather than a *rectangular prism*. The students also offered some of the characteristics and properties of rectangular prisms in their explanations describing how they knew that the shape was a rectangular prism. Ms. Campbell decided to use forward-mapping as she focused their small-group instruction on the above-grade-level concepts of comparing, contrasting, and constructing several types of prisms (including triangular prisms, hexagonal prisms, and octagonal prisms) and pyramids (including triangular pyramids, square pyramids, hexagonal pyramids, and octagonal pyramids).

Students in the yellow group did not yet appear to know about rectangles or rectangular prisms. Several students thought the shape was a triangle. Others did not use any shape names to identify the rectangular prism. The students' explanations lacked support and accuracy. Ms. Campbell used back-mapping as she focused their small-group instruction on the previous grade-level concepts of identifying and describing two-dimensional shapes and connecting the concepts with the on-grade-level concepts, specifically, properties and characteristics for describing rectangular prisms.

The Lesson: Warm-Up and Introduction

Ms. Campbell began the differentiated instruction lesson with the whole group because she knew that the whole-group structure helped the class feel connected academically, socially, and emotionally. For the warm-up, Ms. Campbell played a quick game with the students. She described a shape, and the students used their pointer fingers to sketch the shape in the air.

Ms. Campbell: It has three sides. It is a closed shape. All the sides are straight.

(The students use pointer fingers to sketch triangles in the air.)

Ms. Campbell: What could it be? What could it be?

Students: Triangle!

After two more rounds of the game, during which Ms. Campbell used different shapes, she began the introduction to the lesson. She drew a rectangle on the chalkboard and told a short story about a lonely rectangle who transformed into a three-dimensional shape called a *rectangular prism*. She modeled the story after the well-known story of Pinocchio, the puppet who becomes a real boy. The story included mathematics vocabulary and such concepts as rectangle, rectangular prism, two-dimensional shape, three-dimensional shape, straight sides, and square corners. This introduction was a brief look at some concepts with which the students would work in their small groups.

Before Ms. Campbell called the first group to work with her, she gave directions for the task that the students were to work on when they were not meeting with her. The students would work with partners to construct shapes on geoboards; each dyad, or pair, of students would use shape cards. The students took turns randomly picking a shape card from the pile and constructing the corresponding shape by using geobands on the geoboards. Ms. Campbell encouraged the students to use mathematical language while they talked to each other about the shapes. She also asked them to record each shape that they constructed on geoboard dot paper. Ms. Campbell called it *the independent task* because students worked on this task without her. However, they were not working independently of each other. Ms. Campbell wanted students to work together to challenge and support each other while she worked with the other small groups.

The Lesson: Targeted Instruction

The Yellow Group

Ms. Campbell next called the yellow group to work with her. The students met with Ms. Campbell at the back table. She used the back table for working with small groups because she could work directly with the group yet still see the rest of the students in the class. At any time during the small-group instruction, Ms. Campbell could give a task to the group and leave them to go redirect, support, or challenge other students in the class.

Ms. Campbell sketched several shapes on a large dry-erase board (see fig. 8.1) and then prompted a discussion about the shapes. She encouraged the students to share information about the properties and characteristics of the shapes. She asked the students to decide which shapes were not rectangles. The group quickly decided that circles are not rect-

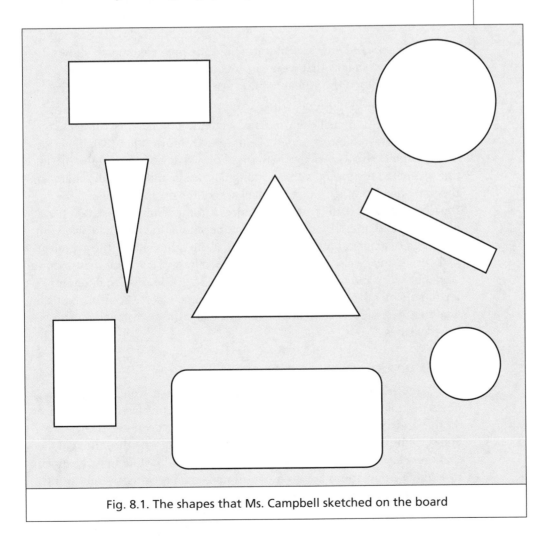

Fig. 8.1. The shapes that Ms. Campbell sketched on the board

Fig. 8.2. Students made rectangles and "not rectangles" from pipe cleaners.

angles and crossed out the two circles. With Ms. Campbell's help, the students identified the triangles and used mathematical language and reasoning to explain why the triangles were not rectangles. One student made a real-world connection when he announced that the word *triangle* sounds like the word *tricycle*. The group discussed the connections between three angles and three wheels. The students subsequently decided that the remaining four shapes were rectangles. Ms. Campbell focused their attention on the shape that did not have any angles. Although that shape resembled a rectangle, it was not a rectangle because it did not have four square corners (right angles). To help the students arrive at this understanding, Ms. Campbell gave each student a pipe cleaner. With her help, the students demonstrated square corners and curves. They attached the pipe cleaners to show rectangles and shapes that were not rectangles (see fig. 8.2). These experiences helped the students build stronger foundations in their understandings of rectangles.

After Ms. Campbell had used back-mapping to help her students understand more about rectangles, she used that information to help her students connect this knowledge with their knowledge of rectangular prisms. She presented the group with a rectangular prism and a cylinder that were the same height. When Ms. Campbell asked the group to explain how the two shapes were different, the students immediately focused on the angles of the shapes. They decided that one shape (the rectangular prism) consisted of angles and rectangles and that the other shape (the cylinder) had curves and circles. Ms. Campbell shared how pleased she was with the students' work and gave them shape cards and geoboards. To differentiate the independent task, she asked the students to sort the shape cards by whether they were or were not rectangles while they constructed the geoboard shapes.

The Blue Group

Ms. Campbell displayed several rectangular prisms and encouraged students to explore the shapes. All the rectangular prisms were different sizes. As the students described the rectangular prisms, they noticed angles and straight sides. Ms. Campbell asked the students why they thought that these shapes were called *rectangular prisms*. The students responded by making connections between two-dimensional rectangles and three-dimensional rectangular prisms and noticed that the word *rectangle* was similar to the word *rectangular*. She asked the students how many rectangular faces a rectangular prism has and whether they thought that all rectangular prisms have six rectanglular faces. Students verified their answers by examining the other rectangular prisms and counting the faces.

The students were then ready to learn about other three-dimensional shapes. Ms. Campbell displayed several cylinders, spheres, and cubes. When the students explored the shapes, they noticed that some shapes roll and others slide. They also discovered that some shapes have angles and others do not. They counted the faces on the shapes and tried to stack them. She encouraged the students to sort the shapes and gave them a piece of chart paper for each group of shapes. With her help, they wrote the name of each type of shape, some specific characteristics, and properties of the shapes (see fig. 8.3). She encouraged students to use mathematical language as they discussed and wrote about the three-dimensional shapes and placed the shapes on the corresponding chart pages.

Ms. Campbell shared that she was pleased with the work that the group had done and asked them to work with the shape cards and geoboards. To differentiate the independent task, she asked the students to make connections with some of the three-dimensional shapes that they used in the small group. When they picked a shape card to make on the geoboard, they needed to tell their partners whether that particular shape served as a face on any of the three-dimensional shapes about which they had just learned. To help with this component of the task, she moved their charts and shapes to a central place in the classroom where the students could refer to the information as needed.

Fig. 8.3. Students sorted cylinders, spheres, and cubes.

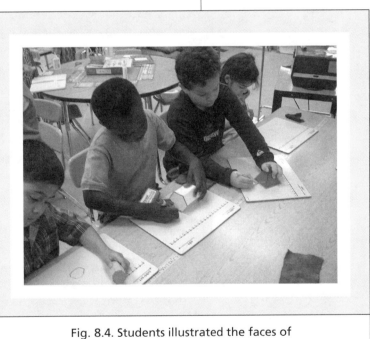

Fig. 8.4. Students illustrated the faces of prisms and pyramids on dry-erase boards.

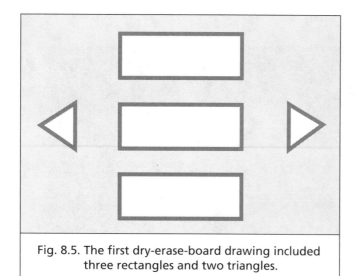

Fig. 8.5. The first dry-erase-board drawing included three rectangles and two triangles.

The Green Group

Ms. Campbell's work with the green group began by displaying the following shapes: triangular prism, rectangular prism, hexagonal prism, octagonal prism, triangular pyramid, square pyramid, hexagonal pyramid, and octagonal pyramid. She invited the students to explore the shapes. After some discussion, she invited each student to take one shape. Ms. Campbell chose the rectangular prism and showed the students another rectangular prism that she had constructed with pieces of cardboard and tape. She next took the cardboard rectangular prism apart as the students described each of the faces, and she then asked the students to think about the two-dimensional shapes that they might need for building the shapes that they had selected previously. She required the students to record these shapes on mini dry-erase boards. Some students traced the shapes, whereas others sketched the shapes (see fig. 8.4).

Ms. Campbell asked the students to place their dry-erase-board drawings on the floor behind them. She lined up the three-dimensional shapes on the table and explained to the students that they needed to match each shape with one of the dry-erase-board drawings. The first dry-erase-board drawing included three rectangles and two triangles (see fig. 8.5).

The teacher encouraged students to use mathematical language and reasoning while they worked together to identify the triangular prism that matched the drawing. Each student showed his or her dry-erase-board drawing. Ms. Campbell guided the group through each possible three-dimensional shape and asked students to explain why it was or was not a match. Ms. Campbell encouraged the students to compare the three-dimensional shapes while they worked to identify the matches.

After the students completed the activity, Ms. Campbell asked them why they thought that some of these shapes were called *prisms* and other shapes were called *pyramids.* After discussing the characteristics and properties of the shapes, students decided that prisms consisted of rectangles and that pyramids consisted of triangles. They were interested to learn that the type of prism indicates the number of rectangles that are needed and that the type of pyramid indicates the number of triangles that are needed. For example, a hexagonal prism needs two hexagons and six rectangles because hexagons have six sides. A square pyramid needs one square and four triangles because squares have four sides. Ms. Campbell asked the students to consider this information when they worked with the shape cards and the geoboards. Each time that they picked a shape card, they needed to identify the shape and the number of shapes needed to transform it into a prism or a pyramid. Ms. Campbell complimented the students on their work and sent them back to the differentiated independent task.

The Lesson: Closure

After each group had worked with Ms. Campbell on its independent tasks, she asked the students to assemble to close the lesson. She typically used a whole-group structure for lesson closure for the same reasons that she used it to introduce the lesson—academic, social, and emotional connectedness. Ms. Campbell also used the whole-group structure to promote reflection, mathematical discourse, and continued learning.

Ms. Campbell asked the students to recall the story about the rectangle that transformed into a rectangular prism and to use what they had learned from the small-group and independent work to describe another two-dimensional shape that could transform into a three-dimensional shape. A student from the blue group suggested that a square could transform into a special rectangular prism—a cube. Another student, from the green group, suggested that an octagon could transform into an octagonal prism. A yellow-group member proposed that a circle could transform into a cylinder and used manipulatives to demonstrate. After each student shared, Ms. Campbell encouraged the other students to ask questions and explain why they agreed or disagreed with the idea. The teacher intended her closure to highlight how all students were working on a common theme, yet each student could bring his or her new knowledge to the experience.

For homework, Ms. Campbell asked the students to create shape transformation stories by using words and pictures. Later, Ms. Campbell planned to use another index question as a postassessment to gauge the students' new levels of understanding about three-dimensional shapes.

Conclusion

Ms. Campbell differentiated instruction by responding to the students' academic needs in ways that are beneficial yet not complicated. On the basis of the evidence in the preassessment, she was aware of what the students knew and what they needed to learn next. She targeted the instruction to meet their exact needs. At times, Ms. Campbell learned that the response that a student gave on the index question was not a complete picture of what the student understood. Ms. Campbell then simply moved the student to a different group for targeted small-group instruction. That capability is the beauty of flexible, purposeful group structures.

One reason that Ms. Campbell was able to differentiate instruction with such ease was that she had command of the content (Taylor-Cox 2008). Having command of the content means that the teacher knows and is comfortable with grade-level concepts, as well as the concepts that come before and after them. The teacher's command of content allowed back-mapping and forward-mapping to drive the targeted instruction. Additionally, command of the content enabled Ms. Campbell to develop index questions that uncovered what students knew about any given mathematics concept.

Ms. Campbell differentiated instruction by responding to the students' academic needs in ways that are beneficial yet not complicated. On the basis of the evidence in the preassessment, she was aware of what the students knew and what they needed to learn next. She targeted the instruction to meet their exact needs.

Another reason for Ms. Campbell's success with differentiated instruction was that she used index questions to guide her instruction. Index questions are a powerful way to find out what students know and what they have learned. Students' responses gave her the information and evidence that she needed to create purposeful small groups and to provide targeted instruction. Thinking about the academic needs of each group also prompted Ms. Campbell to target her instruction in ways that were beneficial to the students. If the small-group activity was not working, she made immediate adjustments. If she found that the group knew more or less than the index question responses indicated, she modified the lesson.

During the lesson, Ms. Campbell did not initially differentiate the independent tasks. All students worked on the same task, that is, they used shape cards to construct geoboard shapes. While Ms. Campbell worked with the small groups, she made subtle modifications to the independent task on the basis of the specific needs of the group. In this way, she offered differentiation through targeted instruction and the independent tasks. When Ms. Campbell first started differentiating instruction, she did not add that component because she wanted to focus on her targeted small-group instruction. As she gained confidence and comfort with differentiating mathematics instruction, she found that differentiating the independent tasks became a natural extension of the concepts that she worked on with the students in the small group. Similarly, Ms. Campbell differentiated homework assignments through specific connections with the small-group activities and the open-endedness of the assignments.

A crucial point to remember is that Ms. Campbell's lesson "is not *the* way to differentiate instruction in mathematics; it is *a* way to differentiate instruction in mathematics" (Taylor-Cox, 2008 p. 61). The teacher has many options when it comes to differentiating instruction in mathematics, because students have diverse and specific learning needs. The teacher's job is to meet the varying needs of diverse classes. One of the best ways to do so is to effectively differentiate instruction.

REFERENCES

National Council of Teachers of Mathematics (NCTM). *Principles and Standards for School Mathematics.* Reston, Va.: NCTM, 2000.

Taylor-Cox, Jennifer. *Differentiating in Number and Operations and Other Math Content Standards: A Guide for Ongoing Assessment, Grouping Students, Targeting Instruction, and Adjusting Levels of Cognitive Demand Prekindergarten through Grade 2.* Portsmouth, N.H.: Heinemann, 2008.

9

Coteaching: Collaboration between an Elementary Mathematics Specialist and a Classroom Teacher

Robert Q. Berry III

THE MATHEMATICS education of students in elementary school has received increased attention because many educators and parents worry about the preparation of elementary school students for rigorous mathematics in the upper grades. Elementary school teachers receive training in all the core subjects (mathematics, science, reading, and social studies); consequently, they may lack the necessary depth in mathematics content and pedagogy to prepare their students for rigorous mathematics in middle school and high school. Shifts in the elementary school mathematics curriculum have led to a substantial increase in the knowledge needed to teach mathematics at that level (Hill, Rowan, and Ball 2005). Not only must elementary school teachers be able to teach arithmetic, but they must also be able to teach geometry, algebraic concepts, data analysis, and probability. In addition, they must be able to teach mathematical reasoning and problem-solving skills, represent mathematical concepts in multiple ways, connect mathematical concepts within mathematics and with other subject areas, and analyze students' thinking about mathematics (Hill, Rowan, and Ball 2005). Many elementary school teachers are uncomfortable with thinking of themselves as mathematics teachers even though they are the primary persons who organize and deliver mathematics instruction for elementary school students (Reys and Fennell 2003).

To increase elementary school teachers' knowledge of, and comfort with, mathematics, they may need a support mentor who can work with them in their classrooms to help them with their mathematics instruction. This support mentor should have specialized knowledge of mathematics content, pedagogy, and assessment. Because of their specialized knowledge, support mentors can serve teachers in several capacities. At times, they can work with teachers to plan and coteach mathematics lessons, model good mathematics teaching, serve as a mathematics content resource, and help teachers assess students' mathematics learning. The literature describes this school-based mentor as an *elementary mathematics specialist* (Nickerson and Moriarty 2005; Reys and Fennell 2003).

Elementary mathematics specialists furnish support for teachers and administrators who want to examine instructional practices within their schools as schools work to improve mathematics teaching and learning (Nickerson and Moriarty 2005). *Principles and Standards for School Mathematics* states, "There is an urgent and growing need for mathematics

Many elementary school teachers are uncomfortable with thinking of themselves as mathematics teachers even though they are the primary persons who organize and deliver mathematics instruction for elementary school students (Reys and Fennell 2003).

To increase elementary school teachers' knowledge of, and comfort with, mathematics, they may need a support mentor who can work with them in their classrooms to help them with their mathematics instruction.

teacher leaders—specialists positioned between classroom teachers and administrators who can assist with the improvement of mathematics education" (NCTM 2000, p. 375).

The purpose of this article is to highlight coteaching as an instructional model that positively affects mathematics teaching and learning in the elementary grades. This article uses an elementary mathematics specialist and a fifth-grade classroom teacher in a case study to discuss tips and strategies for coteaching. Even though elementary mathematics specialists do more than coteach with classroom teachers, this article focuses on coteaching because it is an instructional model that improves teachers' pedagogical content knowledge, positively affects all students' learning, and influences a school's professional community about mathematics.

A Context for Coteaching: Commonwealth Elementary School

Commonwealth Elementary School is located in a rural town with a student body that some would describe as at-risk; however, looking at this school from a positive viewpoint indicates that it is at-promise. Approximately 22 percent of the 349 students at Commonwealth are in the special education program, and nearly 30 percent of the students participate in the federal free or reduced-price lunch program. The racial and ethnic composition of Commonwealth's student body is approximately 71 percent white, 26 percent black, less than 1 percent Asian, less than 1 percent Hispanic, and about 1 percent unspecified (VDOE 2006). Commonwealth did meet the state accreditation benchmark in mathematics but did not meet the adequate yearly progress (AYP) achievement benchmarks in mathematics in 2003–2004 or 2004–2005. After implementing a mathematics specialist position in 2004–2005, Commonwealth Elementary School showed growth in mathematics teaching and learning, as evidenced by the school's meeting AYP in 2005–2006 and 2006–2007.

Susan is an elementary mathematics specialist at Commonwealth Elementary School. She has twenty-one years of teaching experience at the elementary, middle, and high school levels as a special educator and a general educator. She taught at Commonwealth Elementary School for three years before becoming the school's mathematics specialist in 2004. Her role as an elementary mathematics specialist follows the lead-teacher model (Reys and Fennell 2003). She does not have her own classroom; she assumes mentoring and leadership responsibilities. Susan's training as an elementary mathematics specialist came through her enrollment in, and completion of, a graduate degree program that focused on developing elementary and middle-grades mathematics specialists.

Joanne has five years of teaching experience and has taught fifth grade for three years at Commonwealth Elementary School. She is enrolled in a mathematics-specialist graduate program that is similar to the one that Susan completed. Joanne and Susan worked together to coteach mathematics to Joanne's fifth-grade class. This class had twenty-one students; eight received special education services for learning disabilities or behavioral issues, and six received gifted education services (one student received both special education and gifted services). For mathematics instruction, the coteachers used the *Investigations in Number, Data, and Space* (TERC 2006) curriculum. Both Susan and Joanne describe their mathematics teaching as being consistent with the NCTM Standards. They cotaught mathematics at least four times a week and agreed to this teaching arrangement because they both believed that they could meet the wide range of needs of their students in this heterogeneous classroom situation and because they are committed to providing high-quality mathematics instruction to all their students.

Developing a Coteaching Relationship

Mathematics specialists have adapted coteaching, an instructional strategy often found in the special education literature, as a collaborative tool in teaching mathematics. Coteachers jointly plan and conduct instruction in a coordinated fashion to ensure the success of all students (Friend and Cook 2003). This method of instruction is likely to improve outcomes for all students—students struggling with mathematics, special education students, and high-achieving mathematics students. Because some elementary school teachers may be unfamiliar with the mathematics that they must teach, coteaching with a support mentor, such as a mathematics specialist, is a feasible option that helps teachers increase their comfort with mathematics while positively affecting the mathematics learning of students. In the example of Susan and Joanne, both of them were comfortable with the mathematics that they taught and with their relationship as coteachers. However, a collaborative relationship among teachers can be challenging if the coteachers do not develop a comfortable working relationship. Many teachers may be accustomed to teaching in isolation; therefore, coteachers should establish rapport and get to know each other. Teachers can use several checklists in the special education literature to develop readiness to coteach and to allow partners to craft an effective relationship. Figure 9.1 is an adaptation of Murawski's (2003) worksheet for coteaching by a special educator and a general educator. The author adapted this worksheet with primary focus on fostering the relationship between a mathematics specialist and an elementary school teacher. Consequently, the questions on the worksheet deal with mathematics teaching and learning.

Before and during their coteaching collaboration, Susan and Joanne discussed their visions of coteaching in the mathematics classroom. With the support of their building-level and district-level administrators, these teachers established rapport and developed a plan for coteaching. They discussed their teaching styles, expectations for students and themselves, and the mathematics curriculum. These teachers had developed verbal and nonverbal ways of communicating with each other. They developed signals to encourage each other to call on students to share their thinking, they moved about the classroom effortlessly to monitor students' learning, and they developed such transition aids as passing the whiteboard markers and

> Mathematics specialists have adapted coteaching, an instructional strategy often found in the special education literature, as a collaborative tool in teaching mathematics.

Mathematics Attitude, Tasks, and Hopes (M.A.T.H.) Coteaching Worksheet

Directions: Coteaching partners should complete this worksheet individually and be honest in their responses. After completing the worksheet individually, coteaching partners should take turns reading their responses to each other. At this point, you should not comment on your partner's responses; partners should merely read and listen. After reading and listening, partners should write down their thoughts regarding their partner's responses. Finally, partners should come together to discuss and react to the responses. The goal of this activity is for partners to arrive at a consensus.

1. I think that good mathematics teaching and learning is _____.

2. The mathematics content and skills that I enjoy teaching the most are _____.

3. The mathematics content and skills that I enjoy teaching the least are _____.

4. My initial attitude regarding coteaching in mathematics is _____.

5. I would like to have the following tasks and responsibilities for this coteaching situation: _____.

6. I would like my coteacher to have the following tasks and responsibilities for this coteaching situation: _____.

7. My hopes for this coteaching situation are _____.

8. I have the following expectations in a mathematics classroom:

   a. regarding modifications and accommodation for individual students (both special education and general education) _____.

   b. modifying and supplementing curriculum or the pacing guide _____.

   c. regarding planning _____.

   d. regarding use of calculators _____.

   e. regarding use of manipulatives (virtual and hands-on) _____.

   f. regarding use of low-tech materials _____.

   g. regarding conceptual understanding _____.

   h. regarding procedural understanding _____.

   i. knowing and understanding the big mathematical ideas _____.

   j. receiving and giving feedback from students _____.

   k. receiving and giving feedback from the coteacher _____.

   l. regarding cooperative grouping _____.

   m. regarding alternative assessment _____.

   n. regarding standardized assessment _____.

   o. regarding classwork and homework _____.

   p. regarding noise level _____.

Note: Adapted from *Co-Teaching in the Inclusive Classroom: Working Together to Help All Your Students Find Success (Grades 6–12)* by Wendy W. Murawski (Medina, Wash.: Institute for Educational Development, 2003, pp. 36–37).

Fig. 9.1. Mathematics attitude, tasks, and hopes (M.A.T.H.) principles

giving each other high-fives. Because of their rapport, students fed from their energy and engaged in learning mathematics. Establishing a good working relationship is essential for planning and instruction.

Planning is an integral part of coteaching because during planning time coteachers determine the content to teach and the strategies that they will use to meet objectives. A major benefit of coteaching is that each teacher brings his or her own strengths and expertise to ensure that the teachers appropriately differentiate lessons for a heterogeneous class (Murawski and Dieker 2004). As coteachers, Susan and Joanne met at least once a week to formally plan and modify lessons. Because Susan and Joanne were familiar with the curriculum and their district's pacing guide, their planning sessions were approximately fifteen to twenty minutes long. Dieker (2001) found that coteachers who have built a relationship and who have a commitment to the sanctity of the planning time spent an average of between ten and fifteen minutes planning together during each session. Susan and Joanne's formal planning sessions began with a discussion of the mathematics content that they would teach and how they would teach it. They usually used the district's mathematics pacing guide. They reviewed the pacing guide and curriculum materials and decided on the appropriate teaching approaches to use; anticipated students' thinking about, and understandings of, the mathematics concepts; considered modifications and adaptations for students; decided on materials and tools needed; and decided who would take the lead on particular lessons. Although Susan and Joanne did not use the lesson-plan form in figure 9.2, the form models their discussions about planning. Figure 9.2 is a coteaching lesson-planning form that teachers can use to assist in role delegation and to ensure that the teachers make modifications and accommodations for students.

Susan and Joanne also had informal discussions that complemented their formal planning. These informal discussions were significant because of the decision making that occurred during them. Informal planning times usually occurred directly after the lesson, but at times they occurred during the lesson. After a lesson, Susan and Joanne discussed the lesson's successes and shortcomings, next steps, and modifications that might improve the lesson. Informal planning that occurred during a lesson happened as the lesson unfolded. The coteachers sometimes decided during the lesson to use one-to-one or small-group instruction. Or they would decide to pull out manipulatives that had not been in the original plan so that they could introduce greater clarity in their teaching and students' learning of a particular concept. To an observer, these decisions to deviate from the original lesson plans were unobtrusive and flowed naturally with the lesson. After the lesson, the informal discussions took less than five minutes. During the lesson, the informal discussions took only seconds because these teachers had developed a rapport that made them comfortable with each others' decision making about mathematics. These informal discussions were as important as the formal planning time because they narrowly focused on the lesson and on students' thinking.

> **A major benefit of coteaching is that each teacher brings his or her own strengths and expertise to ensure that the teachers appropriately differentiate lessons for a heterogeneous class (Murawski and Dieker 2004).**

Coteaching Planning Form

Coteachers: _____ Date: _____

Day(s):   Monday   Tuesday   Wednesday   Thursday   Friday

Week of _____

Goals, Standards, and Objectives

1. _____
2. _____
3. _____

Coteaching Approaches

_____ One-teach, one-support   _____ One-teach, one-drift   _____ Parallel teaching

_____ Team teaching   _____ Station teaching   _____ Alternative teaching

_____ Other _____

1. Mathematics content	
2. Instructional lead	
3. Role of the other coteacher	
4. Student activity	
5. Instructional modifications	
6. Accommodation strategies	
7. Evaluation or instructional feedback	

Comments: _____

_____

_____

Next planning session: Date _____ Time: _____

Fig. 9.2. Mathematics specialist coteaching planning form

Models for Coteaching

The special education literature documents and describes different approaches to instruction in coteaching situations. Educators can adapt these approaches for coteaching situations that involve an elementary mathematics specialist and a classroom teacher. Friend (1998) lists six models of coteaching for teachers of elementary school students: (1) one teach, one observe; (2) one teach, one drift; (3) parallel; (4) station teaching; (5) alternative teaching; and (6) team teaching.

In the one-teach, one-observe model (Friend 1998), one teacher teaches the lesson while the other teacher circulates in the room observing the students and collecting data. Susan and Joanne used this model to introduce students to new concepts as a method of preassessing students' understanding. For example, Joanne presented the students with a task that required them to find the relationship between the number of triangle pattern blocks and the perimeter. Susan circulated in the classroom observing students' strategies. This model allowed Susan to document students' strategies and develop small groups during the lesson. The teachers grouped students so that they could share multiple strategies. Susan and Joanne both indicated that the one-teach, one-observe model is effective for increasing time on task.

In the one-teach, one-drift model (Friend 1998), one teacher teaches the lesson while the other teacher circulates in the room and helps students. Susan and Joanne used this model to provide direct and focused individual and small-group instruction during the lesson. During a lesson on comparing mixed numerals and improper fractions, Susan observed that Donovan, one of the students, was having trouble using fraction circles to understand that

$$3\frac{1}{2} = \frac{7}{2}.$$

Susan drifted toward Donovan while Joanne continued with the whole-class discussion. All students seemed to benefit from this model because the drifter attended to students' needs immediately without interrupting the entire class. In addition, Susan and Joanne anticipated which students needed more attention, so that the drifter could strategically focus on those students. In some situations, students needed supportive teaching or reteaching attention; and in other situations, the drifter challenged students with enrichment tasks and questions.

In the parallel model (Friend 1998), both teachers teach the same content at the same time. The teachers divide the class and teach each group separately. When the students worked on adding fractions and mixed numerals, both Susan and Joanne used contextual problems. Susan had a group for which she made modifications for readability of the problems, but the mathematics was similar to that taught to the rest of the class. By reducing the teacher-student ratio, Susan and Joanne used flexible grouping to divide the class into parallel groups on the basis of needs, learning preferences, interests, and abilities.

Joanne presented the students with a task that required them to find the relationship between the number of triangle pattern blocks and the perimeter. Susan circulated in the classroom observing students' strategies. This model allowed Susan to document students' strategies and develop small groups during the lesson.

In station teaching (Friend 1998), the teachers divide content and students. Each teacher then teaches the content or does an activity with one group and repeats the instruction for the other group. In many situations, Susan and Joanne created a third station to give students the opportunity to work independently. For example, in one lesson, Susan and Joanne created three stations for fraction multiplication. Susan taught one station by using pattern blocks, Joanne taught one station that focused on contextual problems, and a third station was an independent station that involved the use of virtual manipulatives. All students benefited from the model because it increased time on task and involved several modes of representing fraction multiplication.

In the alternative teaching model (Friend 1998), one teacher directs the class through a lesson while the other teacher takes a small group of students aside. Susan and Joanne created small groups of students on the basis of students' individual needs. This model allowed Susan and Joanne to plan small-group instruction to challenge the students who needed challenges beyond the required curriculum or to plan small-group instruction for students who required reteaching or supportive teaching.

In team teaching (Friend 1998), both teachers deliver the same instruction at the same time. Most coteachers consider this approach the most complex one but also find it a satisfying way to coteach (Friend 1998). When Susan and Joanne team taught, they interchanged roles throughout the lesson. For example, when discussing a problem involving variables, Susan took on the role of a student and Joanne played the role of questioner. Joanne asked Susan to explain her thinking while she worked through a problem, then they reversed roles on a new problem. This modeling allowed students to work in pairs while playing roles similar to those of Susan and Joanne.

Final Thoughts

The six coteaching models furnish opportunities for teachers to adapt and adjust their teaching styles to meet the varying needs of students. These coteaching models allow the coteachers to plan together and implement strategies that match their instructional strengths and meet students' needs. Susan and Joanne were effective across the six coteaching instructional models. Their effectiveness had its roots in the rapport that they had developed over time. This rapport allowed them to meet the needs of students by using a variety of informal assessment strategies across individuals, small groups, and the whole class. For example, in the-one teach, one-drift model, the drifter informally assesses the understanding of individual students and provides real-time intervention. Additionally, in the one-teach, one-observe model, the observer takes notes about students' understanding to facilitate planning future instruction for the unit or to make decisions about methods of intervention. The coteachers used students' work to discuss students' progress and devised a variety of options for assessing students. Coteaching allowed for multiple viewpoints of students' mathematical progress; the multiple viewpoints furnished a more accurate

The six coteaching models furnish opportunities for teachers to adapt and adjust their teaching styles to meet the varying needs of students. These coteaching models allow the coteachers to plan together and implement strategies that match their instructional strengths and meet students' needs.

assessment of what students knew and could do in mathematics. Susan and Joanne's students demonstrated mathematical understandings in multiple learning situations, and all but one student earned a pass or advanced pass on their state's standardized mathematics test. As more elementary schools adopt mathematics specialists, opportunities must allow for rapport to develop so that the coteaching models will be effective.

Susan and Joanne's teaching is an example of a successful coteaching situation involving a teacher and a mathematics specialist. However, not all elementary schools have mathematics specialists. As previously stated, coteaching is an instructional strategy often found in special education. Successful mathematics coteaching can therefore occur in elementary schools that do not have mathematics specialists. Coteaching can use a special educator and a general educator, two special educators, or two general educators. Successful coteaching in mathematics can occur with teachers who are knowledgeable about the mathematics, pedagogically flexible, and willing to invest time and effort in working with a teaching partner.

Successful coteaching in mathematics can occur with teachers who are knowledgeable about the mathematics, pedagogically flexible, and willing to invest time and effort in working with a teaching partner.

REFERENCES

Dieker, Lisa A. "What Are the Characteristics of Effective Middle and High School Cotaught Teams?" *Preventing School Failure* 46, no. 1 (Fall 2001): 14–25.

Friend, Marilyn. *Increasing the Effectiveness of Your Inclusion Program: Successful Co-Teaching Strategies: Resource Handbook.* Bellevue, Wash.: Bureau of Education and Research, 1998.

Friend, Marilyn, and Lynne Cook. *Interactions: Collaboration Skills for School Professionals.* New York: Longman, 2003.

Hill, Heather C., Brian Rowan, and Deborah L. Ball. "Effects of Teachers' Mathematical Knowledge for Teaching on Student Achievement." *American Educational Research Journal* 42, no. 2 (Summer 2005): 371–406.

Murawski, Wendy W. *Co-Teaching in the Inclusive Classroom: Working Together to Help All Your Students Find Success (Grades 6–12).* Medina, Wash.: Institute for Educational Development, 2003.

Murawski, Wendy W., and Lisa A. Dieker. "Tips and Strategies for Co-Teaching at the Secondary Level." *Teaching Exceptional Children* 36, no. 5 (May–June 2004): 52–58.

National Council of Teachers of Mathematics (NCTM). *Principles and Standards for School Mathematics.* Reston, Va.: NCTM, 2000.

Nickerson, Susan D., and Gail Moriarty. "Professional Communities in the Context of Teachers' Professional Lives: A Case of Mathematics Specialists." *Journal of Mathematics Teacher Education* 8 (April 2005): 113–40.

Reys, Barbara J., and Francis Fennell. "Who Should Lead Mathematics Instruction at the Elementary School Level? A Case for Mathematics Specialists." *Teaching Children Mathematics* 9, no. 5 (January 2003): 277–82.

TERC. *Investigations in Number, Data, and Space.* Boston: Pearson Education, 2006.

Virginia Department of Education (VDOE). *Virginia School Report Card.* Richmond, Va.: VDOE, 2005. www.pen.k12.va.us/VDOE/src/vasrc-reportcard-intropage .shtml.

Help One, Help All

Julie Sliva Spitzer
Dorothy Y. White
Alfinio Flores

Now, more than ever before, mathematics teachers are asked to teach students more and better mathematics. When increased instructional demands are coupled with an increase in the diversity in our classrooms—including academic, cultural, linguistic, and socioeconomic diversity—teaching mathematics to all students is quite a challenge. Teachers may believe that they need to make an impossible number of accommodations and modifications to meet the individual needs of all their students. However, the task is less daunting when teachers implement strategies that are proved effective for students with a specific need and benefit other students as well. Teachers find that by helping one student understand mathematics through a particular approach, they also help all their students learn mathematics better. Teachers can employ simple strategies—using multiple representations, making connections, and promoting communication—to address the needs of specific students that will in turn serve all their students.

In this article we discuss the importance of creating a learning environment that fosters the development of every student's mathematical power. We follow with strategies that were initially designed to help one type of student (e.g., English language learners, special education students) but actually help all students learn mathematics. We close with a classroom example illustrating how the strategies can promote the mathematics learning of all students.

> Teachers can employ simple strategies—using multiple representations, making connections, and promoting communication—to address the needs of specific students that will in turn serve all their students.

Create a Learning Environment to Foster Mathematical Development

The learning environment is the most important factor in fostering the mathematical development of all students. The environment communicates to students what "doing mathematics" means and what we value in the teaching-learning process. According to the National Council of Teachers of Mathematics (NCTM) (Martin 2007, pp. 39–40), "the teacher of mathematics should create a learning environment that provides—

- the time necessary to explore sound mathematics and deal with significant ideas and problems;
- a physical space and appropriate materials that facilitate students' learning of mathematics;

- access [to] and encouragement to use appropriate technology;

- a context that encourages the development of mathematical skill and proficiency;

- an atmosphere of respect and value for students' ideas and ways of thinking;

- an opportunity to work independently or collaboratively to make sense of mathematics;

- a climate for students to take intellectual risks in raising questions and formulating conjectures; and

- encouragement for [students] to display a sense of mathematical competence by validating and supporting ideas with a mathematical argument."

All students must have an opportunity to learn and develop a deep understanding of mathematics by participating in a supportive learning environment. To achieve this goal, teachers must have knowledge of mathematics, knowledge of teaching strategies, and knowledge of their students.

In the following sections we address how teachers can create a supportive learning environment by getting to know their students, using multiple representations, making connections, and promoting active communication. Too often, students with special needs, English language learners, low-income students, and ethnic minority students are not afforded an opportunity to engage in these types of environments. However, the strategies outlined in this article will not only make mathematics more accessible for more students but also provide an enriched experience for gifted and talented students, who are usually offered only the opportunity to learn the same content, just faster.

All students must have an opportunity to learn and develop a deep understanding of mathematics by participating in a supportive learning environment.

Get to Know Your Students on Many Levels

Developing a positive relationship with your students begins with getting to know your students and the many facets of their lives. Often students whose backgrounds are different from their teachers' or peers' feel like strangers in school. The differences can be in ethnic group, socioeconomic status, language, ability level, or life expectations. Teachers can help all students feel more like an integral part of school by becoming interested in them on many levels. Teachers can learn a great deal about their students by asking them what they like to do outside of school, their families, their celebrations, and their challenges.

Often students whose backgrounds are different from their teachers' or peers' feel like strangers in school.

Teachers can also talk to other people who can provide important insights about the student, such as parents and guardians, previous teachers, and in some instances, special education teachers, social workers, or English as a Second Language teachers. For example, a previous teacher may share the content the student mastered in a previous grade, how he or she preferred to learn mathematics, or how he or she worked with other students. However, teachers must determine whether the information matches what they notice as students engage in the mathematics classroom, to avoid any unintended misinformation about the student. By learning about students

120

on many levels, teachers can include the students' backgrounds and interest in problems posed and establish better working relationships with students.

Use Multiple Representations

Using multiple representations involves presenting a concept in different ways to promote understanding among more students. For example, when teaching a new concept a teacher may use words, diagrams, concrete representations, graphs, equations, pictures, or symbolic representations. Most students need multiple ways of experiencing a concept to understand it fully. Some may prefer a verbal explanation; others may find that a visual representation helps them understand concepts better.

The concrete-representational-abstract (CRA) method is an instructional approach that research has found can facilitate the learning of students with learning disabilities (Harris, Miller, and Mercer 1995; Mercer and Miller 1992; Maccini and Gagnon 2000). This approach has three components: (1) concrete, in which the teacher models the concept in a concrete manner using manipulatives; (2) representational, in which the teacher transforms the concrete representation into a semiconcrete model, such as a drawing; and (3) abstract, in which the teacher models the previous representations in a symbolic manner using numbers and symbols. An example of this method is illustrated in the context of teaching the addition of fractions. The teacher may initially use pattern blocks to represent the concept concretely by combining blocks, then draw pictures of the pattern blocks to represent the addition in a semiconcrete manner, and finally move into solving a problem such as 1/2 + 1/6 abstractly. The CRA approach supports conceptual learning because it does not focus on the learning of "rules" and can benefit all types of learners.

Mathematical concepts are abstract, and using multiple representations can help students learn. Students should also be encouraged to represent their actions and thinking through multiple representations. The NCTM Representation Standard (NCTM 2000) suggests that students should increase the variety of their representations as they progress through school. More specifically, students in elementary school should represent objects they can see directly; in middle school students should represent objects they cannot see directly, such as rates or rational number; and finally in high school students should make representations of common mathematical structures (e.g., the sum of the first *n* odd natural numbers). By demonstrating concepts—especially new ones—concretely, pictorially, and symbolically *throughout* the grades, teachers can reach a variety of different learners and further their understanding. The most important point to remember, however, is that students move through these different levels of representations at different paces.

Make Connections

Hiebert and Carpenter (1992) suggest that the number, accuracy, and strength of students' connections determine their degree of understanding.

By demonstrating concepts—especially new ones—concretely, pictorially, and symbolically throughout the grades, teachers can reach a variety of different learners and further their understanding.

121

When teaching students mathematics, teachers need to emphasize connections among and within mathematics topics and with other subject areas (NCTM 2000). Students, especially those with learning difficulties, often have trouble making connections on their own and need support in making them (Bley and Thornton 1995; Clements 2000). Making connections explicit and helping students organize their knowledge of a mathematical topic are essential. One way these outcomes can be achieved is with concept maps (see figs. 10.1 and 10.2). Concept maps ask students to reflect on what they are learning and to make connections with new and existing knowledge. Encouraging students to engage in discussions about their maps and highlighting how different concepts, skills, and vocabulary are connected can strengthen the number of connections students can make.

Teachers can also facilitate their students' mathematical connections by tying the content to their life experiences; the method for doing so may be different for each student. The different connections that students make will give their peers a rich network of examples of how mathematics can be relevant in different aspects of life. Students from groups that have not been served well by traditional approaches to mathematics may benefit from examples that make mathematics more relevant to their lives.

Students should also study how mathematics is used in the workplace. In a year-long project, algebra students were asked to find the mathematical concepts and processes they were studying in the workplace of community sponsors (Chazan and Bethel 1998). Students learned how quantities were measured or counted, what quantities were computed, how quantities were represented and related, and the type of comparisons used to compute quantities. Students were able to find places where the mathematics

The different connections that students make will give their peers a rich network of examples of how mathematics can be relevant in different aspects of life.

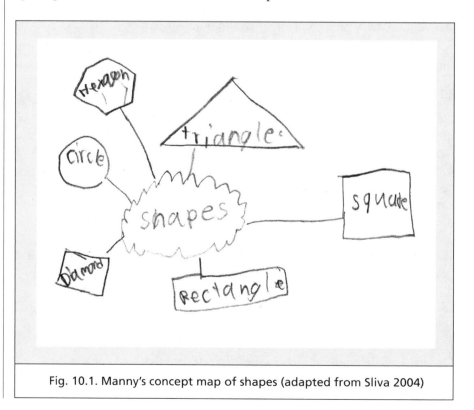

Fig. 10.1. Manny's concept map of shapes (adapted from Sliva 2004)

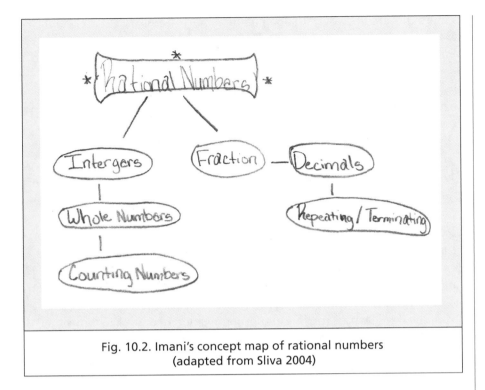

Fig. 10.2. Imani's concept map of rational numbers
(adapted from Sliva 2004)

they were studying was used even in instances in which the sponsors indicated that no mathematics was involved in their work. These students were able to see the relevance of algebraic concepts in very diverse workplaces.

Students tend to find mathematics more interesting and engaging if they perceive relevance to their lives. Helping students make connections, and having them come up with their own and then sharing with their peers, can help all students make more connections and derive more meaning from mathematical concepts.

Promote Active Communication

Establishing a classroom environment that invites all students to participate requires teachers to use various strategies that prompt students to understand and communicate their ideas. When teachers typically think of students who are challenged by communication, they think of students whose native language is not English. However, language barriers can also challenge special-education learners and students whose home language is not "academic English." These barriers may affect students' ability to receive knowledge or express their understandings. While students are explaining their thinking, they need to know that the use of their own words or modes of expression is acceptable. Sometimes these expressions will include the use of words in their native language or nonstandard English constructions. Students need to feel comfortable in sharing their ideas regardless of level of English proficiency or knowledge of academic terms.

As students feel comfortable sharing their thoughts in their native language, teachers can begin to help them develop the academic English proficiency they will need to be successful throughout school. These

Helping students make connections, and having them come up with their own and then sharing with their peers, can help all students make more connections and derive more meaning from mathematical concepts.

As students feel comfortable sharing their thoughts in their native language, teachers can begin to help them develop the academic English proficiency they will need to be successful throughout school.

123

same skills are necessary to open many opportunities in life, and can be fostered by building on students' language rather than by repressing it. Students who are learning English as a second language are often able to communicate better in their first language, or by code switching, that is, by alternating between both languages in the same conversation. If teachers do not speak the language of the student, they can often obtain assistance from classmates who are bilingual. Students may also be allowed to use aids, such as manipulatives or drawings, to help them in communicating their understanding. In such an environment, other students, too, feel more freedom to express themselves mathematically using their own words.

Mathematical terms and concepts are not always easy to grasp. Teachers can support students by simplifying his or her own use of the language. Teachers can speak slowly, enunciate carefully, and write terms on the board or overhead projector in addition to speaking them. Rephrasing and emphasizing important mathematical ideas and concepts may benefit all students by focusing their attention on what they need to remember from the day's lesson. Spelling and pronunciation of technical terms in mathematics are also important to emphasize. Another strategy, word squares, has been used successfully by Winsor (2008) in working with his ELL students. In this strategy, students fold three-by-five-inch cards into four quadrants. In the respective quadrants, they write (1) the mathematical term in their own language, (2) the term in English, (3) the definition of the term in whichever language they understand, and (4) a representation of the concept. These strategies can benefit all students because they have a way to connect the new mathematical term with their current knowledge. By encouraging students to use the terms and important ideas as they share their ideas, teachers will ensure that all students have an opportunity to make connections and develop meaning and understanding of the mathematical terms being used.

Writing is another form of communication for students to share their ideas, reflect on their thoughts, and clarify their thinking. This strategy is particularly helpful for students who are not confident when speaking in front of others. Writing in the mathematics classroom can take the form of personal reflections or journaling. By providing this additional venue of communication to students who may not feel comfortable sharing verbally in the whole group, the teacher also benefits all students by giving them a tool to reflect on concepts and clarify their thoughts.

Students can also write using their peers as an audience. On such occasions, the teacher may make writing a public process. This writing will help students organize ideas so that they can be shared. The class can then discuss examples of students' writing. By trying to make sense of what others have written, readers will also develop a deeper understanding of the ideas being discussed.

Students may also need to communicate through gestures, body language, concrete materials, or drawings, especially when they want to convey meaning. The use of manipulative materials provides a concrete representation of the concept being taught and thus can support learners who have difficulties either processing the information as it comes in or those who are second-language learners and may have difficulties understanding the language.

We next present a classroom example that uses the strategies discussed in this article.

A Classroom Example: The Ice-Cream Survey

In the following scenario we offer a snapshot of a classroom focusing on a data-analysis project. After the short description, we address how each of the strategies we have previously discussed was used in this classroom.

The Problem

Mr. Reilly wanted to involve his fifth-grade students in selecting the ice-cream flavors for the annual end-of-year school picnic. He knew that his students loved ice cream, and he wanted to use this opportunity to assess their knowledge of collecting, analyzing, and representing data. The students in the class were familiar with creating bar graphs and line plots from data presented in their textbooks. Mr. Reilly wanted to determine whether and how his students would apply those experiences in a real school example. He told the students that they needed to develop a plan for selecting the five flavors, and present their findings in multiple ways to convince him of the types and amounts of ice cream he needed to buy and why.

Brainstorming the Process

Mr. Reilly asked the students how they should go about solving the problem. At first students thought it was best to ask their friends and siblings what types of ice cream they liked, and then buy those types of ice cream. However, one student thought that a better approach would be to ask the students in each homeroom and to write down the types of ice cream they liked. Mr. Reilly restated the plan by saying, "So it sounds like you want to conduct a survey of the different homerooms." The class agreed. Mr. Reilly wrote the word *survey* on the board for the class to see.

As students thought about the survey, they cut slips of paper and wrote the question "What is your favorite ice cream?" Mr. Reilly realized that the class needed some guidance for creating the survey, because the nature of the question as posed would yield too many answers. So he suggested that the class conduct a survey in the room to test it out. Students selected all kinds of flavors and quickly realized that they needed a way to narrow down the choices. They decided on the top five flavors and modified their survey papers to read, "What is your favorite ice cream? Pick one: vanilla, chocolate, strawberry, rocky road, or mint chocolate chip." The class was then split into four groups to work on various aspects of the project. Mr. Reilly wanted to make sure that all students participated, so he added a role and responsibilities for each group. The groups, along with the roles, are delineated in the following list.

1. Create a survey for each homeroom to fill out that states the number of students who like the type of ice cream. (Each student votes once.)
   Role and responsibilities of the students: Survey Maker

2. Count the responses from each homeroom.
   Role and responsibilities of the students: Data Collector

3. Analyze the data to determine how much of each type of ice cream should be bought.
   Role and responsibilities of the students: Data Cruncher

4. Decide how much of each kind of ice cream they would like to order.
   Role and responsibilities of the students: Final Data Reporter

Mr. Reilly guided the class's explorations through his questioning. At each point in the lesson, he prompted students to come up with a plan to determine how much of what type of ice cream should be bought. He reminded them that they needed to record their results in multiple ways and to determine how much they would need to buy and why. Mr. Reilly carefully monitored the process and provided feedback to the students as they worked to achieve their goal.

The final product required that students take turns "reporting out" to the teacher and the entire class, both verbally and in writing, about how and why their group made its decisions. For example, the members of the group that had task 1 described how they created the survey so that each homeroom got only one sheet. They defended their choice using numbers (e.g., number of sheets for each class versus number of sheets for each student) and diagrams (e.g., copies of survey sheets). A written description of each of their components was included in the final report to the teacher. Each student was responsible for his or her part as well as understanding the entire project. This requirement was evidenced in a verbal question-and-answer session in which the teacher asked students about aspects of the project for which they were not directly responsible. The students were also required to respond in their journals to specific questions about the experience. These questions were different for each student, but the students did not know about the variation.

Discussion

In this example, Mr. Reilly was focusing on a variety of different aspects of teaching. First, he was interested in involving *all* his students in learning mathematics by tying the experience to something they were all interested in—ice cream. He did so as a means of creating a learning environment that was engaging for all. In this process his students worked collaboratively and selected tasks that they felt comfortable participating in, although ultimately they were responsible for understanding each piece of the project and the final conclusion.

Students were required to use multiple representations of data to convince Mr. Reilly of how much ice cream to buy and why. Some used diagrams, drew pictures, or completed bar and circle graphs. Others crunched numbers, such as mean, median, and mode, or used proportional thinking to explain their answers. All students had to think of different ways to explain their answers. Note that the students used only representation and abstract means to share their ideas. None of them used concrete models because they had developed conceptual understanding and thus had moved to more sophisticated ways of representation.

In addition to connections made with their lives, connections were made among and between other concepts, skills, and areas of mathematics and other subject areas. The students used counting, comparing, analyzing, reasoning, problem solving, and data analysis in this project. These connections allowed Mr. Reilly to note the strength and accuracy of students' mathematical understanding.

Throughout this lesson the students were consistently engaged in the project and communication of their ideas. First, they had to work together as a class to determine a process by which they were going to solve the ice-cream issue. Next they worked in smaller groups to complete their tasks. Ultimately they went back to working with the entire group to complete the final question-and-answer item and write-up. As stated previously, students were permitted to choose their groups, so they could join others they felt most comfortable with or perhaps could work with a student who complemented their best efforts. When they presented their part, they were allowed to do so with their group so that no one individual was singled out. Students were encouraged to use multiple ways to demonstrate their findings so that use of the written language was not the sole avenue to demonstrate what they understood.

Mr. Reilly designed this entire project to help all his students learn mathematics. In designing an activity that would engage all his learners, he promoted a positive learning environment, the use of multiple representations, connections with other areas inside and outside mathematics, and communication among his students.

Summary

The strategies presented in this article are grounded in the NCTM Process Standards (NCTM 1991, 2000) of Representation, Connections, and Communication. We chose these standards to emphasize the importance of using a variety of teaching strategies to teach mathematics to *all* students. Such strategies as learning about your students, fostering a positive learning environment, using multiple representations, and making connections underscore the belief that all students can learn. If a teacher believes that all his or her students can learn, then determining how students learn best and using alternative instructional approaches that capitalize on how students learn best is a must. Our hope is that you, too, believe, that all your students can and will learn mathematics, just in different ways and at different times.

If a teacher believes that all his or her students can learn, then determining how students learn best and using alternative instructional approaches that capitalize on how students learn best is a must.

127

REFERENCES

Bley, Nancy S., and Carol A. Thornton. *Teaching Mathematics to Students with Learning Disabilities.* 4th ed. Austin, Tex.: Pro-Ed, 2001.

Chazan, Daniel, and Sandra C. Bethell. "Working with Algebra." In *High School Mathematics at Work*, edited by Mathematical Sciences Education Board, pp. 35–41. Washington D.C.: National Academies Press, 1998.

Clements, Douglas H. "Translating Lessons from Research into Mathematics Classrooms: Mathematics and Special Needs Students." *Perspectives* 26, no. 3 (2000): 31–33.

Harris, Carolyn A., Susan P. Miller, and Cecil D. Mercer. "Teaching Initial Multiplication Skills to Students with Disabilities in General Education Classrooms." *Learning Disabilities Research and Practice* 10, no. 3 (Summer 1995): 180–95.

Hiebert, James, and Thomas P. Carpenter. "Learning and Teaching with Understanding." In *Handbook of Research on Mathematics Teaching and Learning,* edited by Douglas A. Grouws, pp. 65–97. New York: Macmillan, 1992.

Maccini, Paula, and Joseph Calvin Gagnon. "Best Practices for Teaching Mathematics to Secondary Students with Special Needs." *Focus on Exceptional Children* 32, no. 5 (2000): 1–22.

Martin, Tami S., ed. *Mathematics Teaching Today: Improving Practice, Improving Student Learning.* 2nd ed. Reston, Va.: National Council of Teachers of Mathematics, 2007.

Mercer, Cecil D., and Susan P. Miller. "Teaching Students with Learning Problems in Math to Acquire, Understand, and Apply Basic Math Facts." *Remedial and Special Education* 13, no. 3 (May-June 1992): 19–35, 61.

National Council of Teachers of Mathematics (NCTM). *Professional Standards for Teaching Mathematics.* Reston, Va.: NCTM, 1991.

———. *Principles and Standards for School Mathematics.* Reston, Va.: NCTM, 2000.

Sliva, Julie A. *Teaching Inclusive Mathematics to Special Learners, K–6.* Thousand Oaks, Calif.: Corwin Press, 2004.

Winsor, Matthew S. "Bridging the Language Barrier in Mathematics." *Mathematics Teacher* 101, no. 5 (December 2007): 372–78.

11

Mathematics beyond the School Walls Project: Exploring the Dynamic Role of Students' Lived Experiences

Shonda Lemons-Smith

WITH the release of *Principles and Standards for School Mathematics* in 2000, the National Council of Teachers of Mathematics reaffirmed its commitment to equity and high-quality mathematics instruction for all students. The Equity Principle advocates high expectations and asserts that all students, regardless of personal characteristics, should have equal access to opportunities, resources, and support to learn mathematics. Results from the 2003 National Assessment of Educational Progress (NAEP) and the 2003 Program for International Student Assessment (PISA) provide evidence of the persistent achievement gap that exists, particularly between white students and students of color (black and Hispanic). The achievement gap between white students and students of color has received significant attention and has been the focus of scholarly work within the mathematics education community (e.g., Lee [2002]; Lubienski [2002]; Tate [1997]). Although research related to implementing and supporting high-quality mathematics instruction in diverse classrooms exists (e.g., Strutchens, Johnson, and Tate [2000]; Trentacosta and Kenney [1997]), research that considers the social and political nature of mathematics teaching and learning is limited.

The mathematics education community faces the task of dispelling deficient notions related to students of color and mathematics teaching and learning. Educators must challenge the widely held belief that students of color have—and come to school with—little or no valuable mathematical knowledge. Gergen (1995) refers to this deficiency stance as reflecting an exogenic perspective that views students as tabulae rasae (i.e., blank slates) and treats them as inactive participants in the teaching and learning process. By not valuing students' cultural and lived experiences (i.e., what students bring to the table), educators undermine the very notion of equity and implicitly encourage the silencing of diverse learners. White (2000) affirms this idea and states, "Engaging all students in classroom discussions has direct implications for equity in mathematics education" (p. 21). Thus, teachers should be purposeful and explicit in promoting the full engagement and participation of all students in the mathematics classroom.

This article provides a critical perspective for thinking about mathematical knowledge and considers a framework that can encourage teachers to view diversity as a pedagogical asset rather than as a limitation. It begins with an overview of the Funds of Knowledge framework, which precedes

> **Teachers can employ simple strategies—using multiple representations, making connections, and promoting communication—to address the needs of specific students that will in turn serve all their students.**

129

a description of Mathematics beyond the School Walls, a school-based family outreach project. The article ends with concluding comments and considerations for implementing the described project.

Funds of Knowledge

Moll and Gonzalez (2003) present a framework on which teachers might draw to consider the dynamic role that lived experiences play in constructing children's informal and formal knowledge. This framework, Funds of Knowledge, reflects a sociocultural perspective and builds on anthropological methods. The term *Funds of Knowledge* refers to "the knowledge base that underlies the productive and exchange activities of households" (Moll and Gonzalez 2003, p. 700). The basic tenet of the Funds of Knowledge framework is that educators can use students' social (i.e., home) context to document knowledge. For example, family-generated artifacts can highlight students' out-of-school experiences and informal learning. Funds of Knowledge explicitly dismantles the notion that children from low-income households do not possess valuable knowledge and skills, in addition to providing a backdrop for considering how educators might access, identify, and document children's knowledge.

The research of Moll and Gonzalez (2003) consisted of three primary features: (a) ethnographic analysis of household dynamics, (b) an examination of classroom practices, and (c) the development of after-school study groups with teachers. The project was collaborative, and researchers and teachers visited students' homes together. Through visiting students' homes and conducting observations and interviews, they were able to develop relationships with the family and to document students' knowledge in their home environment. Within after-school study groups, teachers reflected on the visits and discussed how they could use what they had learned to enhance their mathematics instructional practices and the overall learning of students.

Funds of Mathematical Knowledge

In considering how to use the Funds of Knowledge framework specifically within the context of teaching and learning mathematics, the work of Hiebert and others (1997) is germane. Hiebert and his colleagues defined understanding as "we understand something if we see how it is related or connected to other things we know" (p. 4) and identified five dimensions (and corresponding features) of classrooms that facilitate students' mathematical understanding. The dimensions are as follows: the nature of classroom tasks, the role of the teacher, social culture of the classroom, mathematical tools as learning supports, and equity and accessibility.

Blending the work of Moll and Gonzalez (2003) and Hiebert and others (1997) provides a context on which classroom teachers might draw to reconceptualize the nature of students' mathematical knowledge and the role that lived experiences play in constructing that knowledge.

Table 11.1 provides a combined summary of the work of Moll and Gonzalez (2003) and Hiebert and others (1997).

Table 11.1
Funds of Knowledge Frameworks of Hiebert and Others (1997) and Moll and Gonzalez (2003)

Hiebert and Others (1997) Dimensions/Core Features	Moll and Gonzalez (2003) Core Questions
The nature of classroom tasks • Make mathematics problematic. • Connect with where students are. • Leave behind something of mathematical value.	What mathematical content is represented in the various artifacts?
The role of the teacher • Select tasks with goals in mind. • Share essential information. • Establish classroom culture.	How can educators use the information derived from the artifacts in constructing rich mathematical tasks? How can the teacher incorporate the information into an extended learning resource (e.g., family mathematics newsletter)?
Social culture of the classroom • Ideas and methods are valued. • Students choose and share their methods. • Mistakes are learning sites for everyone. • Correctness resides in mathematical argument.	How might the teacher and class use the family-generated artifacts to promote the development of a positive mathematics learning community? Specifically, how might the teacher use the artifacts to promote collective buy-in and create an atmosphere in which students feel comfortable articulating their thinking and sharing work?
Mathematical tools as learning supports • Each user must construct meaning for tools. • Students use tools with a purpose—to solve problems. • Students use tools for recording, communicating, and thinking.	In addition to formal mathematical tools (e.g., manipulatives, calculators), what type of out-of-school resources could the class use as tools to support mathematics teaching and learning?
Equity and accessibility • Tasks are accessible to all students. • Every student is heard. • Every student contributes.	How might teachers use the information derived from the artifacts to promote the full engagement and participation of all students? Specifically, to what extent does using tasks constructed from the lived experiences of students and their families convey the message that all students are equally valued and appreciated? How might educators explicitly communicate that message?

131

Mathematics beyond the School Walls Project

The remainder of this article outlines how teachers in a high-poverty elementary school used the work of both Moll and Gonzalez (2003) and Hiebert and others (1997) to enhance their instructional practices in mathematics. Mathematics beyond the School Walls is a school-based family outreach project that involves fifteen elementary school teachers. As project facilitator, the author worked collaboratively with teachers, students, and families to retrieve, recognize, and record students' mathematical knowledge.

In this project, we wanted to value students' lived experiences by integrating them into the teaching of mathematics. The project consisted of two primary components: (a) collecting family visual and written artifacts, and (b) analyzing and using artifacts in the teaching and learning process. The teacher asked students and their families to document the student's out-of-school mathematics experiences by either (a) taking photographs of objects that they believe reflect how the student experiences or interacts with mathematics in his or her home or community environment, or (b) cutting pictures of objects from magazines, newspapers, and other print sources that they believe reflect how the student experiences or interacts with mathematics in her or his home and community environment. Teachers also asked families to jot down the reasons that they chose each artifact and why the artifact is relevant to the mathematical learning of the student.

To ensure participation, teachers sent home letters explaining the project, allowed adequate time for students to bring in the artifacts, encouraged families to ask questions or seek assistance if needed, and sent reminders before the due date. Most teachers received artifacts from all their students on the due date or within a few days of it. In some instances, students did not have support at home and did not complete the assignment. In those situations, teachers provided magazines and newspapers and allowed students time at school to cut out artifacts. The teachers asked these students why they included the image, and the teachers (or paraprofessionals) documented the rationale. In this project, all students had an opportunity to participate and share their experiences.

After the teachers collected all artifacts, the teachers and the facilitator explored the mathematical content embedded in the artifacts, mapped them to state mathematics standards, and developed corresponding tasks. The teachers could use almost all the artifacts as a springboard for teaching multiple mathematics concepts. The teachers identified relevant mathematical content for each artifact and clustered the artifacts by content strand: Number and Operations, Algebra, Geometry, Measurement, and Data Analysis and Probability. Table 11.2 furnishes a sample of the content mapping and teacher-developed mathematical tasks.

When the teachers had completed the content mapping, they implemented the mathematical tasks with their students. After this implementation, the facilitator asked the teachers to think about the following areas

Table 11.2
Sample of Content Mapping

Artifact	Content Strand	Grade Level	State Standard	Mathematical Task
Powdered drink package	Number and Operations	K	MKN2. Students will use representations to model addition and subtraction.	Alicia and her brother are making punch from a powdered mix. The pack says that it takes 1 cup of sugar to make 2 quarts of punch. Suppose that Alicia and her brother decide to make 4 quarts of punch. How much sugar do they need?
Airplane models	Measurement	K	MKM1a. Students will compare and order objects on the basis of length.	Compare and order the airplane models on the basis of their length. Which airplane is the shortest? Which airplane is the longest? Draw an airplane that is longer than all these airplanes.
Weather data	Data Analysis and Probability	1	M1D1. Students will create simple tables and graphs and interpret them.	Using the weather data, organize high and low temperatures by using tally marks. ▪ 70–79 degrees ▪ 80–89 degrees ▪ 90–100 degrees Then create a bar graph of the weather data.
Grocery advertisement	Number and Operations	2	M2N2. Students will build fluency with multidigit addition and subtraction.	Yesterday, Michael and his mother went grocery shopping. They bought 4 containers of ice cream, 15 cans of soup, and 2 eight-packs of sports drink. The newspaper advertisement lists the following prices: ice cream, 2 containers for $4; soup, 5 cans for $3; and sports drink, 2 eight-packs for $10. Michael's mother gave the cashier one $10.00 bill and four $5.00 bills. Assuming that tax is included, how much change should she receive?

related to their instructional practices and the pedagogical implications of the family-generated artifacts, which are listed in table 11.3, to prepare them for the final session, during which the facilitator posed specific evaluative questions about the teachers' participation in the project.

The following information summarizes the teachers' written responses to six questions indicating what they learned from this process: (1) What insights did you gain from analyzing your students' artifacts? (2) What did

Table 11.3
Instructional Practices and Pedagogical Implications of Artifacts

Areas of Instructional Practice	Guiding Statements
Nature of classroom tasks	Extent to which the artifact-based mathematical tasks contained worthwhile mathematics
Role of the teacher	Extent to which the use of artifact-based mathematical tasks affected the instruction
Social culture of the classroom	Extent to which the use of artifact-based mathematical tasks promoted a positive mathematics learning community
Mathematical tools as learning supports	Extent to which the use of out-of-school resources supported mathematics teaching and learning
Equity and accessibility	Extent to which using artifact-based mathematical tasks promoted the participation and achievement of all students

you learn about how your students and their families view mathematics? (3) Did students bring any artifacts that surprised you? If so, which ones and why? (4) What did you learn about yourself and your view of mathematics? (5) Overall, was this project valuable? (6) Why or why not?

Teachers gained knowledge about their students and their families and became aware of the importance of the family context through the school-based family outreach project. Answering the first question about insights gained, one teacher stated, "From this project I realized that it is very difficult for children to relate math into their everyday lives." Another benefited by learning more about her students. She wrote, "I gained a better sense of who my students are away from school and that helps me reach and teach them better." In writing about how their students and families viewed mathematics, a teacher focusing on the parental role said, "I learned how important it is to help parents see what an important role they can play in helping their children view and interpret math all around them." A second teacher became aware of how her students and their families thought of mathematics, writing, "I learned that most of my students and families view math mainly in terms of number and operations." Another became cognizant of the abstract nature of mathematics in students' experience, writing, "I was surprised at how abstract math is to students."

Most of the artifacts clearly related to what teachers expected for student and family experiences, but one artifact surprised a teacher, who stated, "I was surprised by the picture of the airplanes because it wasn't directly related to the home environment like most of the artifacts." This artifact might motivate the teacher to explore the role of airplanes in the family's life.

The teachers learned valuable lessons about themselves and the mathematics that they teach. One revealed, "I learned that I had a narrow view of what math means to my students in their everyday lives." Another teacher became aware that mathematics is not easy for some of her students and acknowledged, "I learned that I take math for granted because it comes easy to me." Related to the previous comment, a teacher wrote, "I learned that I need to be more explicit in linking my lessons to everyday life." A fourth teacher learned an important lesson about what mathematics is through this project. She declared, "In analyzing the artifacts I realized [my students] have quite a range of understanding of what constitutes mathematics."

All the teachers believed that the project was valuable. One teacher wrote, "I definitely plan to do this project again next school year." Another seemed pleased with the project for her students: "This project was very valuable. By doing these types of projects, students will be encouraged to say, 'I use this all the time.'" And a third teacher spoke about the importance of the project in relation to making family connections, "This project was indeed valuable and reminded me of the importance of making home-school connections when teaching children math."

This project allowed teachers an opportunity to consider the nature of classroom tasks, their role as the teacher, the social culture of the classroom, mathematical tools as learning supports, and equity and accessibility as they relate to mathematics teaching and learning. Together, the teachers and the author explored the teachers' instructional practices and challenged the notion that students living in high-poverty environments lack meaningful out-of-school mathematics experiences. Rather, we focused on using those experiences as a pedagogical asset rather than a limitation.

Concluding Thoughts

This project draws on the work of Moll and Gonzalez (2003) and Hiebert and others (1997) to provide a blueprint for classroom teachers so that they can expand their view of students' mathematical knowledge and integrate students' lived experiences into the instructional scheme. Teachers who want to replicate this project in their classroom should consider the following: (a) a mechanism for ensuring students' participation; (b) the planning time required for examining artifacts, mapping content, and creating artifact-based tasks; (c) the class time necessary to implement artifact-based tasks; and (d) a professional development plan for dialoguing and collaborating with colleagues regarding the project.

This project is very worthwhile for schools, teachers, students, and families. To achieve NCTM's goal of "more and better mathematics for all students," educators not only must value students' cultural and lived experiences but also must function as an integral component of the mathematics teaching and learning process. Simply put, "all means *all*."

REFERENCES

Gergen, Kenneth J. "Social Construction and the Educational Process." In *Constructivism in Education,* edited by Leslie P. Steffe and Jerry Gale, pp. 17–39. Hillsdale, N.J.: Lawrence Erlbaum Associates, 1995.

Hiebert, James, Thomas P. Carpenter, Elizabeth Fennema, Karen C. Fuson, Diana Wearne, Hanlie Murray, Alwyn Olivier, and Piet Human. *Making Sense: Teaching and Learning Mathematics with Understanding.* Portsmouth, N.H.: Heinemann, 1997.

Lee, Jaekyung. "Racial and Ethnic Achievement Gap Trends: Reversing the Progress towards Equity?" *Educational Researcher* 31, no. 1 (January–February 2002): 3–12.

Lubienski, Sarah T. "A Closer Look at Black-White Mathematics Gaps: Intersections of Race and SES in NAEP Achievement and Instructional Practices Data." *Journal of Negro Education* 71, no. 4 (Fall 2002): 269–87.

Moll, Luis C., and Norma Gonzalez. "Engaging Life: A Funds-of-Knowledge Approach to Multicultural Education." In *Handbook of Research on Multicultural Education,* 2nd ed., edited by James A. Banks and Cherry Banks, pp. 699–715. San Francisco: Jossey-Bass, 2003.

National Center for Education Statistics. *The Nations Report Card: Mathematics.* nces.ed.gov/nationsreportcard/mathematics/.

———. Program for International Student Assessment. nces.ed.gov/surveys/pisa/ pisa2003highlights.asp.

National Council of Teachers of Mathematics (NCTM). *Principles and Standards for School Mathematics.* Reston, Va.: NCTM, 2000.

Strutchens, Marilyn, Martin L. Johnson, and William F. Tate, eds. *Changing the Faces of Mathematics: Perspectives on African Americans.* Reston, Va.: National Council of Teachers of Mathematics, 2000.

Tate, William F. "Race-Ethnicity, SES, Gender, and Language Proficiency Trends in Math Achievement: An Update." *Journal for Research in Mathematics Education* 28, no. 6 (December 1997): 652–79.

Trentacosta, Janet, and Margaret J. Kenney, eds. *Multicultural and Gender Equity in the Mathematics Classroom: The Gift of Diversity,* 1997 Yearbook of the National Council of Teachers of Mathematics (NCTM). Reston, Va.: NCTM, 1997.

White, Dorothy Y. "Reaching All Students Mathematically through Questioning." In *Changing the Faces of Mathematics: Perspectives on African Americans,* edited by Marilyn Strutchens, Martin L. Johnson, and William F. Tate, pp. 21–32. Reston, Va.: National Council of Teachers of Mathematics, 2000.

Dynamic Pedagogy in Diverse Elementary School Classrooms: Examining Teachers' Instructional Strategies

Erica N. Walker
Eleanor Armour-Thomas
Edmund W. Gordon

DESPITE the numerous reform efforts to improve students' outcomes in elementary mathematics (National Research Council 2001) and in particular, to address the racial and ethnic disparities of outcomes in elementary school mathematics (NCTM 2000), differences between the mathematics achievement of African American and Latino/a students and that of Asian American and white students still persist (NCES 2004; Tate 1997). In addition to school funding inequities, differential placement of highly qualified and experienced teachers, and continuing patterns of discrimination that all contribute to opportunity, equity, and achievement gaps, researchers and educators have pointed out that important differences exist in the quality of instruction that students from different ethnic groups receive (Schoenfeld 2002; Walker 2003).

We developed an intervention, Dynamic Pedagogy (DP), which we designed to address the issue of instructional quality for underserved students. DP integrates curriculum, instruction, and assessment components in an effort to provide elementary school students with mathematics experiences that, instead of emphasizing basic skills acquisition, focus on students' attaining computational fluency, procedural skill, conceptual understanding, and problem-solving skills (Armour-Thomas et al. 2002; Conference Board of the Mathematical Sciences 2001; NCTM 1989, 2000). Table 12.1 describes the curriculum, instruction, and assessment elements of DP.

Undergirding DP is a five-pronged theoretical framework that comprises Sternberg's triarchic theory of intelligence (1988, 1998), Vygotsky's (1978) sociocultural perspective of cognitive development, Gordon's (2001) concept of intellective competence, Feuerstein's (1979) mediated teaching-learning experiences, and Artzt and Armour-Thomas's (1999) model of teaching as problem solving. The goal is to improve teacher-learner interactions through curriculum, instruction, and assessment, with an emphasis on improving teaching-learning experiences for students of color. Major components of the intervention include on-site professional development[1]

---

1. Walker (2007) more fully describes the DP professional development components.

Table 12.1
Selected Dynamic Pedagogy Elements and Indicators

DP Element	Indicators
Curriculum	In a lesson, teacher provides a variety of tasks encompassing analytical, practical, and creative modalities, as well as tasks that require memory recall, so that students can demonstrate their knowledge.
Instruction	Teacher engages in the following instructional behaviors in interactions with students consistently throughout lesson: scaffolding, modeling, explaining, and regulating.
Assessment	Teacher asks students questions in a variety of modalities: declarative, procedural, conceptual, and metacognitive.

The underlying purpose of the intervention is to ensure that mathematics teaching in the elementary school is not a static, solely teacher-directed enterprise but rather, a dynamic exchange that enables teachers and students to explore mathematics together (NCTM 1989, 2000; Walker 2007).

In this article, we present selected examples of the instructional practice of two teachers, one of whom was among the most effective and the other of whom was one of the least effective DP teachers in the achievement of their students, who were predominantly African American and Latino/a.

targeting teachers' planning, implementation, and reflection; the development of mathematics tasks targeted to students' strengths and needs in different but not necessarily disjoint cognitive modalities (creative, practical, and analytical); the effective use of questioning (or probing) in instruction to gauge students' existing knowledge of a mathematics concept and their readiness for new content knowledge; and to activate students' interest in mathematics. The underlying purpose of the intervention is to ensure that mathematics teaching in the elementary school is not a static, solely teacher-directed enterprise but rather, a dynamic exchange that enables teachers and students to explore mathematics together (NCTM 1989, 2000; Walker 2007).

Background of the Study

In collaboration with district administrators, we worked with a group of ten third-grade teachers and their students in an ethnically and socioeconomically diverse school district, Joytown, to implement DP in 2003–2004. In this article, we present selected examples of the instructional practice of two teachers, one of whom was among the most effective and the other of whom was one of the least effective DP teachers in the achievement of their students, who were predominantly African American and Latino/a. Principals had selected Lorraine and Serena[2], two veteran teachers in Joytown, to participate in the DP project because their principals believed that they were high-quality and effective teachers, especially in the area of classroom management. However, Lorraine's students made the greatest gains in mathematics achievement of all the DP students, as

---

2. These names, as well as the name of the school district, are pseudonymous.

measured by standardized preassessments and postassessments. Further, Lorraine's students outperformed Serena's students by the end of the 2003–2004 school year although Lorraine's students, on average, started with lower mathematics achievement scores. Because Lorraine and Serena both participated in the DP project during the same time period and participated in the same number of professional development seminars, the examples of Lorraine and Serena provide an opportunity to explore how the same reform efforts, as enacted by two different teachers, can have very different results for students' achievement.

In exploring why Lorraine's implementation of DP in her classroom practice was more effective than Serena's, we discovered important differences between the teaching practices of Lorraine and Serena. This article focuses on two elements of their use of DP instructional strategies: from the assessment component, we examine Lorraine's and Serena's interaction with students during selected lessons, particularly their use of questioning; and from the curriculum component, we examine the nature and quality of the tasks that they presented to students. Both elements reflect the instructional focus of the two teachers and provide a sense of how Lorraine and Serena approached specific mathematics content. The goal of the article is to compare the examples of the most effective and least effective DP teachers for African American and Latino/a students and thereby foster insight and provide clear strategies showing how students of all backgrounds can actively engage in mathematics learning in the classroom.

Description of the Study

Lorraine and Serena taught in different schools in Joytown and had different amounts of experience teaching third grade, as table 12.2[3] indicates. Table 12.2 also shows the number of African American and Latino/a students in each teacher's class and the average mathematics scores, pre-intervention and postintervention, for the black and Latino/a students in their classes. Of particular note is that Lorraine's students gained more than 100 points during the school year.

What are possible explanations for the differences between the average performance of Lorraine's students and that of Serena's students seen in table 12.2? As part of our research about the effectiveness of DP, we collected data about teachers' practice. We obtained four portfolios from participating teachers for each DP unit (number sense, fractions, geometry, and measurement). In each portfolio, teachers submitted a representative lesson preplanning template, a lesson plan, samples of students' work, and a teacher self-assessment worksheet. In addition, members of the research team observed lessons during each unit and took field notes. For two units, we also obtained a videotaped lesson for each teacher as part of the portfolio for that particular unit.

Because Lorraine and Serena both participated in the DP project during the same time period and participated in the same number of professional development seminars, the examples of Lorraine and Serena provide an opportunity to explore how the same reform efforts, as enacted by two different teachers, can have very different results for students' achievement.

---

3. Table 12.2 does not include a standard deviation (σ) for Serena's Latino/a "average" because only one Latino/a student was in her class during 2003–2004.

Table 12.2
Achievement Data for Students in Lorraine and Serena's Third-Grade Classes

Teacher	Years of Experience Teaching Grade 3	Total Number of Students (Number of African American and Latino/a)	Average Mathematics Score at the Beginning of the 2003–2004 School Year on Second-Grade Terra Nova Mathematics Assessment		Average Mathematics Score at the End of the 2003–2004 School Year on Third-Grade Terra Nova Mathematics Assessment		Pretest/Posttest Gains	
			Black	Latino/a	Black	Latino/a	Black	Latino/a
Lorraine	Ten years	18 (13)	536.0 ($\sigma = 34.9$)	536.8 ($\sigma = 50.5$)	646.6 ($\sigma = 31.3$)	668 ($\sigma = 28.6$)	+110.6	+131.2
Serena	Three years	19 (13)	552.1 ($\sigma = 32.19$)	574.0	610.8 ($\sigma = 42.5$)	627	+58.7	+53.0

Findings

In examining the work of Lorraine and Serena, we found that although both teachers incorporated DP strategies in their teaching, Lorraine's use of the strategies was more developed and extensive than Serena's was. In curriculum, Lorraine used a wide variety of tasks to engage students and develop their conceptual understanding of mathematics concepts. For example, throughout her lessons, Lorraine provided several examples of activities that encompassed the analytical, creative, and practical modalities and memory activities that are associated with DP (Armour-Thomas et al. 2002; Sternberg 1988). Serena, however, often focused on memory tasks and activities that encompassed low-level practical and analytical modalities. On many occasions, Lorraine's tasks encompassed several modalities at the same time. Further, her tasks included a number of levels of difficulty. For a unit on equivalent fractions, for example, Lorraine used the activities shown in table 12.3.

As shown in table 12.3, Lorraine provided tasks that allowed students not only to demonstrate their knowledge of fractional concepts but also to use their creative problem-solving abilities. The tasks require that students understand what fractions represent, using a variety of models (e.g., set, unit), and that they can tap into their analytical abilities to work with fractions in a number of different contexts. The tasks also have motivational appeal and pique the interest of third-grade students. They include decorating a bulletin board for Halloween, giving beverages to friends, solving a mystery, and using concrete items (measuring cups and crayons) with which students may have had a great deal of experience. The tasks vary in difficulty, and subtasks within the tasks can also have differing levels of difficulty. For example, task 4, subtask (a) is an easier question than subtask (b). Further, subtask (b) allows students to report several different answers, which offers an opportunity for rich class discussion and underscores the concept that mathematics problems can have more than one correct solution.

Lorraine provided tasks that allowed students not only to demonstrate their knowledge of fractional concepts but also to use their creative problem-solving abilities.

Table 12.3
Some of Lorraine's Equivalent-Fraction Tasks

Task Prompt	Selected Subtasks	Modalities Addressed
1. You have been asked to help decorate a bulletin board in your classroom. It is almost Halloween, and the teacher gives you 12 decorations to put on the bulletin board. Come up with a creative plan for decorating the board using the exact amount of the different pumpkins, ghosts, and black cats shown below.	(a) 2/3 of the decorations are pumpkins, 1/4 of the decorations are ghosts, and 1/12 of the decorations are black cats.	Memory, analytical
2. A cake is missing. Solve the clues to figure out the mystery of the missing cake. Use the blanks beside each clue to fill in the letters.	(a) Take the first 1/3 of the letters in **though** and the last 1/3 of the letters in **ate**. (b) Take the last 2/3 of the letters in **bit**.	Memory, analytical
3. Use your set of 16 crayons to answer the following questions.	(a) Write the number that is 1/2 of your set. ____ Write this number as a fraction of the whole set. ____ Explain why this fraction is equivalent to 1/2.	Memory, practical, analytical
4. Imagine that you had to give a cup of soda to one friend and a cup of milk to another friend, but you do not have a one-cup measure. However, you do have a set of measuring cups that includes 1/4-cup, 1/2-cup, 1/3-cup, and 1/6-cup measures.	(a) How would you measure one cup of soda by using the 1/4-cup measure? (b) How would you measure one cup of milk by using both the 1/3-cup measure and the 1/6-cup measure?	Memory, practical, analytical Memory, practical, analytical, creative

In addition to these tasks, Lorraine used textbook-based worksheets with items that required students to use fraction strips to evaluate the size of fractions and to generate equivalent fractions by looking for a pattern, when given a "base" fraction. Although none of these tasks asked students to explain their thinking as Lorraine's self-developed worksheets did, they did encourage students to practice and memorize common patterns of equivalence.

Another hallmark of DP is the focus on ongoing or formative assessment. We worked with teachers during professional development to develop ways to conduct ongoing assessment of students' knowledge before the lesson and their grasp of mathematics concepts during the lesson. Probing was one way in which teachers gauged students' learning before, during, and after instruction. Lorraine's questions to students during instruction showed that she paid attention to what students were thinking and was interested in learning their thinking about mathematics. Serena's questions to students during instruction were often procedural; she asked students to explain how to do mathematical computations but rarely invited them to explain their thinking about a problem.

In contrast, in a unit on equivalent fractions, Lorraine used several different media to engage students' thinking about fractions during one lesson. She next gave the students the questions in table 12.3 to discuss. At the start of the lesson, Lorraine used graham crackers to spark students' thinking about fractions. Figure 12.1 shows an exchange from the start of the lesson that demonstrates Lorraine's range of questioning, her ability to use questions to encourage students to think mathematically and express their thinking, and her responses to what students had to say about the problem that she had posed. Lorraine then used this discussion to enhance students' thinking about the concept of equivalent fractions.

From these exchanges and after observing Lorraine's and Serena's teaching videotapes submitted for DP, we saw that Lorraine used question-

Lorraine:	Now, what we're going to do first, boys and girls, is we're going to see how good you are at sharing something fairly.... Each pair of students is going to share one cracker fairly. Who can tell me one way they might do it?
Student A:	You can break it in half because there are two people.
Lorraine:	Okay. Now I want each of you to break each of the two pieces in half. Break it in half now. So now how many pieces do you have that are equal?
Student B:	2/4.
Lorraine:	She has 2/4. Who can explain what she means by that? That was very smart, but I don't understand what she means. Who can explain it to me?
Student C:	Out of 4 pieces you have 2 equal ones, so it's 2/4.
Lorraine:	But I thought I had 1/2.
Student C:	That's because when it was together that made it one. But when you break it in half, that takes one part of each other and it makes 2.
Lorraine:	Does that mean that I have more now than before?

Some students reply yes, and others reply no. A few say that they are equal.

Fig. 12.1. Lorraine's opening interaction with students during an equivalent-fractions lesson

ing throughout her lessons for a variety of assessment purposes, whereas Serena used questions mainly to elicit basic knowledge or facts. Very commonly, as many teachers do, Lorraine and Serena asked declarative or procedural questions to elicit information from students about a particular problem, operation, or concept (e.g., "How do I divide this equally into three groups?"). However, Lorraine also frequently asked conceptual questions (e.g., "What pattern do you notice here?").

Lorraine also asked questions to further her instructional goals to help her students master mathematical concepts. At the beginning of her lessons, Lorraine probed students to elicit their existing knowledge of a particular mathematics concept. Sometimes Lorraine used questions as a transition from one topic to another; she often used a question as a predictive measure to help students think about where the next lesson would lead them. Lorraine also used questions that tap into students' ability to describe a concept in their own words or by using their own methods, especially to probe how much students comprehend about a certain topic using different media (e.g., "Can anyone draw a picture to explain what a fraction is?" "Can anyone tell me a little story that uses fractions?"). Such questions enabled Lorraine to view students' creative and analytical modalities and gave students an opportunity to demonstrate what they knew in a variety of ways. Lorraine often used metacognitive questions to engage students in explaining their responses or elaborating on their own thinking or the thinking of others. She asked students to explain one another's work (e.g., "Who can explain what she means by that? Can you explain it another way?") and often asked them to explain their thought processes and alternative solutions. Lorraine was clearly interested in developing her students' mathematical problem-solving ability as independent thinkers, so she often allowed students to try problems on their own. Occasionally, Lorraine asked questions that refocused students or encouraged them to stay on task, as do many classroom teachers who demonstrate good classroom management.

Although both Serena and Lorraine had excellent classroom-management skills, presented a variety of mathematical tasks, and used strategies that were effective for students' learning of mathematics, Serena's instructional practice was more limited in scope than Lorraine's. Table 12.4 shows the effective strategies that both teachers employed. Despite Serena's use of effective strategies, however, an important difference in her lessons was the quality of the tasks that she gave and the scope and rigor of the questions that she asked.

Many of Serena's lessons focused on the use of mathematical games or interesting activities. This strategy was an excellent one when coupled with opportunities for students to explore the mathematical concepts underlying the game or activity. However, Serena's students rarely did those explorations. Serena's tasks, although compelling and interesting for third graders, were often time-consuming and provided little opportunity for students to delve as deeply as they could into the mathematics of the task. For example, Serena gave her students the prompt and questions in figure 12.2 during a unit on measurement.

Lorraine was clearly interested in developing her students' mathematical problem-solving ability as independent thinkers, so she often allowed students to try problems on their own.

Table 12.4
Lorraine's and Serena's Effective Instructional Strategies

Effective Instructional Strategies	Teacher	
	Lorraine	Serena
Tasks provided for students encompass several modalities (analytical, creative, and practical).	*	*
Questions posed to students encompass several modalities (analytical, creative, and practical).	*	
Activities for students vary in difficulty.	*	*
The lesson explicitly addresses students' misconceptions and provides activities designed to correct them.	*	
Tasks provided for students have substantial motivational appeal.	*	*
Students justify and explain their thinking throughout the lesson, verbally and in writing.	*	
Students use various games, media, and manipulatives throughout lessons.	*	*
Questions posed to students vary in difficulty and type (procedural, declarative, conceptual, and metacognitive).	*	*
Questions posed to students about tasks, games, and activities are mathematically focused.	*	
The teacher devotes the bulk of instructional time during lessons to mathematics content rather than to the procedure of a game or activity.	*	
The teacher uses questions throughout the lesson to assess students' knowledge and understanding of a mathematics concept or topic.	*	

The stated goals of the lesson, according to Serena's lesson plan and debriefing conversation with two of the researchers after the lesson, were to add pounds and ounces together, so that students could practice converting ounces to pounds, and vice versa. However, the task can be much richer than the one in Serena's lesson. The questions that follow the prompt do not encourage students to predict the number of items they can take along or to estimate the weight of a backpack with certain items in it. The last two questions could have allowed students to explore how they could most efficiently add ounces to pounds or convert pounds to ounces. However, because students worked on the assignment individually, they did not have an opportunity to hear thinking strategies from their classmates that could have helped everyone realize that all the items that are given in ounces are in units of eight ounces, which is one-half pound. Students could have reviewed fractional relationships and learned that doubling an eight-ounce item results in a pound of that item.

At the close of the lesson, Serena could have asked students to think about a question that revisited the relationship between eight ounces and

You are going on a trip. You can fill a backpack with everything that you need for the trip, but the bag cannot weigh more than 15 pounds. Please choose from the following items. Your bag must weigh close to 15 pounds without going over that weight.

Item	Weight
Backpack	2 lb.
Camera	8 oz.
Clothing	3 lb.
Coat	4 lb.
Sneakers	2 lb.
Books	8 oz. each
Video game player	1 lb.
Video games	8 oz. each
Baseball bat	3 lbs.
Baseball mitt	1 lb.

1. Create a list of items that you will pack for your trip. You cannot pack a backpack that weighs more than 15 lbs. What will be the total weight of your backpack when you pack all your items?

2. When you added pounds and ounces together, how did you convert ounces to pounds? Explain.

3. Explain why you chose the items that you packed.

Fig. 12.2. Serena's activity for measurement unit

one pound. She could also have given students a problem that involved a number of ounces that was not a multiple of eight and that encouraged students to think about division, especially remainders. Instead, Serena's questions during the close of the lesson focused on the procedural and peripheral:

- How do you add pounds and ounces?

- How did you decide what to bring on the trip?

- How do you convert ounces to pounds?

In addition to Serena's providing tasks that were less mathematically rigorous than those of Lorraine, her questions to assess students throughout her lessons were limited. For example, in analyzing Serena's videotaped lessons, we found that she very rarely asked students to explain their answers. Most of her questions were declarative or procedural in nature and related directly to the materials or games that she was using rather than to the mathematical concepts underlying them. For example, in a lesson about equivalent fractions, which we observed at the same point in the unit as we observed in Lorraine's classroom, Serena used a game with pattern blocks as the focal point of her lesson. Serena most often asked such questions as "How many triangles would cover the entire hexagon?" and

"How many blue pieces cover the hexagon?" which focused on the procedural aspects of working with pattern blocks, instead of such conceptual questions as "What fraction is one of those blue shapes of the hexagon?" When Serena and her students revisited the game during the conclusion of the lesson, her questions had more to do with the game ("What did you think of this game?" "What was fun about it?") than with the conceptual or metacognitive aspects of the mathematics of the game. Although the observation indicated that Serena's students were enjoying the game, it was not clear that this significant amount of instructional time was giving students opportunities to discover new mathematics concepts or even to review old ones in a significant way.

> Her questions had more to do with the game ("What did you think of this game?" "What was fun about it?") than with the conceptual or metacognitive aspects of the mathematics of the game.

Conclusion

We have shared the work of two teachers who participated in our DP project to demonstrate that teachers who may share professional development experiences and similar goals for the mathematics learning of their students may enact mathematics reform in very different ways. Lorraine's students demonstrated that they learned much more mathematics content during the school year than Serena's students did. Although both teachers showed strengths and limitations in their teaching, Lorraine, in using a wide range of DP strategies, essentially provided more opportunities for her students to learn more mathematics during the school year than Serena's students learned. In addition, Lorraine asked more meaningful questions; used shorter, more relevant mathematics tasks and activities; and engaged in more meaningful teaching and learning interactions with her students. In contrast, Serena provided engaging activities, but they were not necessarily rich in mathematics and had limited scope. They often focused on memorization or practical applications without tapping into students' creative and analytical strengths.

> Educators, researchers, administrators, and policymakers must examine how mathematics reform is enacted at the classroom level so that they can determine what works for all students.

Educators, researchers, administrators, and policymakers must examine how mathematics reform is enacted at the classroom level so that they can determine what works for all students. On the surface, Lorraine's and Serena's students both improved during the academic year. However, Lorraine's stellar results show that examining classroom practice can be useful for gaining insight into methods of providing high-quality mathematics instruction for all students.

REFERENCES

Armour-Thomas, Eleanor, Edmund W. Gordon, Erica N. Walker, and Eric A. Hurley. "A Conceptualizing of Dynamic Pedagogy: A Social-Constructivist Teaching Model." Working paper prepared for the Institute for Urban and Minority Education, Teachers College, Columbia University, 2002.

Artzt, Alice, and Eleanor Armour-Thomas. "A Cognitive Model for Examining Teachers' Instructional Practice in Mathematics: A Guide for Facilitating Teacher Reflection." *Educational Studies in Mathematics* 40, no. 3 (November 1999): 211–35.

Conference Board of the Mathematical Sciences. *The Mathematical Education of Teachers.* Providence, R. I.: American Mathematical Society in cooperation with Mathematical Association of America, 2001.

Feuerstein, Reuven. *The Dynamic Assessment of Retarded Performers*. Baltimore: University Park Press, 1979.

Gordon, Edmund W. "Affirmative Development of Academic Abilities." *Pedagogical Inquiry and Praxis*. No. 2. Institute for Urban and Minority Education, Teachers College, Columbia University, September 2001.

National Center for Education Statistics. *The Condition of Education*. Washington, D.C.: U.S. Department of Education, 2004.

National Council of Teachers of Mathematics (NCTM). *Curriculum and Evaluation Standards for School Mathematics*. Reston, Va.: NCTM, 1989.

———. *Principles and Standards for School Mathematics*. Reston, Va.: NCTM, 2000.

National Research Council. *Adding It Up: Helping Children Learn Mathematics*, edited by Jeremy Kilpatrick, Jane Swafford, and Bradford Findell. Washington, D.C.: National Academy Press, 2001.

Schoenfeld, Alan. "Making Mathematics Work for All Children: Issues of Standards, Testing and Equity." *Educational Researcher* 31, no. 1 (January 2002): 13–25.

Sternberg, Robert. "Principles of Teaching for Successful Intelligence." *Educational Psychologist* 33, nos. 2–3 (March 1998): 65–72.

———. *The Triarchic Mind: A New Theory of Human Intelligence*. New York: Viking, 1988.

Tate, William. "Race-Ethnicity, SES, Gender, and Language Proficiency Trends in Mathematics Achievement." *Journal for Research in Mathematics Education* 28, no. 6 (December 1997): 652–79.

Vygotsky, Lev S. *Mind in Society*, edited by Michael Cole, Vera John-Steiner, Sylvia Scribner, and Ellen Souberman. Cambridge, Mass.: Harvard University Press, 1978.

Walker, Erica N. "Who Can Do Mathematics?" In *Activating Mathematical Talent*, Monograph Series for Leaders in Mathematics Education, edited by Alexander Karp and Bruce Vogeli. Boston: Houghton Mifflin and National Council of Supervisors of Mathematics, 2003.

———. "Rethinking Professional Development for Elementary Mathematics Teachers." *Teacher Education Quarterly* 34, no. 3 (Summer 2007): 113–34.

Acknowledgments

The work reported herein was supported under the Educational Research and Development Centers Program, PR/Award Number R206R000001-04, as administered by the Institute of Education Sciences, U.S. Department of Education. The findings and opinions expressed in this report do not reflect the position or policies of the Institute of Education Sciences or the U.S. Department of Education.

Meeting the Challenge of Engaging Students for Success in Mathematics by Using Culturally Responsive Methods

Emily Peterek
Thomasenia Lott Adams

WELCOME to Oaklane Elementary School. Oaklane is located in the northeast section of an officially rural yet college-town community. In this section of town, one of the oldest African American communities in the city and a recently established African American community have merged because of the addition of a new, affordable housing development.

Setting the Stage

Oaklane Elementary School is central to its merged neighborhood and serves a population of students primarily from the local community, which is 99 percent African American. The school has a Title I classification, with 92 percent of the students receiving free or reduced-price lunches. Many of the students live in a nearby large subsidized housing development owned and operated by an African American church located just a few blocks from the school. Oaklane offers an arts magnet program that is open to any elementary school child in the district, although the curriculum brings little diversity to the school.

In previous years, Oaklane's students had been plagued by such labels as "low-achieving," "struggling," and "at risk." At one point, the district administration considered closing Oaklane, but support from the local community kept the school's doors open. However, the school has recently experienced a change in building administration, a change of philosophy in teaching, and an improvement in parental involvement. These changes have led to a dramatic increase in students' achievement and a campus-wide boost in morale. In just five years, the school went from a grade of F to a grade of A in the state's school grading system, and it is currently maintaining a grade of B. Of particular interest to the authors is that the students' gains and achievements in mathematics are notable. We wanted to find out for ourselves what was happening at Oaklane that produced such dramatic results. In particular, we wanted to know how the teachers at Oaklane were reaching students in mathematics. Thus, we established a relationship with the school's principal and the lead mathematics teacher. After some time and many conversations, we decided to pay Oaklane a visit.

We were not sure what to expect when we walked into what would be one of the most eye-opening experiences of our lives as mathematics educators. As we entered the classroom of Ms. Kay,[1] we were overwhelmed by the sound of students' voices. "A mixed number is a whole number and a fraction!" we heard the twenty African American fifth graders say in unison, with rhythm and enthusiasm. When we entered, we saw several fractions on the whiteboard. The students were focusing on a problem for which they had attained an answer of three-sixths. "Is it in simplest form?" Ms. Kay asked, to a beat that she kept by snapping her fingers, followed by the students' unison response "No! No!" Then we heard her say in a talking-singing voice, "Break it down," to which the students answered with a very audible choral response, "Three on top, three on bottom, three on top, three on bottom...." "What is the answer?", she asked in her controlled rhythm. "One-half," the students responded.

While Ms. Kay continued, she led the students through many other mathematical concepts, including measurement, measures of central tendency, least common multiples, prime and composite numbers, and geometry. The class reviewed every idea by using this oral chant, call-response, and rhythmic technique. We asked her about this style of instruction, and she said, "The students come to me as a 1 [as measured by the state's standardized test], but they leave me as a 4 or 5 [out of 5]." We were awestruck by her confidence but were unsure that she had the evidence to back it up. We decided to return to Oaklane and to Ms. Kay's class for observations and a chance to see how she established mathematics learning as a priority for her students.

Week after week, we observed Ms. Kay teaching fifth-grade mathematics classes. We partially expected that the students' enthusiasm and focus would wane. We also realized that we might return to find that what we had seen was a rehearsed and memorized presentation that lacked real support for conceptual understanding. Yet we always found consistency in her instruction, with the same level of whole-class involvement regardless of the mathematics topic. We saw her genuine gift for teaching mathematics. "I try to relate it to their lives ... I tell a story" she said, as if it is the simplest thing in the world to do—to tell a story with mathematics in a way that the story captures students' imaginations and relates to their daily activities so that they can learn the mathematics.

Ms. Kay is in a unique environment at Oaklane because many in the community had given up on the school, yet she has used her teaching craft effectively to support her students' success. She has learned how to respond to the learning needs of her students. Indeed, our observations of Ms. Kay confirm that she attends to the cultural characteristics of her students as a means of reaching them. We see her as successfully facilitating culturally responsive mathematics teaching. The aim of this article is to present a brief snapshot of the foundation for the pedagogical tools that Ms. Kay uses to teach mathematics.

---

1. Pseudonyms have been used throughout this article.

Culturally Responsive Teaching

Many discussions in the literature center on the needs of learners from diverse backgrounds. Conceptualizing reforms (for teachers and schools to enact) that attempt to meet those needs, however, is not easy and requires innovation, patience, and willingness to change at every level. Oaklane Elementary has accomplished such reform, which has been led largely by reinvented and empowering instructional techniques that reflect culturally responsive teaching (CRT). These practices are a crucial part of this critically needed systemic process of reform.

CRT, which has emerged largely from multicultural assumptions and theoretical underpinnings, is at the core of multicultural education. Its basis is that many current schooling and teaching environments stifle cultural practices, perspectives, and experiences. Culturally responsive educators, however, consider students' diversity as a strength in the classroom rather than a challenge that they must overcome, and they see the incorporation of cultural perspectives as a necessary educational commitment. They view students and teachers as cultural beings with cultural filters (Gay 2000) that sift all information. They see cultural experiences and identities as the foundations for all other experiences and behaviors (Ladson-Billings 1994).

CRT creates learning communities in which members validate cultural practices and values and revere them as funds of students' knowledge. Students of culturally responsive teachers embrace their own culture while learning to respect the cultures of others. For the student and the teacher, the educational experience is liberating and empowering in every sense (Gay 2000). In the process, the student and teacher transcend Eurocentric values on which much of the curricula, disciplinary practices, and pedagogy are based, allowing the use of home cultures as a learning tool in school.

CRT establishes a culturally relevant community endeavor that addresses students' needs. For example, when working with African American children, CRT "uses students' culture in order to … transcend the negative effects of the dominant culture, [and] the primary aim of culturally relevant teaching is to assist in the development of a 'relevant black personality' that allows African American students to choose academic excellence yet still identify with African and African American culture" (Ladson-Billings 1994, p. 17). Culturally responsive mathematics teaching (CRMT) is a natural extension of this theory. This article focuses on this emerging concept and uses an example of success to illustrate our findings.

A Brief Note on the Challenges That African American Students Face

As indicated by statistical evidence, African American students are currently experiencing struggles that prevent success in instructive settings. They include dropout rates that are higher than those in the past, as well as lower academic achievement scores and increased incarceration rates (Pennington 2000; Ladson-Billings 1994). Further, students of color are grossly overrepresented in special education programs (Gay 2002;

Culturally responsive educators, however, consider students' diversity as a strength in the classroom rather than a challenge that they must overcome, and they see the incorporation of cultural perspectives as a necessary educational commitment.

151

Townsend 2003), are more likely to be suspended from school (Ladson-Billings 1997), and are less likely to receive a standard high school diploma. Gay (2000) asks a very poignant question: Why are students of color, who are successful in so many areas outside school, failing in school? This question is worthy of investigation, particularly in the context of mathematics, where the achievement gaps are some of the most marked (Howard 2006). The need for CRMT is undeniable.

Ms. Kay: Foundations in Community

As previously described, we have been fortunate to work with a teacher whose instructional practices mirror many core ideals of CRT. As with all great teachers, the attributes and routines of her instruction are holistic and multifaceted, making them difficult to identify and discuss briefly. Moreover, classroom dynamics are distinct and unique, making our task of sharing this story even more challenging. Clearly, however, Ms. Kay uses her understanding of students' needs and interests as a foundation to make the learning experience meaningful for her students. Further, the nature of this teacher's pedagogical practice deeply interweaves with every aspect of her life. Ms. Kay not only helps her mathematics students with academics, confidence, and self-perception but also involves herself in many aspects of the school and community, thereby putting herself in a position to learn about the cultural context of the community. For example, Ms. Kay offers a night class for parents who are interested in improving their own mathematical skills. Teaching this class gives her an opportunity to (1) motivate parents for parental involvement, (2) learn more about the home and community lives of her students so that she can use this information to connect with students and to use as contexts for mathematics problems that students can explore, and (3) show the students that she cares about them beyond the boundaries of the classroom.

> **Ms. Kay offers a night class for parents who are interested in improving their own mathematical skills. Teaching this class gives her an opportunity to (1) motivate parents for parental involvement, (2) learn more about the home and community lives of her students, and (3) show the students that she cares about them beyond the boundaries of the classroom.**

Similarly, Ms. Kay is visible in the religious community; she realizes and respects that this involvement is also important to the students at Oaklane and their families. Many weeks, she has invited us to attend her church, an experience that has been enlightening to us as researchers and inspiring to us as educators. Most notably, we came to realize that Ms. Kay's style of facilitating instruction with her students closely resembles the way that the minister of her African American church facilitates the service: active participation of the whole audience, leader-audience dialogue, leader-audience call and response, rhythm in repetitions and clapping, and other indications from the leader that he expects an audience response. This same level of expectation is evident in Ms. Kay's active, student-centered, structured classroom. This type of congruence between home and school culture is fascinating to watch and has been immensely successful in her classroom.

Such concern for families' experiences in the neighborhood is one of the hallmarks of Ms. Kay's style. As a result, she is well-respected, visible in the community, and knowledgeable about her students' lives outside school. Her involvement is important to the students because it illustrates that children and families are cared for, looked after, and respected in every aspect of their lives. Moreover, as we subsequently describe in more detail, her involvement enables Ms. Kay to recognize cultural practices and values that help her design effective, empowering mathematics instruction.

As Ms. Kay's extensive involvement in the community indicates, she stays in touch with her students, as evidenced in her instruction through the use of such cultural practices gleaned from students' daily lives as chants, dance, clapping, stories, and choral responses to teach mathematics. Further, she knows what and how much her students are able to engage in, so that each learner reaches the level of knowledge that Ms. Kay is seeking for her or him. Standardized test scores, although a focus and a goal, are not the only facets of education with which she is concerned. She wants students to *understand* what they are doing and to be able to make sense of it in their own lives. She wants students to relate to, and interact with, the material so that they are able to use it, retain it, and be confident in their abilities. Ms. Kay empowers students as learners of mathematics. This article next attempts to put into words specific mathematics teaching practices that Ms. Kay exhibits.

Ms. Kay's Approach to Culturally Responsive Teaching of Mathematics

Ms. Kay is a strong and respected teacher. Her peers, school administrators, parents, and teacher educators praise her because of her ability to reach for and touch the stars with her students. Fully capturing the unique and dynamic pedagogical practices that have produced remarkable results for her students is challenging, but this section attempts to describe aspects of her mathematics instruction.

Chants and Movement

Consistent with the culture of the local community, where the students play in the neighborhood recreation center and on the sidewalks, Ms. Kay's classroom features choral responses, requiring the vocal, physical, mental, and personal involvement of each student. She rarely sits down during class and is continually walking among the students to encourage participation and engagement in mathematics. She is relentlessly moving, snapping, clapping, leading chants, and encouraging enthusiasm. Her energy and passion are contagious, as evidenced by the full engagement of her students.

To further the effectiveness of these chants and choral responses, Ms. Kay uses her vocal talent to engage students, creating rhythms that teach mathematics through musical modalities. Students come to realize that singing mathematics is an enjoyable way to learn concepts and is effective for retention. Further, because Ms. Kay knows that her students enjoy the music of the hip-hop culture, she uses that music as an inspiration for various rhythms and songs and allows students to sing along to their favorite tunes. She has found that through hearing and participating in chants every day, students retain information and continually refine their knowledge. Several students have reported to us that when they hear a song or rhythm on the radio, they cannot help but sing the "math words" instead of the real words. The information is therefore accessible and relevant to students, and receives reinforcement daily outside the classroom.

In addition to the chants, Ms. Kay assigns specific movements to concepts to give students another way to retain the information. For example, Ms. Kay may ask the class to show her a line. First, all students extend one arm fully (open-palmed) and say "this way." Then they extend the other arm, saying "that way." Students do these movements very quickly: "this way/that way," "this way/that way" in a unison chant. Next, she may ask to see a ray. First, each student extends one arm, but makes a fist and says "stop." Next, he or she extends the other arm fully (open-palmed), wiggles his or her fingers, and says "keep going, going." Again, students are chanting in unison "stop/keep going, going," "stop/keep going, going" each time that they make the arm movements. Eventually, students use these movements and others—for such related concepts as right angle, acute angle, and so on—together in a "geometry dance," complete with music and order. This type of movement activity engages the students, builds their confidence in the material, and substantially increases the students' chances of retaining the information. In addition, it gives learners a physical representation that enhances understanding.

This involvement is the type that Ms. Kay requires and encourages. Students are in the rhythm of the mathematical content with her, learning through music, movement, and rhythm: matters that are very much a part of their lives outside the classroom. Additionally, she varies the topics, the order of topics, and the responses that she solicits, so that students do not have a way to rehearse for the experience. Rather, the students must learn what to expect of Ms. Kay's style and must reach a place of comfort knowing that she is interested in their learning. The students are acquiring sophisticated mathematical knowledge in the context of cultural consistency, accepting that Ms. Kay challenges them to do their best, even in the process of having a good time.

Incorporating rhythms, songs, and movements into her lessons is one way that this teacher encourages her students to be full participants in lessons; using specific songs as the basis for projects is another.

Incorporating rhythms, songs, and movements into her lessons is one way that this teacher encourages her students to be full participants in lessons; using specific songs as the basis for projects is another. For example, Ms. Kay grew concerned that her students were spending so much time listening to hip-hop music at home and in other venues that they were not accomplishing as much as they could at school, specifically, in mathematics. To address that problem, she assigned a weeklong project at the end of class one day. Because she had noticed that many of her students knew all the words to the hip-hop song "Laffy Taffy," she asked them to keep track of how many times they heard the song each day for a week. She then required the students to organize their data into a bar graph, complete with title and appropriate labels. The results were amazing. Not only did students produce colorful and artistic bar graphs, but they were also able to analyze the data that they collected, group it in different ways, and discuss why they may have heard the song more on one day than on another day.

This type of continual attention to students' engagement supports Ms.

Kay's goal of capturing students' interest and keeping them interested and invested in mathematics. During class, she encourages students to answer questions in unison, using a strong voice so that they feel empowered by their knowledge and assurance. In fact, if Ms. Kay senses meekness in learners' voices, she continues to ask for an answer until she hears a powerful refrain. The result is truly amazing and unconventional: learners are continually clapping, stomping their feet, drumming on their desks, moving, dancing, and marching in time during mathematics lessons. Moreover, students engage in mathematics at home when listening to their favorite song or when the familiar beat of the geometry dance comes on the radio. One might expect chaos from this type of behavior, but the mood in the classroom is extremely positive, organized, and goal-oriented. Ms. Kay is clearly in control of the situation, but she is like an orchestra conductor who purposefully draws out the best from those she is leading.

Real-Life Examples

Teachers receive continual encouragement to relate the material that they teach to the real world and to students' lives. Truly incorporating a sense of usefulness into mathematics instruction is a challenge in and of itself. Ms. Kay, however, is deeply in touch with the culture of the school and community and makes storytelling a naturally occurring medium through which she conveys real-life contexts.

"You've got two numbers here, two-fifths and one-tenth," Ms. Kay says. "What do you know about them?" Several students say, "They are related." "How do you know?" she persists. "When you count by fives you say ten," respond the students. "So how do you add them?" she asks. There is a pause, and then the students answer, "You find a common denominator." Unsatisfied with the enthusiasm of the class, the teacher rings out, "What?"—to which more students respond enthusiastically, "You find a common denominator!" Ms. Kay then uses a familiar story to access children's existing knowledge of finding the least common multiple as a means of finding the least common denominator. She proceeds to tell this story about five and ten. "We know the numbers are related, and let's say ten is the big brother. If they are walking down the street, who do you see coming first?" All the students respond, "Ten!" "So who decides what denominator we use?" All answer, "Ten!" The students respond with smiles and laughs, clearly understanding the point that the teacher is making and the underlying mathematical idea. Ms. Kay has realized that the students in this school are part of a walking community. Many students walk to school with their brothers, sisters, cousins, and neighbors, so this example relates to the students' real lives. In addition, she asks them to explain concepts to her as if they were explaining them to their little brother or sister. This type of focus on family and interaction is important to this specific population, and students respond with hard work and determination.

High Standards through Tough Love

Brandy was a new student in Ms. Kay's class. We were there on her first day of class. She entered the room with a visibly negative attitude and a smug expression on her face. She sat in the back of the room; and as Ms. Kay quickly discovered, Brandy was unprepared. Ms. Kay tried to be accommodating, asking Brandy what she had done at her previous school and how comfortable she was with the current material. From this brief interaction, Ms. Kay learned that Brandy had not enjoyed her previous school and the idea of having to do such energetic work in Ms. Kay's class did not thrill her. Further, when another student lent Brandy a pencil and paper, Brandy snatched it from his hands and rolled her eyes. This type of behavior pushed Ms. Kay to her limit. The teacher stopped what she was doing and made clear to Brandy that her attitude and actions were unacceptable. She then explained that her students do not disrespect one another, especially when one is trying to help another. Brandy looked angry when Ms. Kay walked away and continued with her instruction.

About a month later, we returned to watch the same class. Brandy, who had been resistant in the beginning, was one of the loudest chanters. She was helping students around her, taking meticulous notes, and smiling. "Finally," Ms. Kay said, "she came around, and she is happy." When we discussed this incident with Ms. Kay, she indicated that for these students, community accountability goes a long way in helping individual students do the right thing. Brandy rose to Ms. Kay's expectations and became a more confident learner.

Such relationships with students are of particular interest to the authors. Throughout the year Ms. Kay makes demands on her students; her expectations for their mathematics learning are clear, high, and unwavering. At the same time, however, she conveys a sense of care for students' well-being and success in school. For example, when a student shows that he or she understands a mathematics concept so well that he or she can explain it to the entire class, Ms. Kay praises the student enthusiastically. However, she does not tolerate wandering attention. She often calls out students who are not engaged and directs them back on task. She tells students who forget their mathematics journal to call home so that someone can bring it to them. Students respond to these lofty expectations by meeting the standard and in some cases, exceeding it. Ms. Kay responds with visible pride in her students, a reward for which they work very hard.

Focusing Students' Energy for Mathematics Learning

What does the perfect classroom look like? Many people believe that it should be full of silent students. However, this definition of *normal* or *perfect* is not consistent across cultures. In other words, traditional school practices are considered normal even if they do not work for students of diverse backgrounds. In turn, students' achievement suffers, appropriate behavior that is acceptable at home is not acceptable at school, and the educational setting devalues household language patterns and practices. Thus, the school setting deems certain cultural behaviors inappropriate, dooming some groups of students to a life of conformation or a life of unfulfilled potential.

What does the perfect classroom look like? Many people believe that it should be full of silent students. However, this definition of *normal* or *perfect* is not consistent across cultures.

Ms. Kay has found her niche in incorporating cultural behaviors into her classroom. She engages students musically through chants and rhythms; she encourages students to speak with loud, confident voices. Students know that they are to respect themselves, their classmates, and their teacher. In her class, all the students' energy focuses on mathematics and the empowerment that they believe keeps them engaged. Ms. Kay empowers students to be confident learners. When she speaks precisely and forcefully with the mathematics through chanting and recalling, the students engage in the same, and the students appear to be developing their own confidence about the mathematics that they are learning.

Conclusion

What can teacher educators and teachers learn from Ms. Kay? They can take Ms. Kay's ideas and successes and begin to evaluate their own practices. She shows teachers that accepting and caring for students as they are is important. Teachers should not force students to conform to values that do not acknowledge their power as learners and as human beings. Rather, educators must remember that each student has a cultural background. In the context of that background, students will make the most progress. The previous statement does not mean that students should not follow rules or think outside their home culture, but it is a call for educators to consider a student's culture and background when making decisions about curriculum, instruction, behavioral intervention, and assessments for him or her. Because each classroom and each teacher are different, no one formula can unlock the secrets of cultural responsiveness; yet each teacher can think about how her or his instructional style affects students. Further, each teacher can engage in conversations about the topic of diversity, sharing ideas and continually improving his or her own craft. These conversations may include colleagues, parents, and students. The question for you is, How can *you* empower students as learners of mathematics?

Although no one-size-fits-all approach to CRMT exists, we have gleaned several ideas from Ms. Kay that have been helpful to practicing teachers.

- Chants and rhythm are an important part of Ms. Kay's instruction. She asks about and notices students' musical interests and uses them as a basic component in creating engaging mathematics lessons. She sets vocabulary to music, sets definitions to music, and sets procedures and algorithms to music. Rhythmic motions punctuate recitation. The class accomplishes practice within the meter of musical accompaniment.

- Ms. Kay constantly communicates high expectations built on tough love to her students. She accepts no excuses and does not tolerate failure. Students must rise to the occasion. She expects all students to participate in every lesson, and she does not allow students to do otherwise. She says, "They can't be in my class if they won't participate." Her no-excuses policy and her endless praise of successful students evidence her tough love. Students learn that this praise, however, does not come easily and that they must earn it.

Teachers should not force students to conform to values that do not acknowledge their power as learners and as human beings. Rather, educators must remember that each student has a cultural background. In the context of that background, students will make the most progress.

- Teacher-mentor is a way to describe Ms. Kay overall. She provides students with what they need to learn and become successful mathematicians. She addresses their attitudes about, and responsibilities for, schoolwork, and she encourages them with praise.

- Storytelling is a means through which Ms. Kay connects mathematical ideas with her students. She uses practical examples from the daily lives of the children (e.g., walking to school or borrowing from a neighbor).

- Review happens in every mathematics lesson. Ms. Kay actually builds this review into the songs and chants that she leads throughout class. She believes that hearing or seeing mathematics one time is simply not enough for students to learn it thoroughly.

- For Ms. Kay, community involvement is an important component in positioning herself to stay in touch with her students and their families. She realizes that the community in which students live greatly influences their culture, and she stays close to the community by offering mathematics instruction to parents and by organizing rite-of-passage programs for her fifth-grade students.

- Empowerment—that is, mathematics empowerment—is what Ms. Kay wants for the students. For example, when the class studies percents, Ms. Kay creates scenarios about the students' planning a shopping budget and shopping. She instructs the students to pay close attention to percent-off sales so that they can make certain that they receive the appropriate discount on purchases. Ms. Kay warns the students that without mathematics empowerment, others can cheat and take advantage of them.

- The language of mathematics is an essential component of Ms. Kay's instruction, as evidenced by her use of chants and songs, her guidance in students' journal writing, and her requirement that students justify their thinking and give articulate explanations for their solutions.

As the large gaps in achievement among students of various backgrounds illustrate, culture is essential to learning. Specifically, heritage, personal perceptions, experiences, and societal norms play roles in processing information and shaping individual thinking processes. CRMT presents a necessary intervention. Through empowering pedagogical practices such as those previously described, educators must bridge the gaps sustained by the status quo while empowering students to bridge the same gaps. What we need now is action that addresses the reasons that teachers are failing to reach much of the minority population in schools. No one holds the patent on "good" mathematics teaching, not even Ms. Kay. So we are confident in proposing that other teachers can also help their students reach for and touch the stars.

REFERENCES

Gay, Geneva. *Culturally Responsive Teaching: Theory, Research, and Practice.* New York: Teachers College Press, 2000.

——. "Culturally Responsive Teaching in Special Education for Ethnically Diverse Students: Setting the Stage." *Qualitative Studies in Education* 15, no. 6 (November 2002): 613–29.

Howard, Gary R. *We Can't Teach What We Don't Know: White Teachers, Multiracial Schools.* New York: Teachers College Press, 2006.

Ladson-Billings, Gloria. *The Dreamkeepers: Successful Teachers of African American Children.* San Francisco: Jossey Bass, 1994.

——. "It Doesn't Add Up: African American Students' Mathematics Achievement." *Journal for Research in Mathematics Education* 28, no. 6 (December 1997): 697–708.

Pennington, Harvey J. "Issues in Mathematics Education with African American Students." *Multicultural Education* 7, no. 3 (Spring 2000): 36–41.

Townsend, Brenda. "Testing While Black: Standards-Based School Reform and African American Learners. *Remedial and Special Education* 23, no. 4 (July–August 2002): 222–30.

Moving from Deficiencies to Possibilities: Some Thoughts on Differentiation in the Mathematics Classroom

Mark W. Ellis

> What the learners conflict with in the mathematics classroom may not only be the mathematical meaning of a particular piece of content or a particular strategy, but the whole act of being taught through processes that ignore, reject or make invisible some students, processes destined to select a few and fail the rest.
>
> —*Núria Gorgorió and Núria Planas*

KATHLEEN Collins' (2003) eighteen-month case study of Jay, a fifth-grade African American student, documents in detail the ways in which those in authority in school "pathologized Jay's family structure, his cultural way of being" (p. 194) such that he was labeled as having low ability and was held to lower expectations by his teacher. Even after Collins shared samples of his work that clearly exhibited cognitive strengths, Jay's teacher "still responded to Jay as though he were less than capable" (p. xiii). The teacher's beliefs about Jay's abilities and, consequently, his academic needs were premised on a deficit model and reinforced by labels applied to him by the schooling process, leading her to discount evidence of his achievements as somehow immaterial. Although perhaps unintentional, the actions of his teacher served to limit the possibilities for Jay's success.

A practice exists in the United States of using school as a location in which to label students according to some perceived "ability" and separate them into various levels of coursework rather than see the potential for success that lies in every student (Oakes 2005). As this article's opening quote describes, this approach has led to practices in the mathematics classroom that often keep students from the mathematics rather than get them into it (Ellis 2007). Efforts to reform our teaching of mathematics such that a broader range of students have access to high standards and are supported in reaching those standards are often at odds with this practice or habit of mind. When thinking about the idea of differentiation in the mathematics classroom, how it is undertaken must be carefully considered—what are the assumptions and beliefs from which teachers work to differentiate instruction? This article is intended to stimulate readers to examine the positions from which their own efforts at differentiation are

> When thinking about the idea of differentiation in the mathematics classroom, how it is undertaken must be carefully considered—what are the assumptions and beliefs from which teachers work to differentiate instruction?

161

enacted. Specifically, notions of ability are examined as social constructions that have a big impact on how efforts to differentiate instruction come to be crafted.

Since the early 1900s, school mathematics in the United States has offered a convenient location for the separation of students by so-called "ability" (Ellis 2008). Although concern about the overall mathematical knowledge of all students has become greater and greater in recent years (Diaz and Lord 2005; National Commission on Mathematics and Science Teaching for the Twenty-first Century 2000; National Council of Teachers of Mathematics [NCTM] 2000; U.S. Department of Education 2003), much of the energy being directed toward mathematics education remains focused on determining students' placement within a variety of leveled courses, planning and implementing separate curricula, and measuring the resulting variations in learning outcomes (Booher-Jennings 2005; Diamond and Spillane 2004). Although these efforts may be socially sought after, they are in large part educationally counterproductive (Ayalon and Gamoran 2000; Boaler, Wiliam, and Brown 2000; Oakes 2005). As long as outcomes in mathematics achievement as measured by standardized examinations (and the resulting inferences about students' abilities in mathematics) continue to be correlated with such demographic markers as economic status, race, and ZIP code, the educational mission of schooling—that of supporting all students in reaching their full potential—has yet to be fulfilled.

At issue are conceptions of mathematical ability and students' potential and the impact that these factors have on teachers' decisions about how best to serve their students. Ample research has documented the ways in which poor academic performance among low-income and African American and Latino students is problematized such that students' characteristics and backgrounds are blamed, whereas such factors as opportunities to learn and access to information are ignored (Diversity in Mathematics Education Center for Learning and Teaching 2007; Oakes et al. 1997; Rubin 2008). Such deficit perspectives persist despite teachers' commonly stated belief that all students can succeed in school (Wilson and Corbett 2007).

Activating Students' Potential

Hearing talk about students who are of "low ability," or who "don't care" about learning, or who "can't do math" leads me to think back to my experiences as a teacher of mathematics in low- to middle-income communities with students who were diverse not only ethnically, economically, and linguistically but also with respect to their existing knowledge of mathematics and their preferred learning modalities (e.g., visual, tactile). In my classroom students who did not care to do mathematics, who were not proficient in English, whose abilities in mathematics had been deemed to be low, somehow found themselves learning mathematics. The cause of this apparent aberration was grounded in my refusal to base expectations for students' achievement on the labels applied to them by schools and society.

As a case in point, Alonso[1] was in my seventh-grade mathematics class along with twenty-four other students whose existing knowledge of mathematics was tenuous at best. The class average on their sixth-grade state mathematics examination placed them at the thirtieth percentile, far from what I considered their potential. Alonso's prior achievement in mathematics was well below that of his peers, in the single digits, a result that seemed inexorably linked with his being labeled as having low ability. Although I realized that he lacked *proficiency* with many mathematical concepts and skills, I did not equate this lack with Alonso's having a low *ability* to do mathematics. In fact, as I got to know Alonso, I learned that he had become accustomed to being left alone in class as long as he was not causing a distraction—left alone and not encouraged to learn to do mathematics (see Rousseau and Tate [2003] for research documenting how students from certain groups are "allowed to fail"). For me this neglect was at the root of his low achievement in mathematics.

Over the course of the two years that Alonso and his peers were in my mathematics class, through the seventh and eighth grades, they grew in every way imaginable—physically, socially, and, of course, academically. The class mean on the state mathematics examination increased to the sixty-third percentile, and Alonso's, to the sixty-fifth. Even more important, the students became doers of mathematics who communicated their thinking, challenged one another to justify strategies and outcomes, and strove to make sense of mathematics. This improvement took place in spite of the labels that had been applied to them by the schooling system and by society. These students' progress was made possible by my connecting mathematics with their lives through contextualized problems; providing multiple pathways to learning important concepts, including the use of visual models; requiring them to achieve proficiency in prerequisite skills while at the same time engaging them in learning grade-level concepts; and holding them accountable for making progress that reflected their potential to make sense of mathematics. Their success was due to the phenomenal response by my students and their supportive families to the challenge to bring their proficiency in mathematics up to and above benchmarks set by the state standards.

Essential to this success was a perspective that a fundamental aspect of a teacher's job is to hold high expectations of every student's potential and to create possibilities for all students to learn in ways that respect who they are and recognize their strengths as learners. Bransford, Brown, and Cocking (2000, p. 6), in their landmark publication *How People Learn: Brain, Mind, Experience, and School*, state quite powerfully,

> Learning research suggests that there are new ways to introduce students to traditional subjects, such as mathematics, science, history and literature, and that these new approaches make it possible for the majority of individuals to develop a deep understanding of important subject matter.

---

1. This is a pseudonym.

Although I realized that he lacked *proficiency* with many mathematical concepts and skills, I did not equate this lack with Alonso's having a low *ability* to do mathematics.

Essential to this success was a perspective that a fundamental aspect of a teacher's job is to hold high expectations of every student's potential and to create possibilities for all students to learn in ways that respect who they are and recognize their strengths as learners.

This philosophy lies at the heart of efforts to make mathematics accessible to all students, a concept exemplified by the cases and strategies shared by the authors in this book. Rather than continue the legacy of separation and leveled expectations, teachers of mathematics must learn to recognize and teach to students' strengths.

Problematizing Differentiation

The *Oxford English Dictionary* (Simpson and Wiener 1989) defines *differentiate* as "To make or render different; to constitute the difference in or between; to distinguish." The term *differentiate* derives from *different*, meaning "not of the same kind; not alike; of other nature, form, or quality" (Simpson and Wiener 1989). The underlying concept within these terms is that of making comparisons with a standard or norm and recognizing objects that fall outside that norm. That "differentiate" came into common use in the mid- to late-1800s (Simpson and Wiener 1989) is indicative of Western imperialistic and rationalistic thought of an era in which dominant groups sought to bring under control those who were "other" than the norm (Willinsky 1998). Given this historical perspective, care must be taken when using a term such as *differentiation of instruction* if the aim is to give all students greater opportunity for meaningful learning to take place.

Indeed, when examining its use in education, one finds that differentiation of instruction is characterized in multiple and often discrepant ways. One well-known scholar of differentiation, Carol Tomlinson (2000), contends, "Whenever a teacher reaches out to an individual or small group to vary his or her teaching in order to create the best learning experience possible, that teacher is differentiating instruction." The central idea within Tomlinson's depiction of differentiation is to *vary one's actions as a teacher to meet the needs of students*. Note that the focus here is on changing instructional practices, moving beyond the standard, or normative, habits that characterize mathematics teaching (e.g., teacher-led lecture and demonstration followed by students' individual work on rote procedures; see Stigler and Hiebert [1997]; Weiss et al. [2003]).

In contrast with a focus on changing teachers' actions, Ayalon (2006) describes how differentiation is often viewed from a curricular perspective: "[A] differentiated curriculum enables students to enroll in courses that are congruent with their interests and abilities. The rationale behind level differentiation and formal tracking underscores the diversity in students' abilities and the need to offer programs that correspond to that diversity" (p. 1188). From this perspective, differentiation involves *changing the curriculum in response to students' perceived abilities*. Particularly in school mathematics, with its history of providing inequitable access to content on the basis of perceived ability, this latter take on differentiation is all too easily embraced—but should be vociferously avoided! Although teacher educators often frame differentiation much as Tomlinson does—as requiring teachers to respond to students' needs to make content accessible—in practice the curriculum is often changed because of perceived differences in students' abilities. I argue that the latter of these responses to differen-

> The central idea within Tomlinson's depiction of differentiation is to *vary one's actions as a teacher to meet the needs of students.*

tiation is a consequence of the term itself that, together with a belief that mathematical ability is both accurately measurable and unevenly distributed, promotes actions that work against our efforts to create classroom environments in which all students learn meaningful mathematics.

Creating Possibilities for Students' Success

The challenge, then, is to move one's focus from "ability" to "possibility" by getting to know students' strengths and preferences with respect to learning modalities, then implementing lessons that activate those strengths and build from existing knowledge. Meeting this challenge requires a new stance toward teaching mathematics that is premised on creating possibilities for students' learning, a perspective that expects students to be successful when provided access to important ideas and that furnishes support in making sense of these ideas. This sort of differentiation, reflective of Tomlinson's definition, shifts teachers' attention away from activities that construct students as able or unable, directing attention instead toward strategies and situations that allow access for all students to learn mathematics. Too many "Jays" and "Alonsos" in our classrooms fall victim to traditional habits of teaching mathematics. Instead, our efforts to make content meaningful and accessible must activate the tremendous potential that lies within all students.

REFERENCES

Alayon, Hanna. "Nonhierarchical Curriculum Differentiation and Inequality in Achievement: A Different Story or More of the Same?" *Teachers College Record* 108, no. 8 (June 2006): 1186–1213.

Ayalon, Hanna, and Adam Gamoran. "Stratification in Academic Secondary Programs and Educational Inequality in Israel and the United States." *Comparative Education Review* 44, no. 1 (February 2000): 54–80.

Boaler, Joan, Dylan Wiliam, and Margaret Brown. "Students' Experiences of Ability Grouping: Disaffection, Polarization and the Construction of Failure." *British Educational Research Journal* 26, no. 5 (December 2000): 631–48.

Booher-Jennings, Jennifer. "Below the Bubble: 'Educational Triage' and the Texas Accountability System." *American Educational Research Journal* 42, no. 2 (Summer 2005): 231–68.

Bransford, John D., Ann L. Brown, and Rodney R. Cocking. *How People Learn: Brain, Mind, Experience, and School.* Washington, D.C.: National Academies Press, 2000.

Collins, Kathleen M. *Ability Profiling and School Failure: One Child's Struggle to Be Seen as Competent.* Mahwah, N.J.: Lawrence Erlbaum Associates, 2003.

Diamond, John B., and James P. Spillane. "High-Stakes Accountability in Urban Elementary Schools: Challenging or Reproducing Inequality?" *Teachers College Record* 106, no. 6 (June 2004): 1145–76.

Diaz, Alicia, and Joan Lord. *Focusing on Student Performance through Accountability.* Atlanta, Ga.: Southern Regional Education Board, 2005.

Diversity in Mathematics Education Center for Learning and Teaching. "Culture, Race, Power, and Mathematics Education." In *Second Handbook of Research on Mathematics Teaching and Learning,* edited by Frank J. Lester Jr., pp. 405–33. Charlotte, N.C.: Information Age Publishing, 2007.

Ellis, Mark W. "President's Choice: Constructing a Personal Understanding of Mathematics: Making the Pieces Fit." *Mathematics Teacher* 100, no. 8 (April 2007): 516–22.

———. "Leaving No Child Behind Yet Allowing None Too Far Ahead: Ensuring (In)Equity in Mathematics Education through the Science of Measurement and Instruction." *Teachers College Record* 110, no. 6 (2008): 1330–56.

Gorgorió, Núria, and Núria Planas. "Cultural Distance and Identities-in-Construction within the Multicultural Mathematics Classroom." *Zentralblatt für Didaktik der Mathematik* 37, no. 2 (2005): 64–71.

National Commission on Mathematics and Science Teaching for the Twenty-first Century. *Before It's Too Late.* Washington, D.C.: U. S. Department of Education, 2000.

National Council of Teachers of Mathematics (NCTM). *Principles and Standards for School Mathematics.* Reston, Va.: NCTM, 2000.

Oakes, Jeannie. *Keeping Track: How Schools Structure Inequality.* 2nd ed. New Haven, Conn.: Yale University Press, 2005.

Oakes, Jeannie, Amy Stuart Wells, Makeba Jones, and Amanda Datnow. "Detracking: The Social Construction of Ability, Cultural Politics, and Resistance to Reform." *Teachers' College Record* 98, no. 3 (1997): 482–510.

Rousseau, Celia, and William F. Tate. "No Time Like the Present: Reflecting on Equity in School Mathematics." *Theory into Practice* 42, no. 3 (Summer 2003): 210–16.

Rubin, Beth H. "Detracking in Context: How Local Constructions of Ability Complicate Equity-Geared Reform." *Teachers College Record* 110, no. 3 (2008): 646–99. www.tcrecord.org/Content.asp?ContentId=14603.

Simpson, John A., and Edmund S. C. Wiener, eds. *Oxford English Dictionary.* 2nd ed. New York: Oxford University Press, 1989.

Stigler, James W., and James Hiebert. "Understanding and Improving Classroom Mathematics Instruction: An Overview of the TIMSS Video Study." *Phi Delta Kappan* 79, no. 1 (1997): 14–21.

Tomlinson, Carol. "Differentiation of Instruction in the Elementary Grades." ERIC Digest (August 2000). Document No. ED0-PS-00-7. Available at ericece.org.

United States Department of Education. "Proven Methods: The Facts about … Math Achievement." www.ed.gov/nclb/methods/math/math.pdf.

Weiss, Iris R., Joan D. Pasley, P. Sean Smith, Eric R. Banilower, and Daniel C. Heck. *Looking inside the Classroom: A Study of K–12 Mathematics and Science Education in the United States.* Chapel Hill, N.C.: Horizon Research, 2003. www.horizon-research.com/insidetheclassroom/reports/looking/.

Willinsky, John. *Learning to Divide the World: Education at Empire's End.* Minneapolis, Minn.: University of Minnesota Press, 1998.

Wilson, Bruce, and Dick Corbett. "Students' Perspectives on Good Teaching: Implications for Adult Reform Behavior." In *International Handbook of Student Experience in Elementary and Secondary School,* edited by Dennis Theissen and Alison Cook-Sather, pp. 283–311. Dordrecht, Netherlands: Springer, 2007.

Inequitable Classroom Practices: Diagnosing Misconceptions as Inability in Mathematics

Daniel S. Battey
Meg Stark

I N OUR work in urban mathematics classrooms, we hear many teachers comment on students' abilities. Many times, the teacher will say that a student's ability is low, average, or far below basic right in front of us—and more important, in front of the student. Slipping into making judgments about students' abilities in mathematics is easy because we often think of the domain as hierarchical and static (Ruthven 1987). When we tell people that we are mathematics teachers, we commonly hear such comments as "I'm not a math person" or "I've always been good at math." These statements provide two boxes for grouping people in terms of innate mathematical ability: "math people" (high ability) and "nonmath people" (low ability).

Mathematics Ability

When educators make such statements as those above about students' ability, they buy into limited views of both mathematics and how "learnable" the content is. If nonmath people exist, why teach them mathematics? We call this way of thinking *deficit thinking* because no matter what, ability levels do not change—they are permanent judgments about the child. Teachers and schools that label children as remedial or far below basic are more likely to diagnose students as having low mathematics ability.

Gee (1992) calls these broad ways of talking and thinking about students *Discourses*[1] with a capital D. Discourses about mathematical ability lead to ways of understanding failure that affect views of who is and who is not mathematically able and who can and cannot do mathematics. They also structure individual interactions with people. When these ways of thinking explicitly or implicitly reference students of color and the poor,

> Discourses about mathematical ability lead to ways of understanding failure that affect views of who is and who is not mathematically able and who can and cannot do mathematics.

---

1. Gee distinguishes *Discourse* from *discourse* with a small "d" by defining *discourse* as the actual words and speech, whereas *Discourse* refers to the broad ideologies, values, beliefs, and ways of thinking that structure discourse.

This research was supported in part by a grant from the National Science Foundation (NSF) (ESI9911679). The opinions expressed in this article do not necessarily reflect the position, policy, or endorsement of the NSF.

167

they are called *cultural deficit thinking* (Connell et al. 1982; Natriello, McDill, and Pallas 1990). Parents, teachers, administrators, and researchers who allow limited Discourses focused on race, ethnicity, class, gender, language, and disability to narrow their view of students' ability are engaging in deficit thinking. Because of the often-limited ways of viewing mathematics ability and the ease with which cultural deficit thinking can guide judgments, mathematics educators run the risk of labeling students according to low ability that coincides with other issues that stratify access in society.

In making these ability judgments, the danger is that we provide a fundamentally different kind of instruction to some student groups, particularly students of color (Diversity in Mathematics Education [DiME] 2007). This article looks at how some teachers unconsciously make judgments about ability and the resulting instruction that students receive. It ends by examining promising classroom practices for teachers to engage in while they teach mathematics.

Misconceptions as Inability in Mathematics

Incorrect answers, mistakes, and misconceptions frequently provoke judgments about students' ability in mathematics (Watson 1999). When students make a mistake while using a standard algorithm, obtain an incorrect answer, or have difficulty generating a strategy on a problem, it is easy to misdiagnose the error as indicating something more broadly about the level of a student's ability in mathematics. Rather than see students' misconceptions as an opportunity for learning more mathematics, educators sometimes view these misconceptions as signs of an individual's fixed ability level (Watson 1999). Framing misconceptions as inability does little to help the teacher determine how to help the student learn more mathematics. In this situation, teachers might either move to different—that is, mathematically able—students or assume that the students cannot do the mathematics and tell them the steps to take. These strategies for diagnosing misconceptions lend themselves to the previously discussed limited views of ability and cultural deficit thinking.

A different approach to understanding mistakes or misconceptions is to view them as opportunities for learning. Students' errors might be attributable to multiple reasons, such as the specific problem or set of problems solved, a broader mathematical misconception, common errors across students, or carelessness. Making a judgment about ability, as previously discussed, wrests responsibility from the teacher. Rather, the mistake can guide the teacher to pose a new problem, pose questions to the student to help him or her discover the error, lead a whole-class discussion about an important mathematical idea, or have the student discuss the mistake with another student in the classroom. These strategies all work to extend students' learning of mathematics. We next make these approaches explicit by looking at two classroom episodes from a larger study on algebraic thinking.

When students make a mistake while using a standard algorithm, obtain an incorrect answer, or have difficulty generating a strategy on a problem, it is easy to misdiagnose the error as indicating something more broadly about the level of a student's ability in mathematics.

School and Classroom Context

The larger work focused on professional development on algebraic thinking as a way to help students transition from arithmetic to algebra (Carpenter, Franke, and Levi 2003). The basis for this work was Davis's (1964) writings about true-false and open-number sentences. It helped teachers rethink the mathematics that they were already teaching related to number facts, place value, multiplication, and fractions, to name a few, in their efforts to support students in using the equals sign more flexibly, as well as in making generalizations about the fundamental properties of mathematics. The professional development focused on their own students' thinking and classroom videotapes, in addition to the important mathematics for students to learn. The study followed the learning of both teachers and students in ten elementary schools engaged in the professional development, as well as nine control schools in the same district. We measured learning through students' written tests, interviews of students, interviews of teachers, and teachers' written tests (for more information see Jacobs et al. [2007]).

The particular work discussed in this article took place in one urban elementary school with more than 1,300 students. All the students at this school were either Latino (85 percent) or African American (15 percent), and the school scored between the tenth and twentieth percentiles in mathematics for the state of California. To help us better understand the choices that teachers make when they adapt mathematics professional development to their classroom teaching, eight fourth- and fifth-grade teachers at the school agreed to participate in a study as they took ideas learned in the professional development to the classroom.[2] We videotaped the teachers in the professional development and in their classrooms and interviewed them after the videotaping sessions. In the classroom videotapes, we noticed a number of practices that the teachers engaged in during their mathematics instruction. The practices discussed in this article are the different ways in which teachers dealt with students' misconceptions and incorrect answers and how those approaches relate to ideas about students' abilities and intelligence in mathematics.

Our goal in this article is not to criticize the teachers with whom we worked. Rather, in spending many hours watching videotapes, generating transcripts, and coding the classroom talk, we realized that teachers' strategies for dealing with misconceptions looked very different. We saw patterns across teacher-student interactions. Sometimes teachers told certain students, but not others, what to do; moved on when a student gave an incorrect answer; and offered very little constructive feedback to students who had made mistakes. At other times, teachers probed students about their thinking, questioned students about what was happening in the problem, or guided students toward substantive mathematical issues. We want to use those patterns to make explicit what sometimes remains a fairly unconscious practice for many mathematics teachers. We chose specific excerpts to highlight teaching practices and the frequency with which

---

2. This research was in addition to the broader study.

they occurred. Rather than characterize the teachers involved, we chose these excerpts to emphasize particular teaching practices to make a point. We therefore believe that we cannot and should not make generalizations about the teachers observed. Still, we believe that we can learn something about teachers' construction of mathematics ability from mathematics classroom practices.

Episode 1: Diagnosing Misconceptions as Inability

Seven of the eight teachers in this study dealt with misconceptions on an individual basis. Although this situation might not sound problematic, issues arose in how teachers judged students as mathematically able or not mathematically able according to whether the students made mistakes. The following episode occurred in a fourth-grade classroom while the class was working on the handshake problem given in Kaput and Blanton (2001):

> Twenty people are at a party. If each person shakes everybody else's hand once, how many handshakes will take place at the party? How many handshakes will occur if the number of people is twenty-one? How does the number of handshakes grow every time someone new arrives at the party?

The class was trying to solve the first part of the problem. As soon as the teacher posed the problem, the students started yelling out answers. Most of the answers were wrong, but no students shared strategies. The teacher decided to bring five students to the front of the class to have them shake one another's hands. While they shook hands, she recorded the number of handshakes for each person. She totaled the number of handshakes and then asked them to solve the problem for twenty people.

Fifteen minutes into the class, the episode took place with students' calling out answers, some raising their hands, and some not raising them. The teacher stood in front of the class at the chalkboard. The thirty-five students sat at eight tables, with either four or five students to a table. To give a richer description of this six-minute-long segment of class,[3] we supplement the transcript with information from the field notes.

T:	Raise your hands if you have an answer. Raise your hands when you have an answer. First right answer. SP?
SP:	Ten.
T:	All the way down to one. That is not the right answer. Nineteen plus eighteen plus seventeen plus sixteen all the way down to one. Add them.
SP:	Oh, I see.

---

3. "Ss" stands for multiple students. If the teacher says a specific student's name, the first two letters appear in capital letters (e.g. SP). If a student who is not named shares, we represent the student with a number (e.g., S1).

T:	Just like what we did over here, guys.
S1:	Thirty-six?
T:	Keep adding. Keep adding. First right answer.
S2, S3:	Ninety, eighty-one.
T:	Where would you go? Over here I see people working together, good job.
Ss:	*(Murmur.)*
T:	Come on, guys. Use your mental math strategies. Choices are right there. Let's go.
Ss:	*(Murmur.)*
T:	Not quite. Don't yell out your answer. Raise your hands. Rather than yell it out. VA?
VA:	109.
T:	TR?
TR:	*(Murmur.)*
T:	Hands, AN?
AN:	104.
S4:	105.
	(Students shout out different answers.)
T:	Quiet, unless I call on you.
S5:	190.
T:	BR, what did you get?
BR:	190.
T:	Good. 190. How did you do it, BR?
BR:	I added nineteen, eighteen....
T:	OK, but did you just add nineteen plus eighteen plus seventeen, or did you find another way? Show me how you did it.
S:	*(murmur.)*
T:	OK, everybody. Stop. Thank you. Show me how you did it.
	(BR explains her answer at her table to Ms. Tinsley and her group while students at other tables continue to talk.)
T:	Shh, shh. Quiet.
T:	Let's see what BR can do.
	(Students continue to talk among themselves.)
T:	OK. That's great. Did anybody else think of a different way to add it maybe? I saw some people writing and grouping numbers together? Right here, what were you doing?

This excerpt begins with students' calling out different answers. The teacher did not talk to students after they answered incorrectly, and she explicitly or implicitly told students that they were wrong by saying, "First right answer," "Not quite," and "Come on, guys. Use your mental math strategies." After students had given a number of wrong answers, the teacher called on a particular student whom she told us in the interview is "a great math student" (that is, a math person). She spent time talking to her in her small group and then asked her to share her thinking with the class. These interactions speak to two markedly different ways of working with math people and nonmath people. In this situation, the teacher explored the thinking of the mathematics person, assuming that if she had the correct answer, she had something of value to share. The other implicit message is that if students do not have the correct answer, the teacher will not ask questions of them, explore their thinking, or provide instructional feedback, since she does not value the contributions from these students. In the mathematics lesson, which took about fifty-five minutes, students with wrong answers did not get instructional time other than being told that their answer was wrong, either explicitly or implicitly. This type of interaction did not allow the teacher to know why students got the wrong answer but instead focused attention on what students could not do. The teacher then made judgments about individual students' ability, since she had no other information to draw on in understanding students' thinking (Watson 1996).

In addition, multiple students often had the same misconception, but when teachers do not address these mathematical issues with the whole class, they support the idea that a single misconception signifies individual inability. In this classroom, several students called out the answer 90. This situation—multiple students giving the same incorrect answer—occurred in all eight classrooms. Even when teachers devoted more time to students with incorrect answers than in this example, seven of the eight teachers dealt with incorrect answers and mistakes individually, although multiple students had the same answer or strategy. Six of the seven teachers who dealt with misconceptions on an individual level told each student the strategy to use to solve the problem correctly. According to their interviews, the seven teachers conceptualized misconceptions as signifying that the problem was too hard for students or that the students were "not good at math" (that is, nonmath people). One fifth-grade teacher stated in her interview, "Some kids have a knack at looking at something and it just comes to them. They're process people or step people naturally, and others are not. It just doesn't come naturally to a good majority."

Instead of seeing common misconceptions as something to discuss and address with students as a learning opportunity for a group, some teachers attached these misconceptions to students' abilities. In the interviews, teachers gave ability as a reason for their decision to make the problem easier, reduce the numbers, or "go back to the basics." If students did not understand the mathematics from the initial instruction, the teachers diagnosed those students as not being ready yet, not being good enough, or not knowing the basics. These diagnoses not only led teachers to attach fault to students but also were the main focus of discussion between teachers during the school day during the two years that we spent at the school. These two issues—devoting less instructional time to students who give incorrect answers and strategies and not publicly addressing common misconceptions—contribute to who we see as mathematically able and mathematically unable in mathematics classrooms.

Some teachers perceived students through a cultural deficit view in making instructional decisions, influenced by the location of the school in an urban community and the history of schooling, which often labels Latinos and African Americans as less able (Hull et al. 1991). When teachers working with remedial, low-achieving, or ethnically underrepresented students in mathematics buy into broad Discourses about who these students are—or sometimes more important, who they are not—they have lower expectations for these students. Consistent with the findings here, researchers have found that teachers are more likely to ignore incorrect responses from students for whom they have lower expectations (Ansalone and Biafora 2004). These Discourses are ways of explaining away failure and making it easier to interpret students' wrong answers and misconceptions as signifying a nonmath person or membership in a culture that "cannot do mathematics."

Episode 2: Equitable Teaching Practices

Although this article has discussed the dominant practices for dealing with students' misconceptions in this school, some teachers also engaged students in other ways. In particular, one fifth-grade teacher never engaged in the preceding practices and avoided diagnosing misconceptions as ability in the interview. This teacher walked around to the different groups and had discussions with both individuals and groups who had generated incorrect answers, correct answers, incorrect strategies, and correct strategies. The thirty-four students sat at six tables, either five or six at a table. The following episode took place at the very beginning of the class, while students worked on the same problem that other students were working on in the first episode. The teacher posed the problem to groups of students, and the students began working with one another instead of calling out answers. Since most of the teacher's interactions took place in small groups and with individual students, the audio recording was inadequate for providing a transcript. However, we used the field notes to build a picture of this five-minute classroom episode with some verbatim excerpts of the conversation.

	(After posing the problem, the teacher starts circulating among the groups.)
T:	You must show your work.
	(The teacher moves to the next group. Many hands go up in the groups.)
S1:	Teacher, we got 400.
T:	So, why did you multiply 20 and 20?
Ss:	*(Students in group talk inaudibly to one*

another.)

T:	Can you shake your own hand?
S2:	Yeah, look *(shakes right and left hand).*
T:	*(Laughs)* How many hands does the first person shake?

(Teacher moves to next group and pauses for about 15 seconds.)

T:	Why did you multiply 20 and 19? What about the second person at the party, how many hands would he or she shake?

After ten minutes, only one group had a correct answer or strategy. The teacher asked the students to drop their pencils and turn over their papers. He then called on five students to come to the front. The five students modeled the problem while they counted the handshakes that each one made; recorded the numbers 4, 3, 2, 1 on the board; and then added them.

In this episode, the teacher's questions addressed the specific issue that students were having difficulty with: realizing that in multiplying 20 by 20, a person would be shaking his or her own hand. Rather than give students a different strategy or a teacher-generated strategy, this teacher asked questions of groups to build on the students' thinking and address the specific misconception. Similarly, later in the lesson, the teacher noticed that another group multiplied 19 and 20 because the students did not realize that this method would result in everyone shaking each student's hands twice. When the teacher saw that multiple groups were dealing with the same issue, he engaged the whole class in shaking one another's hands, modeling the handshakes to find the pattern of 19, 18, and so on. He did not treat mistakes as individual misconceptions or as reflections of students' abilities. When groups raised their hands to give an answer, an incorrect or correct answer by itself was never a good enough explanation. He always prompted students for a further explanation. Rather than deal with misconceptions as an individual problem, this teacher asked questions that engaged groups of students in working through these mathematical issues. Instead of diagnosing misconceptions as indications of inability and attaching them to deficit views of students, this teacher engaged students in the specific mathematics with which they were struggling. He treated misconceptions as a learning opportunity for groups of students and the whole class.

Further, toward the end of class, the teacher combined the incorrect strategy generated previously by students, multiplying 19 by 20, as well as a strategy generated by students after modeling the handshakes, making twenties to get to 190 (19 + 1, 18 + 2, 17 + 3, and so on) to generalize a formula for the problem. The teacher had students count up the groups of twenties and find that the result is 9½, or half of 19. From this result, he adapted 19×20 to $19/2 \times 20$, or 190. He asked students what 19 and 20 represented in their solutions, and they responded that the 20 represented the number of people at the party and the 19 represented one less because

Rather than give students a different strategy or a teacher-generated strategy, this teacher asked questions of groups to build on the students' thinking and address the specific misconception.

the first person could not shake her or his own hand. He then asked students to substitute n for the number of people at the party so that students could generalize their conjecture. They found that they could apply the equation $(n - 1)/2 \times n = h$ (where n = the number of people and h = the number of handshakes) to the problem no matter how many people were at the party. Instead of avoiding incorrect answers and strategies, this teacher used the incorrect answers and strategies to drive the mathematical learning of all students in the classroom.

The teacher asked students to explain their thinking whether their responses were correct or incorrect. On the basis of their responses, he posed questions and asked for elaboration. These explanations allowed the teacher to raise specific questions that led groups of students in rethinking the misconception with which they were struggling. Through modeling the problem posed, he also engaged students as a class in finding the mathematical pattern. These practices spread instructional time across students whether their answers were correct or incorrect, and all students interacted with particular mathematical issues within the problem context. By not buying into deficit Discourses about the students in his classroom, this teacher dealt with students' misconceptions by using more varied mathematical pedagogical strategies than the teacher in the first episode and engaged in high-quality instructional interactions regardless of the answer that the student gave.

Conclusion

The misdiagnosis of misconceptions as inability is problematic across classrooms for many students, even though a select few, similar to BR in the first episode, are seen as having ability. However, the notion of an able mathematics student is often narrow and excludes many potentially talented mathematics students. Because the educational system has a history of excluding, disenfranchising, or providing a different quality of education for students labeled *remedial, low,* or *minority,* educators run the risk of further limiting the participation of large groups of students in mathematics. Because this specific work took place in a low-performing, urban elementary school in which 100 percent of the students were people of color, addressing other issues is also important. In contexts in which broad Discourses set up students of color as "kinesthetic learners," who are unable to think abstractly, or as having cultural deficits, misdiagnoses are all the more dangerous (DiME 2007). Research has found that teachers expect lower levels of achievement from students of color, from girls, and from students of lower socioeconomic status (Raudenbush, Rowan, and Cheong 1993). Because misconceptions and incorrect answers in urban classrooms fit within broader deficit Discourses of students of color and poverty, teachers should avoid them all the more.

We are not stating that educators should avoid dealing with misconceptions. If educators were to avoid dealing with them, they would not serve students in advancing in their mathematics learning. The issue for educators is that tremendous danger exists in establishing fixed views

The issue for educators is that tremendous danger exists in establishing fixed views of ability, because such views limit future instructional opportunities. Instead, teachers should deal with the specific mathematical difficulty as an opportunity for students to learn more mathematics.

of ability, because such views limit future instructional opportunities. Instead, teachers should deal with the specific mathematical difficulty as an opportunity for students to learn more mathematics. Teachers can use the following principles to guide this process in mathematics classrooms:

- Delve deeper than answers (correct and incorrect), and ask for strategies and explanations.

- Handle misconceptions with the same quality of instructional strategies used for students with correct strategies.

- Use common misconceptions as a driving force for learning more mathematics.

- Challenge the thoughts of students whom we see as mathematically able.

To better address issues of equity in mathematics education, educators need to consider the broader educational and cultural contexts that structure the frames of mind of students, teachers, administrators, and researchers. These larger educational and cultural contexts shape such issues in mathematics education as the achievement gap and mathematical ability. Ways of explaining differential achievement by race, poverty, and gender structure larger agendas for addressing equity in schools and affect individual teacher-student interactions. These explanations often frame low-performing students as lacking in ability rather than recognize the institutional, cultural, social, and political contexts that construct achievement differences. Schools have historically made judgments of mental ability from low performance, drawing inferences from behavior to cognition, or put another way, inferring low ability from low standardized test scores (Hull et al. 1991). As educators, we need to be watchful that our informal assessment practices are not increasing differential access to high-quality mathematics instruction.

REFERENCES

Ansalone, George, and Frank Biafora. "Elementary School Teachers' Perceptions and Attitudes to the Educational Structure of Tracking." *Education* 125, no. 2 (Winter 2004): 249–58.

Carpenter, Thomas P., Megan Franke, and Linda Levi. "Thinking Mathematically: Integrating Algebra and Arithmetic in Elementary School." Portsmouth, N.H.: Heinemann, 2003.

Connell, R. W., Dean Ashenden, Sandra Kessler, and Gary Dowsett. *Making the Difference.* Boston: George Allen & Unwin, 1982.

Davis, Robert B. "Discovery in Mathematics: A Text for Teachers." Palo Alto, Calif.: Addison-Wesley Publishing Co., 1964.

Diversity in Mathematics Education (DiME). "Culture, Race, Power, and Mathematics Education." In *The Second Handbook of Research on Mathematics Teaching and Learning,* edited by Frank Lester, pp. 405–433. Charlotte, N.C.: Information Age Publishing, 2007.

Gee, James. *Social Linguistics and Literacies: Ideologies in Discourses.* New York: Falmer Press, 1992.